PRAISE FOR **LOKI'S CHILDREN**

"Nick Brink has been a dedicated practitioner of The Cuyamungue Method that I also teach, using ancient postures in a ritual context to evoke ecstatic trance familiar to shamans among contemporary urban people. In this book he brings his considerable experience and creativity to a fascinating integration of indigenous and modern ways of healing mind and soul. Nick has been inspired to guide his clients in altered states using methods he knows from hypnotherapy and dreamwork along with Ancient Ritual Postures and the myths from his Nordic ancestry. He is blazing a new trail in how to work with clients to help them find deep spiritual and psychological wholeness."
—**BELINDA GORE, PHD, AUTHOR OF** *Ancient Ritual Postures: Oracle Cards with Companion Book,* **FORMER PRESIDENT, THE CUYAMUNGUE INSTITUTE**

"In an act of love, Nick's compassionate heart invites the reader on a journey of self-exploration to remind us of the ancient ways. We are given a valuable opportunity to experience inner healing by honoring the ancestors, becoming stewards for Mother Earth, and listening to Spirit as we embrace what Nick terms the "New Age." Building upon his prior work on ecstatic trance, Loki's Children introduces the reader to a harmonious balance between the clinical application of ecstatic analytic hypnotherapy and mythical storytelling. This work can be of great importance to those seeking to embark on an inner quest and for clinicians interested in learning a novel approach to integrating ancient healing practices with psychotherapy."
—**MANUEL E. VARELA, PSYD, CURANDERO, CENTER FOR IMAGERY AND SHAMANIC STUDIES**

"This fascinating book combines elements of Jungian depth psychology, Norse mythology and Ecstatic Trance into a remarkable and profound synthesis of inspiration and wisdom. It is highly recommended

to individuals seeking to explore their repetitive patterns of self-entrapment and re-connect with their true essence. "
—ROBERT DALE ROGERS, HERBALIST, ASSISTANT PROFESSOR IN FAMILY MEDICINE, UNIVERSITY OF ALBERTA. TEACHERS EARTH SPIRIT MEDICINE, NORTHERN STAR COLLEGE, AUTHOR OF 52 MEDICINAL PLANT BOOKS

LOKI'S CHILDREN

A HEALING STORY OF ANTIQUITY, SHAMANISM AND PSYCHOTHERAPY

NICHOLAS E. BRINK, PhD

FOREWORD BY LEWIS MEHL-MADRONA, MD, PhD

Red Elixir
Rhinebeck, New York

Paperback ISBN 978-1-954744-85-1
eBook ISBN 978-1-954744-86-8

Library of Congress Control Number 2022941564

Book design by Colin Rolfe

Red Elixir is an imprint of Monkfish Book Publishing Company

Red Elixir
22 East Market Street, Suite 304
Rhinebeck, NY 12572
(845) 876-4861
epigraphps.com

CONTENTS

ACKNOWLEDGMENTS

I would like to acknowledge the Cuyamungue Institute. The Institute, founded by Felicitas Goodman in 1978, is on the Pojoaque Pueblo north of Santa Fe, NM. Its purpose is to promote Dr. Goodman's original research and findings in the nature of ecstatic or shamanic trance. Her work, known today as the Cuyamungue Method, focuses on the use of ancient sacred practices and postures of the hunting and gathering cultures that, when properly used, provide an experience that creates a doorway to an ecstatic experience of expanded reality. Dr. Goodman captured the essence of her work and findings in the book *Where the Spirits Ride the Wind*. I received formal training in the history and proper use of the Cuyamungue Method at the Cuyamungue Institute. My own continued research of these shamanic ways has taken me beyond the limits of the "Cuyamungue Method." This book examines how it can be used in the setting of traditional psychotherapy. Though the procedure I offer diverges from the "Cuyamungue Method," it still follows Felicitas Goodman's six basic elements for inducing ecstatic trance.

To learn more about Dr. Goodman's original work in ecstatic trance and her development and use of the Cuyamungue Method, visit the Cuyamungue Institute's website, www.cuyamungueinstitute.com.

FOREWORD

LEWIS MEHL-MADRONA, MD, PhD

In *Loki's Children*, Nicholas Brink presents a route to extraordinary experiences that he calls ecstatic trance. He distinguishes this from other forms of trance by calling it controlled folly, a term coined by Carlos Castenada to describe an attitude in which one understands that nothing is important yet acts as if everything is important. Nicholas says that "*Controlled folly* provides a person with a distraction from their busy mind to carry them beyond their conscious world and into the world of extrasensory knowledge, knowledge that comes from beyond the five senses. By choosing an act that … is unimportant yet *doing* it as if it is important, [it] allows the *stalker* to let go of rational thinking in order to quiet the mind. Choosing to use rapid stimulation to the nervous system with drumming or rattling as an act of *controlled folly* provides … this needed distraction."

Fundamentally, *Loki's Children* presents Nicholas' method of doing psychotherapy, focusing upon three clients with whom he has worked and following their progress using a schema from Norse mythology. The struggles of the gods with each other and with evil powers parallel the process of psychotherapy and the inner struggles that occur within the world of the client.

The namesakes of the book are the three children that Loki fathers with an evil giantess. The three are prophesied to destroy the home of the Norse gods. Removing them and the danger they pose becomes a grand project for these gods. They throw one into an underworld reserved for those who die of illness. They cast another into the sea. They struggle most with the last, a wolf of tremendous size. With the help of dark dwarves, they eventually bind him and place him in a cave on an island. All will return for the final battle.

Nicholas uses the story of Jormungand, the Midgard serpent, as a model for managing fear. Jormungand is the terror of the Norse oceans. Odin had cast this beast into the sea, who sinks to the bottom and grows so large that he circles the Earth, holding his tail in his mouth. To go to sea requires negotiation with Jormungand, whose strength is demonstrated in the story of Thor's wager with the giant, Hymir. Thor, son of Odin, is the strongest of the gods and controls the sky and thunder. He is known to have a mercuric temper and enjoys challenging others to contests. In one such challenge, Thor seeks to win an enormous cauldron used to brew ale from the giant, Hymir, through a fishing contest. Thor encourages Hymir to row farther and farther out to sea. Thor throws his baited hook into the water and the serpent lets go of its tail and swallows the bait. Thor pulls the poison-spitting monster toward the boat. As it reaches his striking zone, Thor raises his famed hammer to smash the serpent's head. Just before he can strike, Hymir cuts the line, allowing Jormungand to return to the bottom of the sea. Hymir is so frightened by this whole episode that he gives Thor the cauldron. This leads Nicholas to a discussion of facing fear that is informed by this story and other aspects of Norse mythology. He presents "four characteristics of fear when one faces threat. First, for some, the fear in facing a threat may trigger increased strength and determination" as portrayed in the story of the strength of Thor in overcoming the threat of Jormungand. Thor teaches us to face the object of fear with great respect and strength.

Second comes the motivation to prove one's strength, to gain fame and notoriety, thereby pleasing the gods (replace with any relevant audience). Brink says, "In the mind of the Viking warrior, only cowards are deterred by fear and thus end up in Hel's realm."

Third, the stories teach us that we must manage our rage and our tempers. Nicholas tells the story of Thor's competition with the giant, Utgard-Loki, in which Thor's increasing rage renders him blind to important aspects of the challenge and his blindness keeps him from prevailing. Thor's humiliation at losing each competition only serves to escalate his rage and prevents him from becoming aware of the tricks being played against him. The challenges and the tricks are also instructive. First Utgard-Loki challenges Thor to see who can drink the most. Little does Thor know that an illusion of magic has caused him to drink directly from the sea. Next Thor is challenged to lift a cat, but when Thor puts his arm under the cat to lift it, it merely arches its back. Finally, they challenge him to wrestle an old woman who turns out to be old age itself.

Fourth, we learn to face threats with a sense of calm strength and even humor. Facing threats with calming laughter allows us to deal with them more effectively. When we take the threat too personally and without humor, we are prone to despair, rage, humiliation, and even death.

Brink mentions American Indian tricksters and European court jesters as being able to make fun of what we might otherwise take too seriously, allowing us to laugh at ourselves. When we value our beliefs, self-concepts, and possessions too much, we become vulnerable should we lose them. We risk our resilience. Fear arises when we cannot laugh at ourselves. We fear the loss of what we are valuing. Brink continues to discuss the importance of facing our fear openly and with humor so as to find the power over that which is tormenting us. He gives the example of the Berserkers, a group of Viking warriors, famous for intentionally working themselves into a frenzy before battle so that they felt invulnerable and fearless. This strategy does not work so well in ordinary life.

Brink tells stories of clients with whom he has worked psychotherapeutically. They are rich, interesting and instructive for those who wish to try Brink's model for doing psychotherapy. For example, Jerry comes to take responsibility for his wife's leaving him. Jerry rescued underdogs. His wife was an underdog, a struggling secretary who couldn't pay her bills. Sadly, Jerry didn't know how to move beyond the rescue, and his wife needed more than just rescue. Paying her bills wasn't enough. Jerry felt fulfilled by helping others, but Brink's approach helped him to see that it stopped there. He lacked the skills to take relationships beyond the rescue phase.

The book nicely illustrates Brink's combination of techniques. He uses the narrative arts effectively in dialoguing with Jerry while Jerry is in an altered state of consciousness. Brink uses trance-inducing postures as a means of reaching an altered state of consciousness and giving direction to the trance experience. He uses what David Cheek called ideomotor signaling for Jerry to identify when he has accomplished a task. He provides a number of therapeutic suggestions for Jerry to use to modify Jerry's identity narrative. He does what is sometimes called age regressions to help Jerry connect with early times in his life and the character who represents who he was at that earlier time. I have italicized parts of the dialogue in which the use of language arts is particularly powerful and effective.

> [In a session with Jerry, three days after his wife left, following nightly dreams that she had returned and was in the house, Brink used the Bear Spirit Posture to provide Jerry with] "increased ego-strength with the *suggestion* of being curious and wondering about the deeper reason that led his wife to leave. As the drumming played quietly, I had him stand with his hands resting on his center

of harmony, feeling it rise and fall with each breath. As he inhaled a sense of increased strength flowed in, and as he exhaled the strength flowed throughout his body. I gave him a recording of the drumming and *instructed him to practice it at home to help him learn to find this focused and increased strength in facing his wife leaving.* During this session his first level of fear had somewhat subsided and he was ready to face a deeper level of fear. As I sat at the edge of my chair with a straight back, grasping my knees with my hands, I suggested that Jerry sit in this way, and asked him what he felt. He reported that he felt that he was anxiously waiting for something. I suggested, '*We are going to take your feeling of fear back through time to see where it began, and it is that answer that you are anxiously waiting for.*' With his fear as the affect bridge,[3] we again stood in the Bear Spirit Posture for a few minutes, while he focused on his breathing, inhaling increased strength and allowing the strength to flow throughout his body, before we sat grasping our knees in the Lady of Cholula Posture, (Fig. 1.2). As I turned on the drumming, I suggested, 'Carry your feelings of fear with you *as you begin to go back through time, curious and wondering. Watch your life go by, year by year, season by season, places you've been, watch your life go by as you carry your feeling of fear with you, curious and wondering. You will soon find yourself at some important place and time in your life. When you arrive at this place and time, lift the index finger of your right hand to let me know that you are there.*'

"When his finger lifted, I asked him of his experience. 'I'm sitting in a reading circle in school. I hate to read. The teacher is going around the circle having each kid read a couple of sentences. I'm scared. It will soon be my turn.

I hate this. I stumble and stammer over every word. I'm next. Everyone is looking at me. I feel so stupid, dumb...'

"He was still in trance, sitting grasping his knees and the drumming continued. After a few moments of silence, I *suggest*, 'Take a few deep breaths. Slowly let yourself again begin to relax. Stay with the spirit of your younger self feeling frightened of reading out-loud. *Your fear has an important message to you. You may not understand that message now, but there will be a time when its importance will become clear.*... Now, they have now passed you in going around the circle. The reading circle is about over. What happens next?'

"'Recess. We get to go out to play kick ball.'

"'Go on. What happens?'

"'The teacher makes me captain. I get to pick my kick ball team. I love kick ball. I'm really good at it.'

"'*Enjoy those good feelings* of playing kick ball. The spirit of your younger self reminds you that he is good at kick ball... Now *let yourself move ahead in time*. You have told me about some of the books you read. *Move ahead in time to an early time when you found that you can enjoy reading.*'

"'I think it was the 8th grade, the teacher lets us pick a book off the shelf and read for the last 10 minutes of class. I still could not read out loud. I would stammer and get the words all jumbled, but I picked a Hardy Boys mystery and read the whole book over a week or two. When I finished the teacher told me I could have the book. That was the first time I can remember enjoying reading. But I still enjoy reading. I think I must have read 50 Hardy Boys books after that.'

"'Good. Okay, with all the wisdom and understanding of your adult-self, your adult-self who enjoys reading, *go back to be with the spirit of your younger self in the reading circle.* If you feel like it, you can put your arm around your younger self and give him a hug. Let him know that there will be a time when he will enjoy reading. You know him better than anyone else. Though he is anxious, even panics when it comes to reading in a circle, you can appreciate his persistence, his willingness to keep on trying. You know that he will eventually learn to enjoy reading. Appreciate your younger self. Help him understand and feel good about himself.'

"After offering this counter-narrative I could see Jerry's shoulders drop and the tension leave him. Jerry continued to share his experience. 'I never thought about it. I know that I practice pitching a lot. I enjoy practicing and I know that is why I'm good. No pain, no gain. I have to work hard to be good. I did work hard in reading too. I hated feeling stupid and wanted to do better.' Though the trauma of the reading circle could be blamed on his teacher, it was apparent that Jerry took responsibility for his poor oral reading ability and had worked hard to overcome it. At least he accepted *my suggestion recognizing his persistence.* This persistence was one of Jerry's assets, and it would be used throughout the course of therapy. His deeper level of fear was the fear of being stupid or dumb. He was beginning to take responsibility for his wife leaving him because of his stupidity or dumbness. Using the affect of the fear of his wife leaving him as a bridge allowed him to make this connection and take this responsibility."

Brink identifies personality types that are driven by guilt, including the codependent, the abuser, the perfectionist, and the suffering servant. I would prefer to see these as roles that a person can play, characters in a story that is being enacted. I do not think they are always driven by guilt; sometimes they are just learned as the only option available to portray. However, that point of disagreement does not detract from the power of the work. Brink identifies Jerry as codependent, in that he needed to be needed and sought others to fill this need. Jerry rescued his wife early in their relationship and then he proceeded to rescue others, including a baseball team.

Brink describes his therapy with Arlene, who plays the perfectionist role. He believes that these individuals feel a need to prove themselves by trying to be perfect. They can also become unbearable by demanding that those around them also be perfect, becoming intolerant of the mistakes or weaknesses of others. Brink describes the 13-year-old version of Arlene who finds her clean clothes in a stack of laundry on the living room sofa. She runs to put them away and bumps into her mother as she goes around the corner. Her mother screams, "Get out of my way."

> Arlene feels frightened and guilty because she can't do anything right to please her mother. As the therapy session continued, I mentioned, "Sometimes when you put away the clothes your mom might be happy, sometimes she might ignore you, and other times she might be angry. You just don't know what you can do to make her happy."
>
> "I don't remember ever making her happy. All I see her doing is being angry. I guess that in between she was ignoring me, but I don't know what she was doing."
>
> "Wow! You have no memory of her smiling at you or of her being happy."
>
> "I was looking through some old pictures the other day

and found one of her smiling and my first reaction was, 'Who's that?' I didn't recognize her."

"That is so sad…to be that unhappy. Tell me about your father in such a situation as when you were putting away the clothes."

"Dad is sitting in the car. I know he is fuming. The horn honks a couple of times. That is going to make mom even angrier."

Mom feels guilty for not getting everything done, for not pleasing everyone, and for not being perfect. Daughter is feeling guilty for not pleasing mom and for not keeping the peace in the family. Within a family, guilt is passed down through the generations.

Brink is doing classic, good psychotherapy in drawing Arlene's attention to a representative situation that explains her continued feelings of needing to be perfect. The more she can recognize that this strategy doesn't work and only leads to more suffering, the less she can suffer. The therapy continues. She discovered that she was behaving in the same manner as her mother, yelling at her own children and husband when they made mistakes and were less than perfect. This awareness led to her feeling angry at herself for being like her mother. Brink notes that she doesn't know how to be another way. I would say, she has no story template for that character to enact. Brink gave her an assignment of expressing appreciation to each of her children and to her husband each day for something they did. As she did this assignment, she became more hopeful. Brink links this to the metaphor of binding Fenrir, the ever-growing wolf, with a chain. When Arlene has a relapse, Brink says, "the chain broke." Fenrir got free. "The family was going somewhere, and all were in the car waiting for Arlene. She was racing around the house doing some things she 'had to do.' Tim honked the horn once, which irritated Arlene, but when she finally got out to the car, 'Tim said that my diddling around in the house was going to make us late. I was furious. I went back into the house and just sat there. Finally, Tim came in and apologized, but I told him to go without me. He refused and disappointed the kids by missing the movie.'

"I suggested, 'That wasn't very nice of Tim, but he does not yet understand. It'll take a lot of patience and strength to change, but you are on the way.' Arlene needed this reassurance."

Next, Brink took Arlene through an exercise in which she absurdly exaggerated her temper by taking on the persona of Donald Duck, who flaps his wings and quacks in anger, but in a way that is quite humorous. Then Brink engages in dream interpretation. Here is the dream:

> "My mother-in-law gave us a sterling silver platter for a wedding gift. It was a family heirloom. In my dream I noticed it was starting to tarnish so I took it down to polish it. When I wiped it with the polishing cloth, it shined for a moment then turned blacker than before. If I stopped for a moment to rest my hand it turned blacker and blacker. I was getting nowhere. I finally got so tired of polishing that I just threw it down and watched as it turned black and then it crumbled into nothing but dust. I screamed at Tim, 'What did you do to the platter?'"

The dialogue follows:

> "There is always something that needs to be done, just one more project."
>
> "Okay, how about naming it, 'Just one more project.' The second is that you need to take a rest and it turns blacker. What's a good name for that part of the dream?"
>
> "I'm always tired. There is always too much to do."

"Shall we name it that, 'Always tired.'"

"That's okay."

"Now the third part, you get frustrated and tired and it crumbles."

"I give up. When I give up everything falls apart."

"Good, and the last part, you yell at and blame Tim."

"I never get any help. I cannot keep ahead of Tim and the kids. They make messes faster than I can clean them up."

Reading from my notes, "We have 'Just one more project,' 'I'm always tired,' 'I give up,' and 'I never get any help.' I stand and place my hands at my waist in the Feathered Serpent Posture, and briefly tell the story of Felicitas Goodman's discovery of the power of these postures…. I then suggest that she stand as I am standing and as I turn on the drumming CD. I begin with, "With each breath you inhale calmness, and as you exhale, the calmness goes deeper inside of you." After these words the only words I said were, "Go back into your dream." I trusted the power of Arlene's dream would lead her to a rebirth experience. At the end of the fifteen minutes I asked her to describe her experience.

"In going back to the dream what stood out was what I felt when my mother said, 'I never get any help.' I saw myself as a little girl. Those words are my mother's. I can clearly hear her voice saying them. I feel myself shaking. I was always trying to help but could never do it right. I could never please her."

"You feel yourself shaking?"

"Um huh. Scared. I don't know what to do. Frozen in fear, afraid to do anything."

"The 'I never get any help' spirit guide from your dream causes you to shake, frozen in fear.

"Bring your kids and Tim into your image. Can you see them shaking?"

Arlene began to cry. She was out of trance and hurting. She was not ready to truly let go, but she had a deeper understanding of how hard she had been on the family and a beginning understanding of the meaning of letting go. She understood the message of her spirit guide.

I added, "Maybe for the family's sake it is important to let go and let the platter crumble." These were the threads with which she would weave the Gleipnir. So often the strength of Gleipnir is found in new insights and understanding.

Nicholas then returns to the story of Fenrir, the giant wolf's binding, and the need for sacrifice. In the story, Skirnir brings a silk ribbon to the Aesir, which he has obtained from the world of the dark-elves. This ribbon is soft as silk but strong enough to hold Fenrir. The gods then invite Fenrir to come to an island in Amsvartnir Lake. They show the ribbon to Fenrir and challenge him to break it. They demonstrate that none of them can. Fenrir does not trust this challenge and believes that the gods will keep him restrained if he cannot break the ribbon. He demands that one of them put a hand in his mouth as a sign of good faith. Tyr volunteers himself. When Fenrir realizes that he cannot break the ribbon, he chomps down on Tyr's hand, severing it from the arm. Nicholas uses this story to say, "The journey into the unconscious has provided each person with the strength to bind their obsessions, but to do so each has to sacrifice something. Any change in a person's life requires giving up the old ways and giving up the old ways is painful…." He then proceeds to use these metaphors with the clients he is using for example. Arlene, for example, had to sacrifice her need for perfect order in order to sustain better relationships with her coworkers, husband, and children.

When the gods are certain that Fenrir cannot escape, they add a chain to his binding, drawing the chain through a boulder which is then driven deep into the earth with a huge stone covering where it enters. When Fenrir opens his mouth as he struggles, the gods effectively gag him by placing a sword in his mouth with the point wedged against the roof of his mouth and the hilt propped against the lower jaw. He proceeds to howl horribly. Nicholas explains this metaphor as meaning that regardless of the strength needed to bind one's obsessions, our obsessions continue to howl in captivity. They remind us that our problems have not completely gone away. Arlene, for example, still felt the howl from her need for perfection and had to work to prevent herself from unbinding her Fenrir. However, we may slide into complacency, and then our inner Loki brings things to a head again, being the part of us who knows that our problem is not completely resolved. Our Fenrir is still alive and howling, and we deceive ourselves when we ignore him. Loki acts to force us to be honest with ourselves, to acknowledge the inner howling and do something about it. Loki finds a way to kill our inner complacency and upset our apple cart. Like an angry Thor who wants to fight and hurt someone in protest for the loss of his complacency and false balance, we are tempted to lash out, and it takes great strength to avoid doing that. Citing Hermod's journey to Hel to gain back the slain part of ourselves, Nicholas writes that the journey to the land of the dead represents a journey into the unconscious mind similar to the journey into the cave of the dark elves. This journey allows us to face a part of ourselves who is hard to relinquish but nevertheless causes us great emotional pain and grief. He addresses this by joining with his client in his or her feelings as a means of trance induction.

Upon Hermod's return to Asgard from the land of the dead, the gods send instructions to every being on earth to weep for the one who has been killed, our complacency. Only one being, Thokk, a giantess, sheds no tears. Nicholas likens that to the part of us who refuses to express remorse regardless of the circumstances. That part of us continues to justify or defend our destructive behavior and refuses healing. Our confronting part continues to force us to recognize something about us that makes us uncomfortable, perhaps the part who is still chained and howling. It brings us to an awareness of a trait or a way of thinking that prevents us from solving our problem. We struggle to change but feel that it is hopeless. Our frustration increases. We become angry for being challenged to change when we no longer want to change. He uses Loki to represent the confronting part of us, the part of us who tricks us into listening when we don't want to hear anymore. "Loki, the trickster and confronting part of us, can also be considered our shadow, those needs that we seek to deny, those traits that we don't want made public that reflect our dysfunctional thinking. He writes," Loki, the trickster and confronting part of us, can also be considered our shadow, those needs that we seek to deny, those traits that we don't want made public that reflect our dysfunctional thinking." Next we must capture our inner trickster, our inner Loki. In the North story, Kvasier, the wisest of the gods, has a vision for how to capture Loki when Loki is in his salmon form. The gods make a net to catch him in the river. He writes, "The wisest part of ourselves knows what is going on and uses this knowledge to assist in the capture of denial of our need to change. With this knowledge and the knowledge of all parties, it is difficult to deny this confronting part of ourselves and the knowledge we have learned from it." Nicholas gives an example of Arlene escaping from her inability to let go of her anger and her impatience. She channeled her anger in the form of assertiveness and she found patience. He illustrates the restraint in Arlene's finding an effective way to control her anger. Nevertheless, she experienced considerable distress when things weren't perfect or weren't as she had imagined.

A series of dreams helped her to understand her need for perfection and control.

Nicholas moves next to the story of Loki's restraint during which three years of great battles throughout the world follow in which all kinship taboos are broken. Then comes three years of endless winter without summer. "The snow drifts from all directions with great frosts and winds, and the sun does no good." He writes that struggle and depression take over once we have gained sufficient will power to restrain our dysfunctional behaviors. The three years of endless winters remind me of Joseph Campbell's dark knight of the soul. The hero goes through the lowest point in the journey before emerging victorious. In the Norse mythology, a wolf suddenly swallows the sun and another wolf catches the moon. "The stars disappear from the sky; mountains shake and trees are uprooted. Fenrir the wolf breaks his bonds. The ocean surges and Jormungand crawls onto the land full of rage. The ship made from dead people's nails breaks free of its mooring. …[T]he stage is set for the final battle." Nick says that something eventually happens to force us to face our problems that we have to hit rock bottom before a solution appears. This process can take years. For his patient, Arlene, it was a matter of months before her impatience and demand for perfection smacked her in the face. This final battle is represented in Norse mythology by the march from the parched lands of the South of Surt, wielding his bright, shining sunsword. Freyr, the protector and nurturer of the earth, who brings rain and gentle sunshine, meets him and is destroyed by the heat of his fiery sword. Once, Freyr had a powerful sword that could fight battles by itself, but he lost this sword when he fell obsessively in love with the beautiful giantess Gerd. His lovesickness keeps him from eating or sleeping and he loses the confidence that he would need to declare his love to Gerd. He sends Skirmir to carry his message of love to her, but in payment, Skirmir takes his sword, leaving him defenseless. For Nick, this represents our state of mind just prior to the breakthrough. He writes that the Freyr within us nurtures Loki's three children – guilt, fear, and obsessive worry. He writes that we must stop nurturing these three before they can die. I would disagree with Nick here, believing that our inner characters never die; we just learn how better to contain them. Instead of replacing unhealthy stories with new healthy stories, we nurture the desired stories, feeding them and allowing them to grow stronger, eventually towering over them instead of killing them. The metaphor of killing the dysfunctional parts of what is within us disturbs me.

The part of Arlene they are trying to kill is the perfectionist, the one who can never do or care enough. Something uncontrollable or uncontainable always breaks through. He returns to the story of the Feathered Serpent as a therapeutic counter-story for her distress about a situation with her daughter (Jessi) that she couldn't control. He tells Arlene, "'Close your eyes and relax as you stand as the Feathered Serpent. Let a mellowness flow through you, a feeling of strength, the mellow strength children need to feel in parents to feel confident and secure. It seems that Jessi has found that confident strength from somewhere. To comfort April and May [her other two children] and to try to comfort you by letting you know she can take care of herself in school, she has that mellow strength. Let that confident mellow strength flow through you. Let it grow.' I then was quiet, a quiet that offered Arlene time to experience the mellow strength of the spirit of caring.

"Arlene was ready to accept these suggestions. A sliver of red tape reminder on her watch showed her the negative side in her attempt to nurture and care. Being mellow, strong and confident was a positive alternative. The negative side to her nurturing was attacked and mortally wounded. Yet this death was not enough. Guilt, fear and obsessive worry still needed to die before her arguments to support her overreactive caring could die. Such overreactive or overinvolved caring can be considered an addiction to nurturing."

Nick turns next to what happens after the death of Freyr, which importantly allows the three monster children of Loki to be faced. Garmr, a monster guardian hound, who has been chained to the gates of Hel's realm, breaks free to confront Tyr, the bravest of the warrior guards, who sacrificed his hand to chain the monster wolf. Now Tyr sacrifices his life to kill Garmr. With their death, the move toward independence can begin. This leads Surt to march from the desert lands of the South toward the final battle. He carries his shining sun-sword. Freyr, the protector and nurturer of the earth, who provides it with rain and gentle sunshine is killed by the fiery sword. Nick sees Fryer and Surt as opposites or members of a duality. He says that both are important and the extremes of either can be unhealthy. Though Freyr nurtures humans by governing the fertility of the crops and the animals and also promotes peace, he can lose himself in his passions. Nick compares this to Arlene's addiction to nurturing, to trying too hard. He says that the Freyr within us nurtures the three children of Loki: guilt, fear and obsessive worry.

Next. Thor, the greatest of all warriors, faces the most fearsome of all beasts, Jormungand, the sea serpent. Thor is fearless and thinks he cannot be defeated. Jormungand, however, is more than he anticipates. Though he kills Jormungand, the sea serpent's poison touches his skin, and he dies also. Again, foolish hubris kills. Thor foolishly underestimates Jormungand's strength. Nick uses this as mirroring the way in which his clients underestimate the strength of their obsession or addiction, which he says, always demands respect. Like the arrogant, strutting Thor, that part of ourselves has no purpose and needs to die. Then, he says, we can move toward regaining our innocence.

Odin's death follows the death of Thor. Odin once again meets Fenrir, the wolf who has not stopped growing. Fenrir overcomes Odin, who dies in the belly of the wolf. Then Vidar, one of Odin's sons tears apart the wolf to avenge his father's death. Odin was aware of the prophecy that Fenrir would harm the gods, and it has come true. Despite Odin's awareness, he could not avoid fate. Even our most logical acts can be foolish. Nick writes that his clients' obsessions are based upon beliefs that we think are true and wise, but that these obsessions live only through our belief in them. They generally have no basis in reality but take on a growing life of their own thanks to our faith in them. Odin represents our belief that we are wise, however unaware we are of this belief. When we discover that the belief behind our obsession has no basis in reality, our newer, younger strength, represented by Vidar, kills the obsession.

The final battle in this epic is that of Heimdall, the guardian of the gods, fights Loki, the trickster and tormentor of the gods. Heimdall justifies and protects the gods, while Loki mocks and scolds them. After a struggle, they also kill each other. Nick links the death of Heimdall to the death of our final justification, the excuse we give for our behavior that demands the scolding by Loki. After this final battle, only the children of the gods survive, including Modi and Magni, the sons of Thor; and Vidar, Vali, and Hod, the sons of Odin. The gentle and sensitive Baldr is reborn. Magni and Modi have exceptional strength. Nick likens this to the completion of the rebirth of strength and innocence, following the removal of all the intimidating monsters. Following their final battle, his clients now live in a new world of strength and innocence. They have a fresh start in managing the stress of their lives without their obsessions and addictions. Therapy has come to an end.

Nick finishes with a very helpful Appendix so that we can keep track of the Norse names and places.

I enjoyed the saga of the Norse gods and appreciated how Nick applied this story to the process of psychotherapy with three clients. However, I wasn't clear the degree to which Nick shared this story with his clients, which would be interesting to know.[1] My own sense of psychotherapy is not so orderly as Nick's. People in my world do not predictably pass through the stages outlined by the saga of the Norse. This is in no way a criticism of Nick. People have different visions of the world, and I feel that I gained enormously from reading Nick's vision and seeing how he does psychotherapy, even if I wouldn't approach it exactly the same. This is the beauty of diversity and the many viewpoints from which we can see the world. This is an excellent book and opportunity for learning a particular style of psychotherapy which is eclectic, drawing upon trance-inducing techniques, hypnosis, the narrative arts, and psychodynamic techniques. I recommend it strongly.

LEWIS MEHL-MADRONA, MD, PhD

A Native American Psychiatrist, Founder of the Coyote Institute for Studies of Change and Transformation, Orono, Maine, and author of numerous books including *Healing the Mind Through the Power of Story: The Promise of Narrative Psychiatry* and his Coyote series: *Coyote Medicine, Coyote Healing, and Coyote Wisdom.* He is a Faculty Physician in Family Medicine Residency at the Eastern Maine Medical Center in Bangor, Maine, Associate Professor in Family Medicine at the University of New England College of Osteopathic Medicine, and a Clinical Assistant Professor of Psychiatry at the University of Vermont College of Medicine.

PART ONE

THE NATURE OF THERAPY

The seven implicit principles guiding traditional healers of all cultures:

- The healing power of spending time with patients, providing them with complete and undivided attention

- The healing power of relationships and the intent of all persons involved to transform illness

- The power of the mind to transform the physical body, encompassing the self-healing response, and the power of the inner healer who lives within us all

- The awareness that healing a major illness requires profound life change—a transformation of one's relationships to all aspects of life

- The healing power of spirit and the spiritual dimension in our lives, including the role of ritual and ceremony in catalyzing change, in connecting us to nonphysical energies, in giving us a view of ourselves as capable of more than we had previously thought, and by enfolding us in the comfort of the Divine.

- The role of family and community in healing physical conditions and in serving as the unit for study for healing, instead of the individual, as mainstream medicine believes

- The shamanic concepts of taking ourselves apart and reassembling the pieces, coupled with a story-based approach; life is a story that we weave, and healing requires an understanding of the story, the plot, and the characters and how to change them

LEWIS MEHL-MADRONA, MD, PhD

Coyote Healing: Miracles in Native Medicine (2003), 8–9.

CHAPTER 1

THE TOOLS OF PSYCHOTHERAPY

LISTENING TO THE SPIRITS

Of the tools of psychotherapy, one is ecstatic trance, trance used by the shamans of the hunter and gatherer cultures, both ancient and contemporary. Another tool is contemporary clinical hypnosis. Both are powerful tools that can be a part of the narrative psychotherapeutic process and for journeying into the unconscious mind.

From earliest times people lived primarily in a dream-trance state, a state of existence that eventually became the domain of the shamanic healer and seer of the clan. Ecstatic trance gave the shamans the power of extrasensory communication to commune with the spirits of the ancestors, the spirits of the land and with members of their village who at the time may be away from the village. This power was and is a major tool in the repertoire of a shaman's ways to heal. This ability that allows shamans to go beyond their five senses was lost as we evolved into the rational era that denied the existence or importance of this sixth sense. Only now, as we enter the fifth era, the era of time-free transparency, are we rediscovering this ability to go beyond our five senses of sight, sound, smell, taste and touch by suppressing them while in a state of trance, thus allowing us to again commune with the spirits of our unconscious as well as our ancestors and of the Earth.

There is considerable scientific evidence for the existence of this universal consciousness that is beyond our individual and personal conscious that is believed to exist only within one's body or brain. This impressive body of evidence has been reviewed in my previous books and comes from the current research in quantum physics on entanglement and nonlocal coherence, and from such researchers as Rupert Sheldrake (1995), Ervin Laszlo (2009), Gregg Braden (2007), and Dean Radin (2006). This research opens the door to the power of dreams, hypnosis, and shamanic or ecstatic trance.

The five eras of consciousness as described by Jean Gebser (1985) can help us understand the place of this power to access the universal mind in the history of human consciousness. These five eras will be elaborated upon further on in this chapter, but briefly they are the archaic, magical, mythical, and rational eras, and the era of time-free transparency into which we are now evolving. Both the archaic and magical eras were eras of seeing beyond our five senses through dreaming and ecstatic trance, the archaic era beginning from 160,000 to 200,000 years ago.

The era that followed these two eras, the mythical era of consciousness, began at about the time of the beginning of recorded history and has offered us many stories or narratives to explain the creation of the Earth and life on Earth. One of these narratives is the Nordic narrative of the three children of Loki. These narratives came from the collective dreams of our ancestors of that era, and some, like this narrative of Loki's Children, offer us direction in healing to overcome emotional and behavioral problems that frequently develop in one's life. Loki's Children will provide us with a map of the course of psychotherapy for the following chapters.

The core of this book is how to regain the power of listening to the spirits, a power that was valued by our ancient ancestors, whether through our dreams or the trance experiences of hypnosis or ecstatic trance. Listening to the spirits of our unconscious mind and the universal mind that comes from beyond brings us the power for healing and personal growth. Prayer has been suggested as a way of listening to god or to the spirits, but prayer is us jabbering and not listening. I was taught that there are five features of prayer, praise of god, thanksgiving, seeking forgiveness, petitioning or requesting something from god, and intersession or praying for others. None of these features are for taking the time to listen. Only when I began to value my dreams and trance experiences did I realize the importance of these ways of listening. Once the process of healing is in full swing through listening to the spirits of our unconscious mind, we find ourselves going beyond to listening to the universal mind, showing us the avenues for personal growth and self-actualization.

Another major tool in this therapeutic process is the stories or narratives told by the client and the counter-narratives or healing stores told by the therapist. The narratives of greatest depth or importance are the stories that arise while in the state of trance, whether in dreaming, hypnotic trance or ecstatic trance. A major contributor to the field of narrative therapy is Lewis Mehl-Madrona, MD, PhD. (2003), a native-American psychiatrist and storyteller.

NARRATIVE THERAPY

Stories are the core of psychotherapy. The stories of the trials and suffering told by the person who comes for therapy define the purpose of and give direction to the therapy session. These stories likely have embedded within them misconceptions and distortions about life that prevent the person from rising above his or her suffering. The counter-stories told by the therapist are told to give the client new direction to overcome the misconceptions and experienced suffering.

These stories told by the client and the therapist are the narratives and counter-narratives that provide the basis for narrative therapy. Such narratives have been used since ancient times to provide direction in living a healthy life.

There are different levels of stories. The narratives that come from dreams and trance, whether hypnotic or ecstatic, come from a deeper source within the person, the unconscious mind, and likely uncover deeper beliefs that are not at first remembered but repressed because of their painful nature, learned preverbally thus never put in words, or otherwise forgotten. The stories that arise from the unconscious are a more direct source for uncovering the misconceptions and distortions of the consciously held stories the client initially tells in therapy, and they can give new directions for therapy. The characters and images that come from these dream and trance experiences I call spirits or guiding spirits that can lead the client to the changes that are needed to rise above the suffering.

THE COUNTER-NARRATIVE

The counter-narratives are generally stories that have imbedded within them messages or suggestions for change, change that leads to a healthier way of thinking or behaving. When the counter-narratives are told in a hypnotic manner they register within the client at the deeper unconscious level. It is this hypnotic trance-inducing manner of storytelling that is one major theme of this book, the telling of stories that will reside within the person for years.

Hypnotically, the counter-narratives used may be newly created by the therapist like those used in traditional narrative therapy, but often they may be much briefer, just subtle hypnotic suggestions, suggestions that can lead clients to rewriting their own stories with the needed healthy changes. These counter-narratives may be in the form of the therapist hypnotically retelling the client's own narrative but with a subtle or brief suggestion. For example, the counter-narrative may be the retelling of the client's initial narrative but with an emphasis on the feelings or affect of the client's narrative. Then the suggestion is made for the client to carry these feelings back through time to an early incident of when he or she first experienced the same feelings. The suggestion then may be made, "Let your adult-self go back and be with your younger self, and with the wisdom of your adult-self, help your younger self explore what your younger self needed." Sometimes I do create a new story that offers suggestions for change, but my focus of attention is generally more on the client's own story and the details of the story that I recognize as needing to change. Whether in the form of a newly created story or retelling the client's own narrative with an imbedded hypnotic suggestion, the counter-narrative is important in the process and becomes a more lasting part of the person's unconscious way of thinking.

The lasting nature of the counter-narrative was described by one of my teachers of hypnosis, Kay Thompson, DDS, of the University of Pittsburgh's dental school and the first woman president of the American Society of Clinical Hypnosis. As she reported of Milton Erickson, the father of American hypnosis, "He taught by parable, but often it would be years before the story would be recognized for the profound lesson it contained, … Milton knew that the individual does not need to defend against story, that he can listen to them as a child would, wondering and curious…"[1] These narratives and the trance they induce are central in the process of psychotherapy.

INDUCING TRANCE

There are ways of formal trance induction that may be used when the person in therapy requests or expects the use of hypnosis, but trance is easily and commonly induced in most all therapy sessions without a formal induction. The way a therapist speaks can be trance inducing.

This is evident when a fifty-minute therapy session may seem like much less than fifty minutes to the client. This time distortion is a sign that the person was in trance.

What is this therapeutic way of speaking? The therapist's words are trance inducing when they are selected such that the client can respond to them consistently with, "Yes, that's right," whether or not the response is spoken aloud. The words of the therapist need to accurately reflect the experience of the client, the feelings accompanying these experiences, or other observed behaviors of the client. This is referred to as the *yes-set*,[2] the mental set of consistently thinking "yes, that's right." In addition to the *yes-set* the therapist needs to speak these words slowly, a rate matching the client's rate of breathing, thus again *joining* the somatic experience of the client. This way of speaking does not require a formal trance-induction procedure yet easily leads the person into trance. As this way of speaking becomes a habit to the therapist, all therapy sessions occur with the client in a state of trance.

This way of speaking becomes most obvious when a more formal trance induction is used. A formal trance induction may begin with such words as, "Sit back and relax. As you sit, relaxing in your chair, feel the warmth between your back and the back of the chair," or "As you sit there with your legs crossed, feel the warmth between the back of your right leg resting on the knee of your left leg, feel the roughness of the material of your jeans as it passes tightly over your right knee. As you breathe feel your chest rising and falling and feel the slight movement of your shirt against your chest." As the client focuses attention on these truisms, on these sensory or somatic experiences, relaxation and trance is induced. As the session progresses, elements of the client's initial narrative can be repeated along with their associated feelings in this same trance-inducing manner.

DOES EVERYONE GO INTO TRANCE?

Generally, most everyone will go into a state of trance, for some people into a deeper trance than for others. Research has indicated that a person who is learning disabled is less likely to go into trance. It is my belief that people who tend to be anxious or hyper, or who are driven for a quick solution to their problem may not go into as deep of a hypnotic trance as others, but the depth of trance is not necessarily of greatest importance. With practice and experience even these more anxious individuals will soon find themselves going into a deeper trance.

How do I tell their depth of trance? Some clue such as the slowing down of a person's breathing rate, or the obvious relaxation of muscles indicate a deepening trance, but while in trance I quickly find myself also in trance and at a depth equal to that of the client. In this way I experience and feel what they are experiencing and their depth of trance. Very early in the therapy session I find my breathing rate changes to match the rate of the client's, which in turn directs the pace of my spoken words.

At times I can feel a client's resistance to trance. Clients sometimes resist trance because they fear what they might have to face while in trance, maybe something they may not want to reveal or some painful memory. Again, as such resistance and fear arise, the *yes-set* is used by reflecting to the client this resistance or fear.

ECSTATIC OR SHAMANIC TRANCE

I first started using hypnosis in the middle 1970s. Only in 2007 was I first introduced to ecstatic trance. These two forms of trance produce similar experiences but are induced in different ways. The *yes-set* is effective with both, but with hypnosis, words are spoken softly, following the rate of the person's breathing. Ecstatic trance is induced with many less words and with rapid stimulation to the person's nervous system by the beating of a drum or the shaking of a rattle at about 210 beats per minute. This rapid beat distracts clients from their thoughts and resistance. For the anxious or hyper person, the rapid stimulation to the nervous system is closer to and joins the person's more rapid thoughts or heart rate, thus the beat becomes more one with the person. *Joining* a person's somatic experience in this way is another example of the *yes-set* and is trance inducing.

I first learned about the power of ecstatic trance by reading the books by the anthropologist Felicitas Goodman and her student Belinda Gore, a clinical psychologist. As I explored the use of ecstatic trance, I contacted Belinda, and she was open to giving me considerable direction in my use of this form of trance. She soon convinced me to take her workshops at the Cuyamungue Institute to become a certified instructor of ecstatic trance. The story of Felicitas Goodman and her study of ecstatic trance are inspiring.

Felicitas Goodman was born in Hungary and educated in Germany. She was fluent in approximately twenty languages, so when she came to the United States after the Second World War she initially worked as a scientific translator. In 1965, at the age of fifty-one, she decided to return to academia to pursue a graduate degree in cultural anthropology at Ohio State University. There she had met Dr. Erika Bourguignon, a professor of anthropology who was researching religious trance states in small primitive societies. Bourguignon's research caught Goodman's interest and led her to pursue religious and ecstatic trance for her doctoral dissertation. The subjects of her research were members of several Apostolic Churches of the Spanish-speaking and Mayan-speaking churches of Mexico. She sought to determine the necessary conditions that led the members of these churches to be possessed by the Holy Spirit such that they spoke in tongues. She concluded that there are five such conditions:

- Participants need a private physical space separate from their activities of everyday life.
- They need to come to that space with the expectation of a non-ordinary state of consciousness.
- They need to believe that the experience is not crazy, but normal, enjoyable and pleasurable.
- Meditative techniques need to be offered to help each participant quiet their mind, such as prayer or the technique of counting one's breaths.
- Rhythmic stimulation of the nervous system is required, such as that provided by the clapping of hands, the shaking of a rattle, or the beat of a drum.[3]

From these necessary conditions Goodman developed a ritual to induce trance that includes smudging as an act of cleansing and calling the spirits from each direction, acts to define the sacred space. But first, through discussion and answering questions concerning ecstatic trance, the participants learn what to expect in trance. To meet the condition of a meditative technique to quiet the mind she had the participants pay attention to their breathing for five minutes. These acts set the stage for the ecstatic trance induction which then occurs by stimulating the nervous system rhythmically with the beating of a drum or shaking of a rattle at the rate of approximately 210 beats per minute for 15 minutes. She then used this ritual with her students at Dennison University and found that though trance was induced, the trance experiences lacked direction.

Sometime later she read an article by a Canadian psychologist V. F. Emerson (1972) that examined the effect of different body postures on the trance experiences. This article led her to search the works of primitive art found in books and museums for postures that she believed were used by both ancient and contemporary shamans of hunting and gathering cultures. She identified approximately fifty such postures that she had her students sit, stand or lay in while in trance and found that the postures gave direction to the trance experience. Some postures are found to draw a healing and strengthening energy into the person's body, while others are for divination, i.e. answering questions or looking into the future. Others are for journeying into the underworld, while some are for journeying in this world, possibly back through time or into the future, and some for journeying into the upperworld. Then there are postures that provide initiation or death-rebirth experiences and some are for metamorphosis or shape-shifting.[4]

THE ECSTATIC POSTURES

In this book I address the challenge of how to bring these five necessary conditions of ecstatic trance and the use of different body postures into the process of psychotherapy so as to meet the expectations of the client of traditional psychotherapy. Of the postures described in the books by Goodman and by Belinda Gore (1995 & 2009), I selected five, postures that are comfortable to use and clearly express what needs to happen in the therapy session at the moment. The first posture of standing with hands on the abdomen Goodman first found among the

Figure 1.1

Figure 1.2

Indians of the Northwest Coast of America. She called it the Bear Spirit Posture, and it is used to relax, and bring a sense of healing strength into one's body when breathing from one's diaphragm.

The second posture used is a divination posture to find an answer to a question, the Lady of Cholula Posture from a figurine she found from Cholula, Mexico. The lady is sitting at the edge of her chair, grasping her knees, expressing a sense of alert waiting for the answer.

The third posture is for journeying into the underworld of your unconscious mind. Laying on one's back with the back of the left hand resting over the eyes is the Jivaro Underworld Posture, found in a book on shamanism, a posture used by the Jivaro of the Amazon basin, a posture akin to lying upon the psychoanalyst's couch.

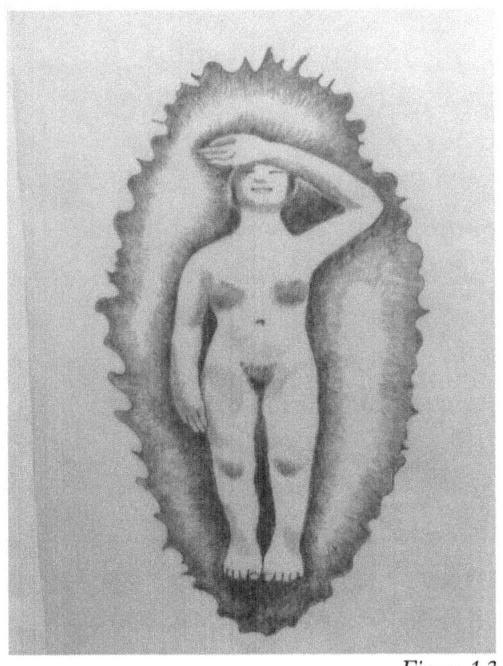

Figure 1.3

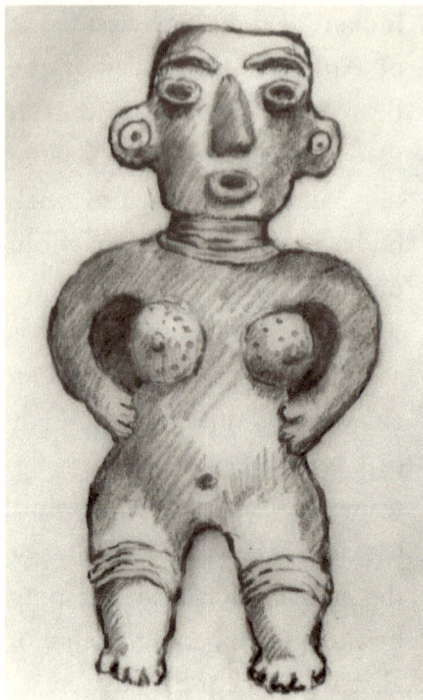

Figure 1.4

The fourth posture is the Feathered Serpent Posture that provides a death-rebirth experience, i.e. it offers the feeling of determination to let an unhealthy part of the client die along with the birth of a newer healthy way of thinking. The figurine of this posture was found in Mexico and is now in the Los Angeles County Museum.

The fifth posture, The Olmec Prince Metamorphosis Posture is for shape shifting, allowing you to become and experience the life of a spirit guide, thus bringing you clearer messages from your guide. While sitting cross-legged in this posture from Mexico with the knuckles of the hands resting on the floor in front of you, you may feel as if your arms are the forelegs of a four-legged animal, though in this posture I have become a snake, a bird and even a tree. In my research of medicinal herbs, of seeking the herbs as spirit guides, I use this posture but with fingers splayed as if they were roots of the plant.

Figure 1.5

I initially do not tell clients the story of these postures, but after experiencing their strength in the healing process, telling them this story likely opens them to the broader world view, a world of greater diversity that exists around them. Initially the clients are very self-centered in dwelling upon their problems, but as they begin to find resolution, they become more open to appreciate a world of greater diversity that the stories of the postures offer them.

INCORPORATING THE ECSTATIC POSTURES IN ANALYTIC HYPNOTHERAPY

The school of hypnosis that I use most is analytic hypnotherapy. There are five steps in the manner in which I use the analytic hypnotherapy process, and the intent of each of the four postures is reflected in these steps:

- First, soon after listening to the client's initial narrative I teach a relaxation and ego-strengthening exercise to give the client the necessary ego-strength to face the potential painful issues in therapy that may be uncovered. This exercise is to be practiced at home and is used in each session of therapy to help lead the client into a state of trance. This relaxation and ego-strengthening exercise is facilitated by the Bear Spirit Posture of standing with hands on your abdomen such that you can feel your stomach rise and fall with each breath.

- Second, having listened to the client's initial narrative, the feeling(s) or affect(s) elicited by the problem the client brings to therapy needs to be identified. Identifying these feelings or affects is facilitated with the use of the Lady of Cholula Divination Posture.

- Third, hypnotic age regression is used to carry the feeling(s) or affect(s) hypnotically back through time to identify the source of the problem, a procedure referred to as the affect bridge.[5] Journeying into the unconscious mind to identify the source of the problem is facilitated by laying in the Jivaro Underworld Posture.

- Fourth, while journeying in the underworld the search begins for hypnotic counter-suggestions that can lead the client to the healthy and healing ways to deal with the source of the problem. Using the Jivaro Underworld Posture helps facilitate finding the appropriate counter-narrative with the use of such suggestions as "Let the wisdom of your adult-self go back and be with your younger self and help your younger self find the words that are needed to overcome the problem." As we shall see in the following case studies, this can be stated in many different ways and depends upon first identifying the source of the problem.

- Fifth, the healthy and healing new ways in thinking are hypnotically incorporated within the client with the help of the death-rebirth Feathered Serpent Posture. This step involves the hypnotic suggestion of the death of the unhealthy way of thinking and the birth of the new.

Edgar Barnett, in describing the process of analytic therapy, did not use the ecstatic postures, nor did he use drumming to assist in inducing trance, but besides using the postures I find that the use of drumming for those who have some difficulty in relaxing into a state of trance increases the effectiveness of the therapeutic process. Also, Barnett generally uses only the first three steps of this process to identify the source of the problem and then uses the suggestion, "Let your adult-self go back and help your younger self understand," thus relying on the cathartic nature of reliving the experience to provide the healing. I have added to this process the final two steps of identifying what was needed to avoid the problem caused by the source experience and to offer the suggestion of the death of the old way of thinking and the birth of the new.

HYPNOSIS VS. ECSTATIC TRANCE

Carlos Castaneda writes of two ways to pursue extrasensory knowledge: *dreaming* and *stalking*. These two ways of pursuit reflect the distinction between hypnosis and ecstatic trance. As *stalkers,* the practitioners of ecstatic trance face the pursuit of this knowledge with the attitude that nothing is important yet act as if it is important, an attitude that Castaneda calls *controlled folly.*[6] *Controlled folly* provides a person with a distraction from their busy mind to carry them beyond their conscious world and into the world of extrasensory knowledge, knowledge that comes from beyond the five senses. By choosing an act that the *stalker* knows is unimportant yet *doing* it as if it is important, allows the *stalker* to let go of rational thinking in order to quiet the mind. Choosing to use rapid stimulation to the nervous system with drumming or rattling as an act of *controlled folly* provides the *stalker* with this needed distraction.

As opposed to stalking, the practitioners of dreaming and hypnotic trance pursue this knowledge by *not doing*, i.e. they are more able to intentionally let go of their rational thinking to quiet the mind. Both *dreaming* and *stalking* are ways of pursuing knowledge, knowledge that comes from the unconscious mind or from the world beyond. For both *dreamers* and *stalkers* "Once they lose their rational side, they are peerless *dreamers* and *stalkers*, since they no longer have any rational ballast to hold them back."[7] This knowledge is presented in the form of the stories or narratives that arise from one's unconscious or from beyond, from the spirit world of the universal mind, a world of the spirits that I will soon describe.

While in hypnotic trance the heart rate slows, blood pressure drops, and the body responds with relaxation, i.e. the response is of the parasympathetic nervous system. In ecstatic trance, though the blood pressure drops, the pulse rate increases, a characteristic of the sympathetic nervous system. With the rapid heartbeat yet with the drop in blood pressure, ecstatic trance is sometimes recognized as a characteristic of a near-death experience.[8]

Whether with dreaming, hypnotic trance or ecstatic trance, paying attention to these altered states of consciousness, valuing these states and appreciating the spirits that these states bring us, the spirits will again begin to come alive and begin to show themselves as they did for our ancient ancestors.

FROM THE UNCONSCIOUS AND FROM BEYOND

As a psychologist I initially learned that the stories that arise in hypnotic trance come from the unconscious mind, and as such, are "deeper," more relevant and honest to a person's true or hidden feelings than the narratives initially told in a therapy session from one's conscious awareness. Occasionally a person tells of a "past life" experience that I would treat as if it was metaphorically expressing an unconscious issue. Though there are practitioners of hypnosis who believe in past lives and consider hypnotic trance as a way to accessing past life experiences, I did not put much credence in the reality of a past life. But with time things happened to opened my mind to the possibility that this knowledge did come from past lives, from the ancestors, or from the spirits of the Earth. This belief developed from my reading of current concepts in modern physics, of nonlocal coherence, the relativity of time and causality, and of entanglement. Also, the explanations of Rupert Sheldrake (1995) and Ervin Laszlo (2009) of a world beyond the self made considerable sense to me.

Sheldrake believes that just as the universe is held together by gravitational fields and the atom by an electromagnetic field, our cells, being composed of atoms, are held together by what he calls morphic fields. Each cell, each organ, each person or animal as a whole, and all within a species are held together by morphic fields, fields that contain all information from the beginning of time. Ervin Laszlo calls these fields Akashic fields, holographic fields of information that are available to us through the sensory receptors of the 10^{18} microtubules of the cytoskeletal structure of the brain and accessed when in a state of trance. These fields are called the divine matrix by Gregg Braden (2007), the collective consciousness by Karl Jung (Campbell, 1971), and world of the spirits by our ancient ancestors. I have generally referred to this source of information as the universal mind, a source of information that comes from beyond the unconscious, information that comes from the world of the spirits. Review of this research can be found in my previous books, research that I find very exciting and convincing.

Robert Waggoner, in his book on lucid dreaming tells the story that while within a lucid dream he has asked the question of the dream, "What is behind the dream or where does the dream come from?" What he has received as an answer from the dream is seeing a blue light,[9] a blue light that I consider coming from an energy field, the divine or holographic matrix, or from the universal mind.

Our expectation as we enter a state of trance may limit where it takes us. If we believe that what comes to us in trance comes only from the unconscious, then it is from the unconscious, but if we believe that there is a spirit world beyond then we begin to experience and learn from the spirits, the spirits of our ancestors and the spirits of the Earth. With the massive amount of information available to us from the beginning of time, what we experience is filtered by our expectations and the information we pursue at the moment. One of my personal expectations has restricted my experiences to what we need to do to survive the global climate crisis and live sustainably on our one and only Earth.

THE SPIRIT WORLD

To this point I have described the nature and tools of therapy, but where does this therapy take us? One place is to a new place of understanding of the world within and around us, the world of the spirits. In this therapy we talk of the spirit guides brought to us by our dreams and trance experiences. What is this spirit world? It seems that many people who are caught up in the rational world do not relate to what we are doing in using ecstatic trance for visiting the world of the spirits. I would like to offer a bridge from the world of rationality to the beauty and power of the world beyond, the world of spirits. The bridge I suggest is to recognize that our nighttime dreams are from our unconscious mind and/or of this spirit world, from a world beyond our five senses. These dream experiences are something that we all experience. The dream world is normal and can be powerful in helping us gain a deeper understanding of our lives and the world around us, i.e. if we open ourselves to them. The characters and elements of our dreams are the spirits or spirit guides, spirits that most all of us have experienced. These characters and elements of our dreams are extrasensory, i.e. they come to us from beyond our five senses.

Similarly, these extrasensory experiences that arise in both hypnotic and ecstatic trance are of the unconscious mind and/or the spirit world of the universal mind. Again, I generally refer to the characters and elements of these experiences as spirit guides. These experiences lead us to new information about ourselves and the world around us.

I have offered ecstatic trance workshops at five of the conferences of the International Association for the Study of Dreams and have found that the hundred-plus participants of these groups have quickly resonated with their ecstatic trance experiences. There is a clear connection between dreaming and ecstatic trance. They both take us into our unconscious mind or into this world of the spirits, the spirit world that was so alive to our ancient ancestors of the archaic, magical and mythic eras of consciousness and can again become alive within us today.

RECONNECTING WITH OUR HUNTING AND GATHERING ANCESTORS

What are the archaic, magical and mythic eras of consciousness? From the writing of Jean Gebser (1985), we are currently moving into a fifth era of consciousness, the era of time-free transparency, or in my words, the New Age. The first era, the archaic era, was the era of the hunter and gatherer that began around 160,000 to 200,000 years ago, of a people who lived in a dreamlike state of consciousness. Sometime more recently within these 160,000 to 200,000 years the human consciousness mutated into what Gebser calls the magical age of consciousness, an age when the hunter-gatherers found ways to cope with life and the environment through the magic found in listening to the spirits while being one with the Earth, listening primarily through the community shaman while in trance. This was the "time when our ancestors moved with the animals and sang with the wild symphony of the natural world—the swoop of a hawk, the roar of a waterfall, the whisper of evening breezes, the kiss of moonlight. We lived *in* the world, responded to its *felt* and subtle messages, understood its deeper meanings. We not only communed with nature, we were in open communication with all its great variety of sounds and rhythms. In short, we understood and spoke the *language* of nature."[10]

During these first two eras the spirits were very much alive, first within their dreamlike state of life and then when they began to experience and value the oneness of all life and all that is of the Earth. Humans did not see themselves as superior to other life. They saw other life as being their ancestors and, as such, they were part of and continually learned from this life. They called upon the spirits of their ancestors to show them how to live, often calling upon their earliest ancestors of different life forms or species, the animals they lived with and knew well. The spirits came to them through their dreams and trance states, trance often induced by their drumming and dancing.

Then came that which Gebser called the mythic era, the era when answers to the questions of life were provided through mythic stories. This era began around 10,000 years ago, the beginning of recorded history, the beginning of the era of agriculture and domestication of animals. These stories that explained the phenomena of life and the Earth again came from the dreams and trance experiences of these people of the time. As these dreams and experiences were shared and retold by others of the time, they developed to a level of coherency of the creation and other mythic stories that we listen to even today. These mythic stories were designated as archetypal by Karl Jung and arose in the collective unconscious or the universal mind of the world of the spirits. The narrative of Loki's Children is one of these myths from the mythic era of consciousness that well describes the process of healing, of dealing with the fears, guilt and obsessions that are found in the dynamics of many emotional problems. This story that arose from the universal mind can be considered of very deep relevance in the process of healing and provides the outline for the case studies presented in this book. During these eras, spirits were very much alive, valued and meaningful to the people of the time, spirits that came from their dreams and other trance states of consciousness and eventually from the myths that were told and retold.

Then came the fourth era of consciousness, the rational era, an era that considered anything not perceived through the five senses, the senses of sight, hearing, smell, taste and touch, as superstitious and untrue. Experiences of dreams and other altered states of consciousness were given a thumbs-down and rejected. We lost the magical power provided us through communing with the spirits. With this loss we have found ourselves believing that we are superior to all other life of Earth. We believed that we have dominion over the Earth and can use it out of greed and for profit without consideration for the rest of life on Earth. This loss has brought us to the edge of destroying our own species and much of the Earth. We sometimes talk of a sixth sense, a sense of intuition, intuition that is brought to us by the spirits, but that, too, has been ignored. Gebser believes that this rational era began approximately 2,500 years ago and peaked at about the time of Leonardo da Vinci, but it is now waning as we begin a journey of mutation beyond the three- dimensional world of DaVinci into the four-dimensional era of time-free transparency.

Gebser wrote his book, *The Ever-Present Origin,* in 1949, and since then it has become increasingly clear that this journey into the new age of time-free transparency is happening. As classical physics wanes in the face of modern or quantum physics, a state of the science that even Einstein called *spooky,* we recognize that things do not happen in the mechanical and linear ways of classical physics. New discoveries are rapidly developing. One such scientific development is the theory of non-local coherence, that is when an atomic particle is split something that happens to one part of the split particle that exists in one particular location and time also instantaneously happens to the other portion of the particle that now exists at some other distant location in fourth dimensional time. Also, another new discovery is that when an atomic particle splits, the split particle sometimes goes backwards in time. This adds to and expands the meaning of the relativity of time. We do not exist only at one point in time, i.e. the now, but we can journey freely into the past and the future as experienced in our dreams and trance experiences as was experienced by our hunter-gatherer ancestors. Another new discovery is that the observer of some subatomic phenomena can have an effect or influence the outcome of the observation, i.e. entanglement. Such discoveries of which there have been many are indeed spooky and open the door to a new era of consciousness, the era of time-free transparency, the new age. As we move into this new age these beliefs and ideas are becoming more and more reputable.

With this new knowledge, as we regain the power of the spirits in our newfound understanding of these earlier eras of consciousness, as we move into the New Age, we recognize a new level of maturity, a spiritual maturity of again being one with the Earth.

BRINGING CLIENTS IN THERAPY TO NEW HEIGHTS FOR THE NEW AGE

The goal of psychotherapy and that sought by insurance companies has been to simply relieve clients of their emotional pain and torment, pain and torment experienced by them and the people surrounding them, a goal that leads them to a state of acceptability in their narrow community and not necessarily in a world beyond them that is of much greater diversity. For us to survive into this coming New Age this limited breadth in the goal of therapy is not sufficient and needs to include appreciation for the world of greater diversity beyond the narrowness of their community. The self-actualized person, or in the words of David Korten,[11] the cultural and spiritual creative, is one who can function as an elder to all those around him, as did the elders of the communities of our ancestors in teaching those younger people of the community to live in harmony with the Earth and all life of Earth. Yet, functioning as an elder now in our much more diverse and complex world is a much bigger challenge than for the elders of the world of our ancestors. This new image reflects the filter I have been experiencing in what has been arising in my ecstatic experiences, experiences that search for the ways to overcome the threat of climate crisis and to live in harmony and sustainability with the Earth and all life of the Earth. In this new age we cannot live a life such that we see ourselves superior to all other life; we need to live a life of oneness with all other life, recognizing that each species depends upon all other species, that each species has something important to offer for the sustainability of all other species in our interdependence with one another.

CHAPTER 2

THE PROCESS OF PSYCHOTHERAPY

The process of ecstatic analytic hypnotherapy is just one tool, though a major tool, in the process of psychotherapy. This tool will be used repeatedly throughout the process of psychotherapy. This chapter will begin by describing the process of analytic hypnotherapy. Then with the use of the ancient myth of Loki's Children as an outline, the process of psychotherapy to overcome these three tormenting children—fear, guilt and obsessive worry—will be described. It is these three tormenting children that torment the clients in the three case studies of this book.

ECSTATIC ANALYTIC HYPNOTHERAPY

When a person comes for therapy for the first time, the first step is for the therapist to listen to the person's story of why he or she is seeking help. This story, the first narrative, is of what is going on in the person's life, and embedded in this narrative are numerous feelings that occur as a result of what is happening. My first counter-narrative is to restate what is happening in the person's life, emphasizing the feelings that arise. For example, a woman, Maple, 34 years old, has been married for eight years and now complains that she is unhappy in her marriage. She is considering leaving Tom, her husband. She describes him as a good and hard-working person who helps around the house and in caring for their four-year-old daughter, but she feels something is missing. She is unable to pin-point what is missing, but as she continues with her story she reports that she feels lonely. Though she is unhappy she does not want to take their daughter away from her father, who loves her dearly. He is so good with her that she does not hesitate running to him when she is in need. "She more likely will run to him than to me."

I would likely reflect, "You really have no specific complaints about your husband, but for some reason you are feeling lonely." These words begin to establish the *yes-set* and set the stage for pursuing the cause. As the narrative continues, I might add, "You appreciate the way he helps in caring for the house and your young daughter." I might ask, "How does it make you feel when your daughter runs to him?" These feelings are central to the therapeutic process. Listening to Maple's story and reflecting the feelings would likely take the entire fifty minutes of the first session. If there is sufficient time, I would teach her a relaxation and ego strengthening exercise, explaining to her that learning to relax and to feel an internal strength is something important to learn in life and to use regularly. This relaxation and strength are also important in therapy and will be used regularly as therapy continues.

To introduce this relaxation exercise I would stand, turn on some quiet new age music, and place my hands on my abdomen, motioning for Maple to stand, and do the same thing. I then would say, "Feel you abdomen rise and fall with each breath," or if she is not breathing from her diaphragm but from her chest, I would suggest that she move her breathing down to her abdomen, explaining that this is a more natural way to breathe, and that breathing from your chest is restricted by the rigidity of your ribs, thus adding to the feeling of anxiety. We then would practice this breathing for a few minutes depending upon the availability of time, and I would occasionally speak softly and at the rate of her breathing, "As you inhale feel a sense of relaxation enter your abdomen and as you exhale let the relaxation spread throughout your body." At the end of the session I would give her a CD of the new age music and suggest that she practice this daily. The new age music on the CD lasts for 15 minutes, and by giving her a copy increases the chances that she will use it. If the time does not allow for this relaxation exercise during the first session I would teach this exercise during the second session.

During the second session, again I would first listen to Maple's narrative of the week and her experience in practicing the relaxation exercise. If I saw her relax deeply in last week's relaxation exercise and she reports that she was able to effectively relax during the week, I would continue using the new age music as the background music, but if I sensed that she has difficulty relaxing, I would switch to a CD of rapid but quiet drumming.

As the session progressed, we would focus our conversation on her feelings of unhappiness and loneness. Soon in this session or the next, after the relaxation exercise is taught, I would sit up straight at the edge of my chair, and grasp my knees while motioning for her to do the same thing. I would then ask her to describe her feelings while sitting in this manner. As we discuss these feelings, she would eventually come around to saying that she feels as if she is alertly waiting for something. I would suggest, "I will have you sit in this way as we explore why you feel lonely by having you take this feeling back through time to find where it began or times when you did not feel at all lonely, but first stand and we will spend a few minutes relaxing." After about five minutes of standing with hands on our abdomen with the soft new age music playing, I would then sit up, grasp my knees and nod for her to do the same thing. I then would begin to speak, "Carry the feeling of loneliness with you as you continue to relax. Think about and wonder about where the feeling of loneliness began or when you did not feel at all lonely. Let yourself go back through time with these thoughts and see where they carry you." I would repeat these words a few times quietly and at the pace of her breathing, soon adding, "When something about your feeling of loneliness comes to mind, you can tell me about the experience."

After a few minutes Maple begins to speak while still in trance, "When I was in school, I had a couple of girlfriends I was really close to. When one of them moved out of the area I felt quite lonely, but I had the other girlfriend, and I became even closer to her. We talked all the time about how we felt about different boys in school and about many other things."

Her deep trance narrative of a memory that she pulled from her unconscious mind seemed very relevant to her feelings of loneliness with Tom, so we will work with this experience, though I could have had her carry the feeling of loneliness further back in time while she was still in trance to find other examples of her feeling of loneliness. As she was still in trance I suggested, "Bring together your feeling of loneliness with your husband and your feeling of loneliness and closeness with your girlfriends. Listen to what these spirit guides have to teach you. After a few minutes I would then say, "With the wisdom and understanding of your adult-self, what can you say about this feeling of loneliness?"

Maple was ready and quick to answer, "We do not talk about our feelings, or at least Tom does not talk about his feelings."

Adding to the counter-narrative, I suggested, "You don't have any close girlfriends now with whom you can talk about your feelings." I could see her subtly nod, "Yes."

Again, Maple begins to speak, "When I was married, I stopped spending time with my girlfriends. None of them were married. My life changed. I was supposed to give my time to my husband, and I then had different interests from my girlfriends."

I added, "You have not found any new married girlfriends," a subtle suggestion that might help in filling her feelings of loneliness.

Again, she subtly nodded yes and added, "But I am supposed to give my time to my husband." It was time to end the session, so I just looked at her with a facial expression that carried the message, "Oh yeh!"

The next session Maple was ready to talk about a couple of women, neighbors who were married but were friends and did a lot together. I brought up the idea of unconscious beliefs that give direction to one's life and suggested that we take a journey through her unconscious mind to find what prevents her from having a close girlfriend. Maple seemed ready with a quick answer, but I cut her off by putting up my hand, suggesting that she wait before telling me. This time I had her lay down on the couch with the back of her left hand resting on her forehead and explained that laying down will help her in going into her unconscious mind. But again, we first stood for a few minutes with our hands on our abdomen to relax our minds. While standing I knew her mind was racing to tell me her thoughts, so I suggest specifically, "As you exhale, let the feelings of relaxation and harmony flow into your head, quieting the words that are floating around in there." Then as she lay down with the new age music playing in the background she soon began to speak, "My mother was always with Dad whenever he was around. She had no girlfriends, and I know she believed that all her time should be with her husband. "I don't remember her ever saying it, but he was her life. After I was married, once one of my old girlfriends, who married and moved away, was back in town to visit her family and came over for a visit. When I told my mother about the visit, she didn't say anything but had a strange look on her face, maybe of disapproval."

I suggested, "The way she looked at you stuck with you, even until today. The spirit guide of your mother has an important message that you now feel as her disapproval of you having a girlfriend."

In the next session as this discussion continued, I found it an ideal time to introduce her to even another posture, a fourth posture that I use in therapy. I stood with the back of my hands on my waist, fingers pointing upwards, and my elbows sticking out to either side. As she stood in the same posture, I asked her how it felt. She first reported that it is how her mother stood when she was angry. I asked, "Do you feel angry standing that way?" She was unsure, but as the discussion continued she identified the feeling of determination, and I suggested, "Determination to give up your mother's belief that all your time should go to your husband, and rediscover the value in having a girlfriend, a new relationship that would take away your feeling of loneliness and help you value what your husband gives to the marriage. Again, after using the relaxation posture, I had her stand in this posture of determination for the fifteen minutes of the new age music. At the end Maple reported, "One of my neighbor friends invited me to go on a walk with her, and I am ready to take her up on it. The other girlfriend is away visiting family, so it will be just the two of us."

The next week Maple came to the session in a happy mood, telling of her new girlfriend, and some enjoyable time she spent with her husband.

LOKI'S CHILDREN AND THE PROCESS OF PSYCHOTHERAPY

The above story brought to therapy by Maple was quite understandable, simple to resolve, and well illustrates the process of analytic hypnotherapy along with the use of the ecstatic postures. The case studies offered in this book are considerably more complex. They have many more levels of struggle and numerous feelings with which to deal, especially the feelings of fear, guilt and obsessive worry, the three children of Loki. These feelings are a central part of the ancient

Nordic story of *Loki's Children* to overcome the torment caused by these three children. This archetypal narrative of *Loki's Children* well describes the process of therapy and is used as an outline for the three case studies presented in this book. As with most mythic narratives, this myth comes from beyond the world of our five senses and reflects the processes of the unconscious mind as well as the world of the spirits that comes from the universal mind. Each character in the myth is an important spirit guide who takes us on the healing journey of *Loki's Children.*

This ancient myth leads us to overcome the obsession-driven compulsive behaviors that have caused us so much fear, guilt and obsessive worry, leading us to experience the rebirth of our innocence. Who are Loki's children? Loki is married to Sigyn with whom he has two sons, however, he has other children with Angrboda, an evil giantess whose name means Sorrow Bringer. His affair with Angrboda produced three monster children—Jormungand, our fear; Hel, our guilt; and Fenrir, our deep obsessive and automatic thoughts that compel us to commit dysfunctional compulsive acts. We need to deal with these three children before change and emotional growth can occur. The *Loki's Children* narrative shows us how to deal with these children, the emotional pain and depression they cause, and the subsequent emotional growth that comes with their death. The story provides us with a guide for exploring these emotions as we journey deep into the unconscious mind. It furnishes a map for the process of change in the course of psychotherapy. This journey into that dark shadow part of us over which we think we have no control can be more direct and efficient with the help of this map.

Many stories of the Norse gods were lost or destroyed during the spread of Christianity into Northern Europe. The stories of these ancient gods were mainly passed down orally through the generations. Some elements of these stories have been preserved in ancient wood carvings and other artifacts of the Bronze Age. The main source of Norse mythology was recorded in Iceland, the last stronghold of this ancient culture, by Snorri Sturluson (1179–1241) in *The Prose Edda*. Another source was the writing of Saxo Grammaticus in *Gesta Danorum* (circa 1215), a sixteen-volume Latin history of the Danes. Saxo Grammaticus was an ecclesiastic whose "stories are badly told in complex, pompous Latin, and are frequently muddled, repetitive, and spoiled by moralizing."[1]

Writers who have translated this myth into English during the twentieth century include Jean Young (1954), Arthur Brodeur (1916) and Anthony Faulkes (1987). Most recently, Jesse Byock (2005) added his translation to this list. The stories have been retold by Kevin Crossley-Holland (1980) in *The Norse Myths* and again most recently by Dag Rossman (2005) in *The Northern Path*.

Although Loki was apparently one of the more popular Norse gods, as noted by the large number of stories about him, he was also the most misunderstood god. In *Gods and Myths of Northern Europe*,[2] Hilda Roderick Ellis Davidson (1964) describes Loki as one of the "enigmatic" gods. Loki, the trickster, is always getting into trouble and causing problems for the other gods. His "ungodlike" behavior is not well-understood in modern culture, which takes life and power very seriously, yet he is part of our heritage. As seen through the eyes of a psychologist, Loki is the psychologist of Asgard. Asgard is the dwelling place of the gods, the Mt. Olympus of the Norse. Loki attacks the self-importance of the other gods, makes them feel uncomfortable, and tries to force them to take life less seriously. Loki and his three children were and are important forces in the lives of the gods and the Norse people until Ragnarok, the final destruction of the mythological Norse world. Since myth is timeless and the past, present and future are all now; the present is before, during and after Ragnarok. Though the gods were destroyed at Ragnarok, the final battle has yet to happen, is happening and has passed. Thus, the gods that died are still alive. Myths, like dreams, are time-free.

The worship of these ancient Nordic gods continues today in the northern countries. In June of 2004, I had the opportunity to be part of the Midsummer Solstice blot (celebration) of Forn Siðr, the worshipers of the Old Religion, at Glavendrup on the island of Fyn in Denmark. One of the Danish worshipers commented to me, "It is Loki that brings us life."

In retelling the story of Loki's Children in Chapter 3, I have relied upon the sources previously cited and have attempted to maintain the original story. Read this story with the intent of finding each character within yourself, to find that part of you represented by the character. By internalizing the characters in this manner, we can recognize a flow of emotional energy which follows the process of personal change and growth. Each detail describes the process of change in overcoming Loki's discontent and our discontent.

As we face discontent in our lives, we face three monsters. As we examine this story, we will discover that the first two monsters are energies that initiate the process of change, our fear and guilt. Jormungand, the Midgard serpent, is our fear. Hel, the guardian of those who have died from illness or old age, is our disgust or guilt. With greater understanding of our discontent, we are ready to face Fenrir, the third child. This ever-growing wolf is our obsessive thinking and, at a deeper level, the thoughts and images of the unconscious mind. As Fenrir grows, chains or will power will not hold him, so the gods of Asgard are called together by Odin, our internal wisdom, to find a solution. Odin seeks help from the dwarfs in the cave of the dark elves, the unconscious mind. The elves produce a solution, Gleipnir, but for Fenrir to accept Gleipnir, a sacrifice, Tyr's hand, is required from the warrior within. Thus, Fenrir is bound.

Chapter 4 through Chapter 20 will then take us on a journey using this myth, step by step, to uncover the dysfunctional automatic thinking of three clients in their course of therapy. Then, with the death of these feelings and the associated faulty thinking, the three clients will experience the rebirth of peace, freedom and innocence. As you read this book, I hope that it will provide you with an emotional experience of growth to health and freedom. For the therapist, I hope that it can provide you with experiences and techniques to better help your clients. Let the gods come alive within you. Let them live again.

CHAPTER 3

THE NARRATIVE OF LOKI'S CHILDREN, A HEALING NARRATIVE

Of the twelve Norse gods, the ones of importance to this story of Loki's children in order of appearance are Loki, Odin, Tyr, Baldr, Thor, Freyr and Heimdall.

Loki, the son of the giant Farbauti, is the mischievous trickster who can change his shape into a fly or flea and go places he would be unable to go in his usual handsome human form. On one occasion he borrows a falcon skin from the goddess Freyja, transforms himself into a falcon and travels far and wide. As we shall see in this story, in an attempt to save his own life, he changes himself into the shape of a salmon, and on another occasion, into the shape of an old woman. Even though Loki makes many enemies because of his trickster ways, he is also skilled at making amends through his cleverness.

Odin, the Allfather, is the most powerful of the gods, the god of gods. The god of poetry, battle and death, Odin watches and protects all the worlds from his high seat in Asgard. He is wise and understanding as well as punitive. He lives forever and ever and created the earth, the sky and everything within them. The greatest of his works is that he made man and gave him a spirit of life that shall live and never perish, though the body may decay to dust or burn to ashes.

You may ask from where did Odin come. To digress for a moment, the creation story says that before Odin was the ice and cold of the North. The South was and is called Muspell. It is bright and hot. The one called Surt defends Muspell with his flaming sword. Surt will be an important figure at the end with the demise of the gods. The land between the North and the South, called Ginnungagap, is mild with soft air that thaws the ice of the North. From this thawing ice life appeared, and Ymir, the first frost giant, grew in the likeness of man. As he slept, from under his left arm came a man and a woman and from his foot a son. These are the beginnings of the race of frost giants.

Formed from the melting ice was also a cow who fed these frost giants with its milk. The cow lived by licking the salt-stones, and as the cow licked the stone the first man, named Buri, was uncovered. He had a son Borr who married a woman called Bestla, the daughter of the giant Bolthorn. Borr and Bestla's first and greatest son was Odin. They eventually had three sons who together killed Ymir, the frost giant, and when he fell, different parts of his body formed the mountains, ocean, sky, trees and rocks.

Returning to the gods, a third god important to this story is Tyr, the god of war and the bravest warrior of them all. This son of Odin, most famous for having only one hand, loses his hand in the story of Loki's children which is about to be told.

The most loved and gentle son of Odin is Baldr. He is the wisest and sweetest-spoken of the gods, greatly loved by everyone, especially his mother Frigg, the wife of Odin and foremost among the goddesses.

The one god with whom you are likely most familiar is Thor. This son of Odin, and second only to Odin, is the strongest of the gods. He carries the great hammer, Mjollnir, that when swung its crash causes the lightning and thunder.

Freyr, the brother to Freyja and the son of Njord, is the god of fertility. He brings the sun and soft rain to the fields for growing crops.

Heimdall is the protector of the trembling bridge, Bifrost, the bridge between Midgard and the upper world. He is the watchman and protector of the gods. He needs less sleep than a bird, can see a hundred leagues, whether during the day or the night, and can hear the growth of grass growing on earth and the wool growing on sheep.

As the story of Loki's Children unfolds, we will meet other gods and goddesses, giants, elves and monsters/tormentors, but first we need to learn of the setting of this story.

The Norse universe consists of three levels. Asgard and Valhalla comprise the upper level. Asgard is the home of the gods, while Valhalla is the home of slain Viking warriors. This upper world is ruled by the Æsir, the council of gods led by Odin. Vanaheim, the home of the Vanir, the fertility goddesses and gods, is also part of this upper world.

Midgard, the middle world, is the home of humans. Located in this middle region are Jotunheim, the home of the giants, and Svartafheim, land of the dark elves. The gods are able to travel from Asgard to this middle world by crossing the flaming and trembling bridge called Bifrost.

Niflheim, the lower earth ruled by Hel, is the home of those who died from illness or old age. In this story we learn about the guardians/tormentors of the upper, middle and lower earth: Fenrir, Jormungand and Hel.

LOKI'S CHILDREN

Loki, in his discontent, in his need to stir up trouble for the gods by making the gods face their inconsistencies and hypocrisies, travels to all corners of the Norse world. His ventures frequently take him to

Jotunheim, the land of the giants. With Sigyn, his devoted and faithful wife, he has two sons, yet Loki spends enough time in Jotunheim with Angrboda, an evil giantess, to sire three children.

When the gods learn of these three children, they know through prophecy that they will bring them great harm and misfortune. Because their mother is an evil giantess and their father is even worse, these three children can be nothing but monsters. The oldest, Fenrir, is a wolf. The second child, Jormungand, is the greatest of sea serpents. The third child, Hel, is a symbol of death in life. Although half of her body is of healthy pink flesh, the other half is black with decay. Her whole being is gloomy and grim.

In his alarm, Odin sends some gods to Jotunheim to capture these children of Loki and Angrboda and bring them to Asgard. Odin, in his wisdom, knows what to do with Jormungand. He acts quickly and throws this child of Loki into the ocean that surrounds the middle world. Jormungand sinks to the bottom of the sea where he grows and grows until he reaches a length that completely encircles the world and is able to bite his own tail. This monster of the sea becomes a great obstacle and tormentor to those who venture out into the ocean.

Odin, in his wisdom, also knows what to do with Hel, Loki's only daughter. He acts quickly and throws this girl of gloom and decay into the darkness of Niflheim. In this lower world of those who die of illness or old age, Hel is given the authority over nine worlds on the condition that she look after its inhabitants and share whatever food she has with whoever comes to her. There she builds a great hall with high walls and a huge pair of gates. Her hall is called Eljudnir, her plate, Hunger and her knife, Famine. Her bed is Sick Bed and the bed hangings are called Glimmering Misfortune. Her servants, called Borders-of-sorrow, move so slowly that some would think they are not moving at all.

Odin allows Fenrir, Loki's first born, to roam freely in the woods and fields around Asgard. But, as Fenrir grows and grows, only Tyr, the god of war, has the nerve to approach him to feed him. The gods begin to worry because of Fenrir's great size and continual growth. Remembering the prophecies that the wolf will be the cause of Odin's death, their alarm becomes great, and they call a meeting of the Æsir to decide what to do.

The council of the gods decides to bind Fenrir with a chain instead of killing him, to prevent his blood from polluting their sanctuary. They forge this iron chain with strong links and call it Lœðing. The Æsir take the chain to Fenrir and challenge the wolf to see if he is strong enough to break it. He accepts the challenge and lets the gods bind him in the chain. The wolf then expands himself, strains against the chain and breaks it. So, Fenrir is free of Lœðing.

The Æsir make a second chain which is twice as strong as the first. They call this chain Dromi. The Æsir again challenge Fenrir, suggesting that if he can break Dromi, he will be truly famous. Fenrir had continued to grow while the second chain was being forged. Now, having grown to be twice as strong as before, he feels confident that he can break this stronger chain. Realizing that he will have to take a chance and expose himself to danger in order to be famous, he allows the chain to be wrapped around him. After Fenrir is fettered, he strains, digs his heels into the ground and knocks the chain against the earth. In the end, Fenrir shatters Dromi. Because of this story, a maxim exists that when someone does something extraordinarily difficult, he "breaks loose of Lœðing" or "battles out of Dromi."

The Æsir's fear greatly increases, fearing that they will be unable to find a means to restrain the wolf. All turn to Odin, hoping for a solution to this problem. Odin sends Skirnir, the messenger of the god Freyr, down into the abode of the dark elves. There, the dwarfs devise a binding which they called Gleipnir. They consider this binding for Fenrir very special and magical because it is made of substances no one has heard of before. The gods accept the unusual nature of this binding because they realize that it will take something very special, something that no one knows of or understands, to bind Fenrir. The substances used to make this fetter are six in number. They include the noise a cat makes when it moves, the beard of a woman, the roots of a mountain, the sinews of a bear, the breath of a fish and the spittle of a bird.

Skirnir brings the binding back to the Æsir, who thank him for going on this mission to the world of the dark elves. Odin describes this binding as soft as a silk ribbon yet stronger than one can imagine because he knows that it is the only binding that can hold Fenrir.

The Æsir beckon the wolf to come out to Lyngvi, an island in Amsvartnir Lake and show Fenrir the silken ribbon, challenging him to break it. Although each god who tests the ribbon is unable to break it, the gods suggest that the wolf can break it easily. Fenrir answers that it will be no challenge and the task will not add to his fame. He adds that if it is a trick, he will most certainly not let them wrap it around him. The challenge of the gods continues, "This ribbon is so slight that you can break it easily and if you cannot, you should not be afraid because we will be here to free you." Fenrir laughs, "If I cannot break it, you will just go away and leave me. I cannot trust you! But I cannot let you accuse me of being a coward. If one of you will put your hand in my mouth, I will trust that your test is done in good faith."

The gods, looking at one another, realize their dilemma. No one is willing to accept the wolf's challenge until Tyr puts out his hand and places it in Fenrir's mouth. Fenrir then lets the gods wrap the ribbon around him. As Fenrir tugs and strains, the ribbon becomes tighter and tighter. Suddenly Fenrir bites down, severing Tyr's hand from his arm.

When the gods are certain Fenrir is securely bound by the ribbon, they fasten a chain to the ribbon. They draw the chain through a boulder, which is then driven deep into the earth. A huge stone is then used to plug the hole, thus holding the boulder in place.

As Fenrir struggles, he widely opens his mouth. When he does, the gods quickly gag him by placing a sword in his mouth with the point wedged against the roof of his mouth and the hilt propped on the lower jaw. The bound and gagged Fenrir howls horribly, the saliva from his mouth running to form the River Von.

Fenrir remains restrained on the island until Ragnarok, the final battle of the world, at which time he is freed from his fetter. Jormungand, Loki's son, the terrible sea serpent, comes out of the sea. Hel and all the dead rise from Niflheim to participate in this final battle. But first, to make sense of this final battle we need to examine another story of Loki, The Death of Baldr.

Loki's mischief-making is far from over. Baldr, a son of Odin, is loved by everyone and is considered the most sensitive and gentle of the gods. One night he has a dream that predicts his death. Fearing Baldr's death, the gods consider all possible ways he could die and his mother, Frigg, goes on a journey to obtain from every substance that could kill him a sworn oath that it will do him no harm. Oaths are made with fire, water, iron and all kinds of metals, stones, earth, trees, ailments, beasts, birds, poisons and serpents. When Frigg returns with these promises, everyone rejoices and begins to celebrate by testing these oaths, throwing every imaginable substance at Baldr, who stands unharmed. This demonstration of Baldr's invulnerability becomes a great sport of amusement for all those of Asgard.

Loki finds such hypocrisy in this sport that he disguises himself as a woman to visit Frigg. While talking to the disguised Loki about how the gods find this sport amusing, Frigg exclaims that she received an oath from everything except from a little bush called mistletoe, a bush so young that it could hurt nothing. Loki then leaves to find some mistletoe, makes a dart of this substance, and finds Hod, Baldr's blind brother, standing at the edge of those amusing themselves by throwing things at Baldr. He helps Hod participate in the sport by giving him the dart and aiming him in the direction of Baldr. Hod throws the dart at Baldr, and Baldr falls, killed by mistletoe. The gods are horrified and weep but do nothing, knowing that they cannot desecrate their home with the evil blood of Loki by killing him.

With the help of a giantess, Baldr's ship is launched and upon it the funeral pyre is set. Nanna, Baldr's wife, dies of a broken heart as she watches Baldr's body being carried out to the ship. She and Baldr's horse are also placed on the pyre. All are present for this burial at sea as Thor consecrates the pyre with Mjollnir. To express his love for his son, Odin lays his golden ring on the pyre, a ring that makes eight new rings of equal value on every ninth night. Thus, Baldr is prepared to make his journey to the domain of Hel, Neflheim.

Frigg in her grief then asks for someone to go to Niflheim to ask Hel for Baldr's release. Hermod, Baldr's bold brother, agrees to make the journey. After traveling nine nights and longer upon the back of Sleipner, Odin's eight-legged horse, Hermod arrives at Hel's hall. In seeking Hel's permission to take Baldr with him back to Asgard, Hermod mentions that everyone is weeping for his return. Hel agrees to Baldr's release with one condition, and that is that everything upon the earth, alive or dead, must weep for Baldr. After a brief visit with Baldr and Nanna, Hermod receives from Baldr the gold ring to return to Odin.

Upon Hermod's return to Asgard, the gods send messengers to every person, animal, plant and stone. All do weep but one. The giantess Thokk has no tears for Baldr. Some believe that Thokk is in reality Loki in disguise.

Loki, knowing he went too far and that the gods will be after him, runs and finds a hiding place in the mountains. There he builds himself a house with four doors so that he can see out in all four directions. During the day though he turns himself into a salmon and hides beneath a waterfall. He tries to anticipate every possible way that the Æsir can catch him. While sitting by his fire he thinks of a kind of net that the gods might use to catch him beneath the waterfall and he knots string in a manner to make such a net as nets are still made today. He then sees that the Æsir are almost upon him, throws the net into the fire and jumps into the river as a salmon. Kvasir, the wisest of the gods, arrives with the Æsir, sees the ash remains of the net in the fire and understands that it is for catching fish. The gods make a similar net to catch Loki. After two escapes by jumping over the net Loki is caught in the net of his own design.

The gods then find Vali, one of Loki's sons, and change him into a wolf. This wolf tears apart Loki's other son, his brother, Nari. The gods know that to bind Loki the only binding that will hold him is the entrails of Nari that will turn to steel. Loki is then tied to three stones in a cave with a poisonous viper fastened above him dripping poison on his face. Sigyn, Loki's wife sits next to him with a bowl to catch the dripping poison. When the bowl is full, she removes it from the cave to empty it. During these unprotected intervals, the drops of poison on Loki's face cause him to writhe so violently that he shakes the earth, causing what we know as earthquakes.

This binding of Loki begins, the three years of great wars throughout the world with the slaughter of brother by brother and father by son. These great wars are followed by the three endless winters, Fimbulvetr, with no summers between of continual strife and starvation for the Norse and their gods. Finally, everything comes to a head. One wolf swallows the sun and another the moon. The stars disappear from the heavens and the earth shakes. Trees are uprooted and mountains fall. Fenrir and Loki break lose, Fenrir with his upper jaw against the sky and his lower jaw against the earth. Jormungand crawls out of the sea in a rage, and the dead rise from Niflheim, including Baldr. Surt leads the sons of Muspell with burning fire. Heimdall, the guardian of Bifrost, blows his horn, calling the gods to come forward. The final battle, Ragnarok, begins.

In this fierce battle Freyr faces the fire of Surt and falls. Garm, the guardian dog of Hel's hall, attacks Tyr and they fight until both lives come to an end. Thor kills the serpent Jormungand, but as he steps back Jormungand's poison kills him. Fenrir swallows Odin but in turn, Vidar, one of Odin's sons tears the wolf apart to avenge his father's death. To do this Vidar places one foot on the lower jaw of Fenrir and with one hand grasp his upper jaw. Finally, Loki battles with Heimdall, each causing the other's death. The only survivors are several children of the gods; Modi and Magni, the sons of Thor; and Vidar, Vali and Hod, the sons of Odin. Baldr also survives—the gentle and sensitive Baldr is reborn. Thus, through the cycle of death and rebirth, a cycle that is initiated and completed by Loki, the rebirth of innocence is finally complete.

When I attended the midsummer solstice ceremony on the Island of Fyn, the Danish worshipers of the Old Religion praised the gods that are important to them with Hil! Odin, or Hil! Freyja. Loki rarely if ever receives such praise, though he deserves it. Hil! Loki.

PART TWO

THE BEGINNING OF THERAPY

Coyote as clown reminds us to laugh at ourselves and our problems. Laughter can come only when we gain perspective—a worry that isn't funny to us in the moment may be in a few years, once we are out from under its shadow…

Coyote as trickster can be useful in generating a healing surprise, a shock that moves a patient from habitual state of illness into another, more precarious one, from whence he or she can "fall" into wellness…

What about Coyote as survivor? The coyote that has extended its domain across the continent is an animal who is adaptable, who will try anything. If we truly want to be healers, we must be willing to use anything that works, regardless of our theoretical positions. Because if it works, it's good medicine. (286-287)

I had only to be faithful, and willing to stir things up a little, like Coyote. (75)

LEWIS MEHL-MADRONA, MD, PhD

Coyote Medicine: Lessons from Native American Healing (1998), 286-287, 75.

CHAPTER 4

LOKI'S DISCONTENT: BEGINNING THE NARRATIVE OF HEALING

Loki's discontent is not only with his faithful wife, Sigyn, but with everything he faces. He frequently causes the gods embarrassment and trouble by making them face their inconsistencies and hypocrisies. In creating such turmoil, he frequently travels to all corners of the Norse world. His ventures take him to Jotunheim, the land of the giants where he spends enough time with Angrboda, an evil giantess, to sire three children.

Thus, Loki's discontent is the basis for much personal emotional pain and torment. Each god of these ancient stories plays some role in the drama of the unconscious mind. What, then, is the role of Loki?

LOKI THE TRICKSTER

Loki is the coyote to the Nordic people. Moore and Gillette in the book *King, Warrior, Magician, Lover* suggest there are four archetypes which comprise the mature healthy male: the king, the warrior, the lover and the magician. Each of the Nordic gods represents one of these archetypes. The healthy king is generous and patient. He is the one who maintains order and bestows blessings upon his people. He is the employer who, by encouraging his employees, brings out their best. He is the father who, by loving his family, brings out the best in his family.

The healthy warrior is a doer. He is energized and motivated to aggressively perform tasks and work towards goals. The healthy warrior is the part of us that is self-disciplined and thinks clearly, the part who is unemotional in performing tasks because he knows emotional involvement leads to vulnerability.

In contrast to the warrior, the healthy lover is in tune with feelings. The lover is deeply sensual, passionate, and committed to his interests and causes in life.

The healthy magician has the knowledge and ability to effectively wheel and deal with people and to solve their problems. He is the healer. The knowledge of the magician requires awareness and insight. He is the archetype that has knowledge of the unconscious— of that which is not immediately apparent to our conscious mind.

Each archetype has a bipolar shadow side, a side that is immature, unhealthy and/or destructive. At one extreme of the shadow side of the king is the tyrant, and at the other extreme, the weakling. One extreme of the shadow side of the warrior takes advantage of others in attaining goals (i.e., the sadist) and the other has no direction or goals in life, is self-punishing (i.e., the masochist). Tyr, in sacrificing his hand, might be considered the masochist, while Thor, with his impulsive anger, could be said to be the sadist. On the one hand, the shadow of the lover is addicted to a cause, and on the other, impotent, with no causes in life.

The poles of the shadow of the magician are the manipulator and the naive person. Using Moore and Gillette's model, Loki could be considered the manipulator, the trickster, the sly one. Heimdallr, in his protection of the gods, could be labeled the naive god and will play that role in his final battle with Loki. Most writers suggest that Loki uses his magical powers to gain attention by manipulation. He has been compared to the devil, the personification of evil. In the Prose Edda,[1] Odin says to Loki, "You're insane, Loki, and out of your senses." In the same book, Loki is described as follows:

> Also reckoned amongst the gods is one that some call the mischiefmonger of the Æsir [i.e., the aggregation of Norse gods led by Odin], the father-of-lies and the disgrace-of-gods-and-men... Loki is handsome and fair of face, but has an evil disposition and is very changeable of mood. He excels all men in the art of cunning, and he always cheats. He is continually involving the Æsir in great difficulties and he often helps them out again by guile.[2]

Although Loki is described as the manipulator shadow side of the magician, he also displays characteristics of the healthy magician—the healer—which is covered in the next section of this chapter. Loki's discontent, his crazy actions that cause a person emotional pain, is what brings this person to therapy.

For a client I will call Arlene, from her initial narrative, her behavior of disorganization, of always losing things, of never being able to get out of the house on time for wherever she has to go, drives her husband crazy. This "crazy" behavior, her Loki within, is what brought her to therapy. She herself knows she has a problem but feels she can do nothing about it. Though she has always been this way to a degree, this disorganized behavior has become much worse in the last several years and she now sees it in her stepchildren—Tony, 5 years old, Josh, 7, and Jessi, 8. Her own two daughters, April and May, are younger yet still respond to mom's behavior with clinging and screams, sometimes attributed to April being 2 years old and May being a baby. This crazy behavior, Arlene's Loki within, is saying something important and is confronting her. But what? We have yet to discover her dysfunctional thinking.

Moore and Gillette's model of archetypes suggests that shadow archetypes are immature and unhealthy. In contrast, Robert Johnson[3] proposes that much "gold" can be found in a person's shadow, and thus the shadow side of a person is not necessarily all evil. According to Johnson the shadow side develops when an adolescent makes commitments to certain values in life and rejects others. The rejected values, which may yet have value, compose the shadow.

In considering the gold in Arlene's shadow, two possibilities come to mind. Arlene's disorganized behavior and her husband Tim's preference for routine and organization have polarized. It may be that Arlene just wants unconditional acceptance and is rebelling, testing Tim's unconditional love. Or, she may have great underlying distaste for structure and organization and greatly prefers spontaneity. At this point the gold in her shadow is a matter of speculation, but Arlene came to the next session with a dream, and from the depths of this narrative she found the gold in her shadow that refutes both speculations. Such speculations, though useful, can lead a therapist astray:

"I was trying to ready up the house. Everything I picked up jumped out of my hand and flew back to where I had picked it up. I was racing around the living room like a chicken with its head cut off, grabbing everything and things were flying everywhere."

This dream suggested that her disorganization had nothing to do with Tim, representing neither a power struggle between her and Tim nor a reaction to Tim's preference for organization. What are the spirits found in this dream, the image that comes from beyond her five senses? The spirits are the things that are jumping out of her hands. These spirits have a message that we will soon explore.

Moore and Gillette's archetype model defines the shadow in a general sense, separate from the individual. For Jung[4] and Johnson[5] the shadow can only be described specific to an individual as opposite the individual's persona. Though the shadow and the persona are psychological constructs that may be limiting in maintaining a person's integrity, they are a way of recognizing the denied or hidden conscious part of the person that interferes with healthier ways of thinking and behaving. When kept in perspective, Moore and Gillette's ideas are useful therapeutically to help clarify personal understanding.

The later stories of the Norse gods—the stories of Baldr's dream and his death, the binding of Loki, and the story of the final battle—demonstrate that the Æsir's narrow view of Loki as totally evil is their downfall. When the gods perceive Loki—our shadow—with no gold or redeeming qualities, as we will see in Chapter 15, the problem is brought to a crisis level. Johnson's concept that there is gold in our shadow opens the door to allow light to shine on the shadow.

The misconceptions and distortions in a person's thinking have many of the attributes of the shadow, and the two concepts, the misconceptions and the shadow, are very much related. Each is to a degree nonconscious, whether learned nonverbally, accepted uncritically or repressed because of its painful nature. Both need to be uncovered, and both are likely to contain some truth or value. Both represent beliefs or concepts that we hold about ourselves, and thus are a part of self.

LOKI AS THE HEALER

In looking across cultures, other names for the magician or the Loki archetype are the trickster, clown, jester or contrary. Native Americans regard the trickster to be the clown who functions as a healer. The Heyoehkah of the Plains Indians and the Koshare or the Koyemsi kachinas of the Hopi are tricksters who look at the rituals of life and perform them in an opposite or backward manner. These clowns, sometimes called contraries, are healers who help people laugh at themselves. In describing the Heyoehkah, Lame Deer says:

Heyoehkah does strange things. He says "yes" when he

means "no." He rides his horse backwards. He wears his
moccasins or boots the wrong way. When he's coming,
he's really going. When it's real hot, during a heat wave,
he will shiver with cold, put his mittens on and cover
himself with blankets ... complaining that he is freezing
to death.[6]

The clown causes emotional pain and becomes a threat when a
person begins to take life too seriously. A person with too much
self-importance or ego-involvement is vulnerable to hurt or humiliation. Personal power is gained when we are able to perform daily
tasks without personal involvement or self-importance. The clown
most effectively fulfills his role when he forces us to experience life
with an unsettled state of mind, making us question our values and
our own self-importance. Tricks of the contrary are staged to shock
an individual into a new stage of awareness and are akin to many
of the devises used by Carl Whitaker (Napier & Whitaker, 1978)
in his experiential therapy, and Milton Erickson (1985). Changing
a person's self-awareness through a narrative that offers a shocking
reframing experience has been considered a form of hypnotic trance
induction by changing a person's experience of his or her usual
reality.[7]

Although the ancient narratives portray Loki as insecure and jealous, the god of mischief and lies, they also reveal his healthy magician side as the effective healer who causes the emotional pain and
grief that supply the energy to promote change and personal growth.
The Loki within us creates a problem that forces us to face the feelings of self-importance. When our introspection leads to change,
Loki can be considered kin to our conscience. For example, Thor's
wife Sif was notorious for her pride in her golden hair. One night,
Loki crept into Sif's bedroom and cut off her gleaming hair.[8] Loki's
mischievous deed caused a great disturbance among the gods and

goddesses, demonstrating to Sif her obsession with hair and her own self-importance.

Another example of Loki's confrontational personality is clearly found in Loki's Flyting from the Poetic Edda.[9] The gods come to a feast in the great hall of Gymir to sample the ale Gymir brewed in his new great cauldron. To the horror of the gods, Loki shows up for this feast. With Gymir's ale the gods begin to feel joyful and praise highly Gymir's two ale servers. Later in the evening Loki begins to attack the self-importance of each god and goddess in their ridiculous and drunken praise for the ale servers. He insults Bragi, the god of poetry, with "You offer a horse you don't have. You offer gold rings you don't have." To Idunn, Bragi's wife and the keeper of the golden apples of eternal life: "You showed love to you brother's murderer." To Gefjon, a fertility goddess: "You seduced a young boy for the necklace he gave you." To Odin: "You never fight fairly, often allowing the weaker man to win." To Frigg: "You were born a whore. You shared a bed with Odin's two brothers." To Freyja: "You've slept with every god and elf." To Njord, the god of the sea: "Everyone knows the giant Hymir's serving-maids squatted over you and pissed in your mouth." Finally, after Loki kills one of the ale servers, the gods are so outraged that they chase him from the hall. Loki, knowing he went too far, runs to find a hiding place in the woods.

The Loki within creates problems that force us to face the real issues and thus promotes change. The tricks of our Loki within generate the emotional energy we need to explore our unconscious, the cave of the dark elves, as will be seen in Chapter 8. The search of the unconscious mind to uncover the dysfunctional thoughts provides us with a deeper and greater understanding of the reasons for discontent.

WHAT IS OUR DISCONTENT?

We first see the results of discontent. Discontent leads Loki to having an extramarital affair that produces three monster children. Discontent leads to maladaptive behavior such as extramarital affairs, alcoholism, excessive eating and gambling. Other behaviors that can originate in discontent are explosive anger, depression, anxiety, obsessive compulsions, and even schizophrenia, as we will see with Carl. The list could be endless. These maladaptive behaviors are our Loki within playing tricks on us. They produce emotional and even physical pain. The emotional pain caused by these tricks is characterized as the three monsters: fear (Chapter 8), guilt (Chapter 9) and obsessive worry (Chapter 10). When maladaptive behavior becomes monstrous and emotionally painful, we begin to look for a solution. The search may lead us to self-exploration through therapy. The purpose of the challenging journey of therapy into the unconscious mind is to uncover our dysfunctional automatic ways of thinking or our shadow, the source or cause of our discontent. The energy that drives us on this journey to find a solution to our problem comes from the three monsters, our emotional pain and torment.

In therapy and while the client is in ecstatic trance, I frequently use the phrase or command, "Face your tormentor!"—a phrase used by the trickster Don Juan from the writing of Carlos Castenada. As I use this phrase for facing one's emotional pain, I generally picture, in my own mind, some form of monster. This pain or torment is important and valuable. I reassure the client of the healthy nature of this pain with a brief counter-narrative suggesting, "If you dropped a brick on your foot, you should hope that the incident would cause some pain; otherwise, you might continue walking, not realizing that your foot was injured, and causing greater damage."

The complaint that Carl brought to therapy was that his wife was having an extramarital affair. His belief in this affair offered a narrative that was a delusion of psychotic proportions. He believed that his wife got out of bed in the middle of the night and went to the bed of the man who lived next door. He had never caught her out of bed at night, and the girlfriend of the guy next door frequently spent the night. Though Abby was not unattractive for her 50 years, the couple next door appeared to be in their 30s. One night the next door neighbor left in the evening, and still Carl believed that Abby went next door, adding to the story that from his bed he saw the lights of his neighbor's car returning home, though the neighbor was not there even the next day.

Behind such delusional beliefs is truth, the truth in this case being that Carl did not feel lovable and therefore could not believe that his wife loved him. It could have been that his wife had indeed withdrawn her love from him, but I saw no evidence of that. A lot of emotional energy or pain is necessary to sustain a delusion. I believed that Carl had done something that caused him to feel bad enough about himself to believe that his wife could not love him.

If we do not experience emotional pain, problems may grow and cause much greater damage in our life. The maladaptive behavior can lead to divorce or loss of employment. We need to respect and appreciate both emotional and physical pain because they focus our attention on our problems and provide motivation for us to seek solutions. Because of the great changes they are ultimately able to achieve in their lives, many clients have gone through the process of therapy to eventually thank the Loki within for causing the maladaptive behavior and emotional pain.

Jerry came to therapy with a narrative that caused him to feel in a state of total confusion, anger, pain, fear and depression. As he walked into the house the previous night after work, he knew something was wrong. The house seemed empty and dead. It took him a few moments to start noticing what was missing. First, he had noticed a picture missing from the wall of the entryway of his wife and daughter, a picture he had taken of his daughter wearing a baseball cap two years earlier, when she was about four.

As he walked through the house towards the kitchen, he found that other things were missing—his wife's easy chair where she sat to read stories to Beth, an afghan from the sofa. In the kitchen he noticed an empty space on the crowded book shelf. Then he saw a note on the table: "I've left. You were never here so I guess you won't miss me, Liz"

Jerry was dumbfounded. He didn't understand. The discontent that would change his life to help him grow up came from outside of himself.

OUR INNER RESOURCES

When the gods learn of Loki's and Angrboda's offspring, they know they have to act. Since Angrboda is an evil giantess and Loki is even worse, these three progeny can be nothing but monsters. The oldest is Fenrir, the wolf. The second child is the greatest of serpents. His name is Jormungand. The third child is a daughter called Hel. Though half her body is of healthy pink flesh the other half is black with decay, her whole being is gloom and grimness.

In their alarm, the gods call a meeting to decide how to prevent the monstrous children from bringing harm to the world. Similarly, within ourselves, we pull together all of our emotional resources to find strength in an effort to deal with our problems.

Arlene and Jerry were each in a state of panic. They each called upon their inner wisdom by seeking therapy. Each was wise enough to know something was wrong, and each wanted to do something about it.

OUR INNER WISDOM

What resources do we find in the gods? The first resource is Odin's wisdom and farsightedness. Odin was well known for his ability to look out over all the worlds from his high seat called Hlidskjalf. From Hlidskjalf, Odin was able to watch Jotunheim, the land of the giants, and to follow the actions of the monstrous children. We too have this wisdom, though we tend to ignore it at times.

Carl's inner wisdom was more subtle. At some level, whether conscious or unconscious, he knew his delusional beliefs were metaphoric for his feelings of inadequacy, feelings that he was initially unwilling to face consciously. I do not want to call these beliefs false because at an emotional level, they are true and honest. Carl needed to blame someone else for his feelings of inadequacy, of being unlovable, and/or for his guilt feelings for something he did, whether real or imaginary. The wife of his delusion is a spirit, a spirit with a message to him that he needs to do something to bring his life back together.

Odin is our wise and powerful inner self which provides us with greater understanding and insight when we open ourselves to it. When we recognize the Odin within, we find a positive and powerful part of ourselves that supports the feeling, "I am not all bad. I have the strength within me to begin to deal with this problem and to overcome discontent." This realization in itself is strengthening. When clients decide to come for therapy, it is Odin within who speaks and makes the call for action. The therapist who reassures clients that they have made the correct decision to come to therapy reinforces the clients' sense of strength.

OUR INTUITION

Odin's farsightedness, a power provided him by his high seat, Hlidskjalf, allows him to predict the future. In Crossley-Holland's retelling of this story,[10] he adds two of the three Norns, Urd and

Verdandi, the goddesses of destiny. Urd notes the evil in Angrboda, the mother giantess; Verdandi proclaims Loki as even worse. The three Norns sometimes provide prophecies in other Norse stories. Whether because of his high seat or because of the prophecies offered him by the three Norns, Odin has the ability to predict the future. The power to predict the future resides in our intuition, which provides us with a deeper sense of the consequence of emotional pain and leads us to undertake the journey into the unconscious mind. Each person has great potential for the insight and intuition that allow us to look into the future. We often ignore or deny such intuition. One purpose of therapy is to sensitize the client to and facilitate this intuition.

Some individuals who find it easy to call upon the three Norns are readily able to access intuition. For others, people who wear the blinders of guilt or fear, intuition is unavailable to them and must be nurtured through therapy. The blinder of fear manifests itself in many men who feel that it is unmanly to experience the emotion of fear. When a man admits fear in therapy, it is frequently a significant turning point.

Many people seek therapy for anxiety or panic. One of the most common symptoms of anxiety is a tight feeling in one's chest that produces a feeling of suffocation. People with these chest and breathing problems often believe they are having a heart attack. They believe their fear of having a heart attack is justified, but this fear is the blinder preventing them from seeing the deeper, real fears in their lives.

One man, wearing blinders to his intuition, sought therapy because of an obsessive fear that he had cancer. It became apparent in therapy that when his mother sought his attention and time, he felt angry and resentful. However, he also felt guilty. This guilt, like cancer, was eating at him. His emotional involvement with his mother greatly interfered in the relationship between the man and his wife.

Although his wife recognized the cause of her husband's problem, the husband did not intuitively see the connection between his mother's dependency on him and his guilt. He was finally able to make the intuitive connection when he realized that he did not experience anxiety when his mother was away visiting her other children.

The blinders we wear sometimes take the form of believing we have all the answers. Believing we have the answer, whether right or wrong, can diminish our fear. The hypnotic suggestion of "being curious and wondering" can begin to change the "know it all" attitude in a positive and less confrontive manner than attempting to convince the client that his or her idea or belief is wrong. Being "curious and wondering" along with "gentle and patient" are words of suggestion in therapy that can open a client to his or her unconscious, counter-narrative words that can lead to greater self-understanding.

As we learned earlier, Jerry, 31 years old, came home from work to find that his wife had moved out. He was dumbfounded. He had no idea that Liz was unhappy, that she was serious about leaving. She had left a couple of nights before with their daughter Beth but with only an overnight bag. His narrative continued with the thought, "Go ahead and leave. You'll be back; you can't survive on your own." A couple of sessions later, it became clear that his identity as a baseball pitcher was his set of blinders. He has pitched for a baseball team since before he was married seven years ago. He had been a high school hero for his pitching ability. Pitching was his identity. He had started dating Liz when she worked as a secretary in the hospital where he worked as a physical therapist. While they were courting, she had come to most of his games, but once they were married, she had complained that he was never at home. He didn't really hear her complaints, believing instead that she loved him because of his fame as a pitcher. He was blind to her needs. As her complaints grew, he became more determined in winning ball games, believing that winning would impress her and stop her complaints. His intuition was wrong. Her leaving had been a great shock to him, but only since she left had he begun to examine the situation more openly and without blinders.

Though Arlene didn't want to admit it, her five-year-old stepson had been acting up lately, and she sensed that it was her fault. When she would become hyper and, in a hurry, not only would Tim complain, but Tony would become defiant and the problems would escalate. "If only he would listen and do what I asked, then I would be able to get things done."

Arlene's intuition that she was to blame opened a door to a counter-narrative, a hypnotic teaching tale. The therapeutic dynamics of such a tale will be discussed in the next section of this chapter, but briefly, such tales are easily listened to, nonthreatening and easily remembered. Though Arlene was tentatively taking blame for the boy's unruly behavior, I believe she did not want to take responsibility and was looking for my empathetic support to let her let go of her guilt. For now, I offered the following teaching tale: "When my five children were young, one evening when I asked them to put away their toys before they went to bed a flash in insight struck me. When I asked them to brush their teeth for bed, they would run off to brush their teeth with no great problem. But when I asked them to put away their toys there was chaos. Why? The difference was when I asked them to brush their teeth, I said it in a loving and patient manner. But when I asked them to put away their toys, I was unnecessarily saying silently to myself, 'Why do I always have to ask them to put away their toys?' Children hear feelings before words. Even though I was not aware of irritation or frustration in my voice, my children heard, 'Dad is upset.' They didn't hear, 'Put away toys.' The next couple of nights I relaxed and said in a patient and loving way, 'Put away your toys,' and it worked. There was a world of difference in their response. Children react to feelings before they hear the words."

This hypnotic monologue supported Arlene's intuition by

clarifying her self-blame and offering her an alternative, though I knew that it would take some time for her to be able to implement this knowledge.

OUR INNER STRENGTH AND COMMITMENT

Another resource utilized by the gods is Tyr, the strongest of warrior-gods. The strength of Tyr is our inner will power. This will power allows us to act decisively, to make decisions and to move aggressively towards meeting our goals in life. As will be discussed in greater detail in Chapter 7, the warrior within, our will power, can also interfere with our ability to access our unconscious and to use our intuition. Again, offering the suggestion of curiosity and patience can lessen the interfering influence of will power and employ a more positive energy in moving towards resolution of discontent.

The aggregate of gods, the Æsir or the total self, gains sufficient emotional strength to face its tormentors by combining their resources. The initial process of therapy enables an individual to begin to pull together the resources necessary to face their pain or torment. Some people, however, deny or ignore their problems or pain. They are unable to find independently the avenue that can lead to a solution to their problems or a cure for their pain. By continuing this denial, they diminish the prognosis for change and emotional growth. These people may have been forced into therapy by the spouse, a physician or the courts.

As a result of their meeting the gods decided to kidnap the three children. As ordered by Odin, a group of the gods travel to Jotunheim, break into Angrboda's hall at night, and take the three children back to Asgard where the gods are able to face them, to see them clearly in order to deal with them. When we summon emotional strength from these resources within us to face our tormentors and emotional pain and see them clearly, the initial process of therapy is concluded.

THE BEGINNING OF THERAPY

When Loki committed adultery, he confronted some weak, inconsistent or hypocritical part of the Æsir. When we act in an unwise or dysfunctional manner we are confronting or revealing some weak, inconsistent or hypocritical part of ourselves. Although we may not be ready to identify this part by our willingness to ask, "What is this part?" we are beginning the therapeutic journey to discover the source of our discontent.

In considering two types of psychological problems, those caused by the attitudes and behaviors of others in a person's life (the topic of my first book, *Grendel and His Mother*) and those caused by the unwise decisions of the individual (the focus of this book), the difference in therapeutic energy is quite evident in development of rapport. Since the issues in a person's life stem generally from both causes, and therapy flows back and forth between these issues, the therapist needs to be sensitive to this flow of energy and ready to change it at any one moment. The words that characterize the energy in therapy when the issues are caused by others in a person's life include "empathy" or "emotional support" for facing one's tormentor, "trust," and "laying down weapons or defenses." Though these words are also important when the problem is caused by the unwise decisions of the individual, the therapist needs to be careful not to show empathy or emotional support for the unwise decision, or even for the emotional "truth" behind the decision. For example, offering emotional support for having an extramarital affair is most likely inappropriate; offering emotional support for the feelings of emptiness or fear of being alone that may stand behind the affair may be more appropriate but can still be perceived as supporting the affair. A client who blames his or her problem on some feeling rather than taking responsibility for the action is like the alcoholic who uses what drove him or her to drink as an excuse for drinking. Challenging this person to find healthy alternatives for achieving satisfaction or fulfillment is likely more appropriate.

The therapeutic energy when the problems are caused by the individual's unwise decisions need to be more confrontive, challenging and assertive with varying degrees of gentleness, depending upon how hard the person is being on him or herself for making the unwise decision. This confrontation and challenge can still be considered empathetic but with a different tone of voice or emotional energy in how the empathy is offered. Yet, if the energy is too confrontive of and divergent from the client's own experience, the client can be lost. The gods of the Æsir—wisdom, intuition and will power—are supported or encouraged within the client. The language of therapy is to be supportive of the client's wisdom in recognizing that the decision was unwise and in the wisdom of seeking therapy; supportive of the individual's intuition regarding the potential negative consequences of the decision or of the intuition that he or she needs help to change; and the will power or the client's determination to change and be different in the future. As therapy progresses, wisdom, intuition and will power then apply to deeper and more central personal issues.

In the case of Jerry the baseball pitcher, again, such a story is appropriate to plant a seed.

"Jerry, when you were young you probably did not play house, at least like the little girls did. You did other things to improve your skills in life, to get ahead. One skill was in baseball, especially pitching. Most guys have dreams of what they want to become: doctors, lawyers, firemen, policemen, all ways to provide for the family. But you didn't practice or think much about what it means to be a husband and a father like girls practice being a mother and a wife. So many men begin marriage with two thoughts in mind: working to make money, often not with the thought of supporting a family but more with the thought of impressing a woman; and the thought of sex, of enjoying a bed partner, and with the thought that the wife is supposed to do the cooking, cleaning and raise the family. But these days, this is not fair or realistic, because the wife also has to work for the family to survive, and the children need a father's love in more ways than just as a provider. Not many men think about these things, things that are very important to a family.

"I recall one person who after he got married still went to the bar with his friends after work most every night and would get home after his wife and the children had finished dinner. This lasted seven years into the marriage until one night while he was at the bar, from somewhere inside of him came the thought, 'What am I doing here? I have a family. I am a husband and a father.' He went home that night seeing his family differently and didn't go back to the bar. He was the lucky one because his wife had hung in there with great patience, waiting for him. So many marriages end before this light goes on inside of the husband." We sat there silently for a few moments before I got up to end the session.

As I told this counter-narrative to Jerry I spoke words or made statements to which I was quite certain he could answer "Yes, that's true." This way of speaking creates a *yes-set*, a technique that is considered the core of inducing a hypnotic trance by Milton Erickson.[11]

Arlene has the wisdom and insight of knowing that she has a problem. She blames herself rather than blaming it on her plate being too full. She feels out of control, yet she believes that if she would relax and focus, she would not get everything done. She holds the false belief that multitasking is efficient.

"Who can you think of who is efficient in getting things done? You are afraid that if you focus to get one thing done, you will miss other things that need to be done. Just too many things, too overwhelming. If you focus, you are afraid you will miss something. Let's try this exercise, an exercise I often use near the beginning of therapy." As I stand, I turn on a recording of quiet drumming and model the Bear Spirit Posture, (Fig. 1.1), though I do not use this name for the posture. I suggest, "Arlene, stand tall with your hands resting on your abdomen on the spot I call your center of harmony. Inhale a sense of calmness. When you breathe correctly from your diaphragm you feel your center of harmony rise. Then as you exhale, feel you center of harmony drop while you let that calmness go deeper inside you. Start counting your breaths. With each breath inhale calmness and with each exhale let that calmness spread to your whole body.'"

After about ten breaths I continued. "Imagine yourself just about to leave the house. You and Tim have to go somewhere, and Tim is in the car with the children, waiting for you. You are trying to leave, but you see several things that need to be done. What do you see that needs to be done? Take a few moments to let this picture develop..."

"...There's a coat on the couch. I need to hang it up. A coffee cup on the end table I need to take to the kitchen. I need to grab the milk bottles to return to the dairy that have been sitting around for months. I cannot stand seeing them sitting around any longer. I need to throw the bag of newspapers into the trunk to recycle. I cannot stand the mess."

"Now stop for a moment and think about how you are feeling. Tell me how you feel."

"I feel pressured, overwhelmed, confused. I'm racing and feel confused."

"Feel the pressure, you need to hurry. You're overwhelmed. Feel yourself racing and confused. Tim and the kids are sitting in the car, waiting. When under the pressure of Tim sitting in the car, you can get a few things done you would not have done otherwise, but there is always more to do."

"Yeah. I get so much more done under pressure."

"You could have started earlier to do these things, but earlier you were not under the pressure of Tim being in the car, waiting. Even though you know that Tim is becoming more and more upset and the kids are more and more restless, that pressure helps you get a few things done. I wonder, I'm really curious, what is going on here. Don't be in a hurry to find an answer, be patient, but think about why you need such pressure to get things done."

Thus, while using the Bear Spirit Posture, Arlene, age 29, was offered a seed to open the door of wisdom and intuition, of awakening the Odin within and the goddess Frigg, Odin's wise wife.

Finally, consider Carl's belief that his wife goes next door at night for her affair with the neighbor. Where does the responsibility lie? Is Carl's problem caused by the attitudes and behaviors of others, which would mean that therapy should be more understanding and empathetic? Or is Carl's problem the result of some unwise decision he had made and for which he needs to take responsibility? The picture becomes clearer during the next session. In keeping with the belief that even though the content of Carl's thinking was delusional, the emotional support of this belief would be honest, I was able to say to Carl, "You worry that you might be losing Abby. You fear for some reason that she does not love you."

Carl answered, "Yeah. I can't help myself. I know Abby loves me, but I can't get it out of my mind that she goes next door at night. I don't know where that idea comes from, but I keep thinking it. I know that it upsets Abby when I tell her what I think, but I can't help myself."

The light now changed. Carl's belief was not delusional but an obsessive-compulsive thought. He knows his wife is not having an affair, knows she is not going next door, and he is taking responsibility for what he thinks and does. Because he is taking responsibility, I join him in a more confrontive manner, which, as we will eventually see, is the correct way to go. "You are angry with yourself for what you say to Abby that upsets her. You don't know what to do about it. You know you are wrong in giving her such a hard time."

CHAPTER 5

JORMUNGAND: DEALING WITH FEAR

Jormungand, the Midgard serpent, is the terror of the Norse seas. Odin in all his wisdom decides to cast this monster into the ocean. There he sinks to the bottom and grows bigger and longer until he encircles the Earth and is able to hold his own tail in his mouth. Any seafarer who attempts to venture out too far over the ocean knows he will have to deal with this creature. The story of Thor's wager with the giant Hymir[1] illustrates the strength of Jormungand. Thor, the son of Odin, is physically the strongest among the gods and is the god of the sky and thunder. Well-known for his temper, Thor is quick to challenge one or more of the giants in competition or in battle.

In one such challenge, Thor seeks to win a fishing contest competing with the giant Hymir, the prize being the giant's enormous cauldron used to brew ale. As they row out into the sea, Thor encourages Hymir to row farther and farther. When Thor finally throws his baited hook into the water, the serpent of Midgard lets go of its tail and takes the bait. Thor pulls in the line, dragging the poison spitting monster up onto the boat. When the monster is within range, Thor raises his famed hammer to drive it into the serpent's head, but at that moment Hymir cuts the line and Jormungand escapes to sink back to the bottom of the sea. Terrified by this event, Hymir gives Thor the cauldron.

THE CHALLENGE OF FACING FEAR

An expected response in facing the threat of Jormungand is fear. Norse mythology portrays four characteristics of fear when one faces threat. First, for some, the fear in facing a threat may trigger increased strength and determination, the strength of Thor in overcoming the threat of Jormungand as portrayed in the above story of the fishing contest with Hymir. Following Thor's example, Norsemen, long renowned as great fishermen, world travelers and conquerors, face the threat of the sea and its monster inhabitant, Jormungand, with great respect and strength.

Second, the fear in facing the threat of Jormungand creates a challenge for the Viking warrior to prove his strength. To gain fame and notoriety and to please the gods, the warrior repeatedly accepts the challenge to face Jormungand. If he should die, entry into Valhalla is the warrior's reward for accepting this challenge. In the mind of the Viking warrior, only cowards are deterred by fear and thus end up in Hel's realm.

Third, for others the fear instilled by a threat may trigger a blinding rage or loss of temper. This rage can cause blindness to important aspects of the threat, and thus lead to failure in overcoming it. In the following story of Thor's competition with the giant Utgard-Loki, Thor's humiliation in losing each competition causes his rage and blindness to the giant's tricks to escalate, thus insuring further failure. Though Thor would deny he was afraid, his fear of humiliation is evident in his escalating anger. On the other hand, the power of such rage can be channeled and controlled as seen with the Berserkers, those who train themselves to use such a frenzied rage to give themselves super strength.

The story of Thor's competition with the giant, Utgard-Loki,[2] begins with Thor and Loki traveling together to Utgardr, a citadel of the giants, to confront and challenge these giants and their leader, Utgard-Loki. Upon their arrival, the giants challenge Thor to various contests. In one contest, the giants challenge Thor to see who can drink the most. The cup-bearer brings Thor a drinking horn filled to the brim and he drinks, but in three tries and with increasing frustration, he cannot empty it. Utgard-Loki is using an illusion of magic such that Thor is unwittingly drinking directly from the sea. Now, people say that when the tides recede Thor is drinking. Next, Thor accepts a challenge to lift the giant's "cat." When Thor puts his arm under the cat to lift it, the cat simply arches its back. As Thor continues to lift, the cat's back forms an arch like a rainbow over the giants' heads, but only one of its feet is lifted from the floor. Again, Thor loses the challenge because of Utgard-Loki's ability to use deceptive illusions—the "cat" is Jormungand. As the giants continue to make a fool of Thor, he becomes increasingly angry. Thor is next challenged to wrestle an old crone giant. The old woman quickly gets the upper hand over Thor, and Utgard-Loki brings the match to an end. It so happens that the old woman was old age itself and nobody can beat old age. Though Thor is a god, he is blinded by his anger and rage so that he is unable to see that these tasks are illusions.

The fourth characteristic may be the most powerful. One may face the threat of Jormungand with a sense of calm strength and overcome it. Realizing that Jormungand represents some internal threat and that this threat is maintained by the person's dysfunctional thinking based on false premises, facing this monster within with calming laughter puts it in a place where it can be dealt with more effectively. The downfall of the gods of Asgard is that Loki's antics and Utgard-Loki's tricks do not produce laughter. Instead, because the gods take the tricks too personally, these episodes cause them great despair, lost tempers, humiliation, and in the end, death.

In contrast the American Indian tricksters, the Heyoehkahs and Koshares and the court jesters of Europe similarly do things to make fun of what you might otherwise take too seriously, but hopefully you are able to laugh at their antics. Like the gods, in our Western culture, at times we may value beliefs, self-concepts and possessions too highly, and thus, we become more vulnerable to being hurt if we should lose them. When we are unable to laugh at ourselves, the alternative is fear. We fear the loss of what we consider valuable. The gods' inability to laugh at Loki is the story's lesson to us.

As expected of Thor, in therapy, fear is often denied. Lost in the excitement of the moment of the affair, The Berserkers, a group of Viking warriors, were famous for intentionally working themselves up into a berserk frenzy before battle, a state that made them feel invulnerable and without fear. As we shall show shortly, each of the three clients found ways initially to avoid the feelings of fear that might have otherwise prevented them from making their unwise decisions or committing their unwise acts. Only when they face their fear openly and are able to laugh will each client be able to find power over his or her tormentor.

There is more than one level of fear. The first level of fear is the fear that would be expected in making an unwise decision. Jerry's fear of his wife leaving him, and Carl's fear of his wife having an affair. The second or deeper level of fear is much more abstract, a fear that is sometimes difficult to put into words. Yet, this deeper fear needs to be uncovered and faced in therapy. I would be getting ahead of myself if I now offered examples of the deeper level of fears.

THE FIRST LEVEL OF FEAR

JERRY'S FEAR OF LOSING HIS WIFE

Jerry's first level of fear was the fear of losing his wife, but he was slow in accepting even this fear. When Liz told him to leave, he insisted that he would not and suggested that if anyone was going to leave it had to be her.

Liz again complained, "You're gone so much of the time, it is as if you're not here anyway. What difference does it make? Why don't you just leave?"

As he argued back, she went to their bedroom to grab an overnight case, already packed. It was apparent that she was prepared to leave. As she walked out the door with their 6-year-old daughter, he continued in his bravado, "Go ahead and go." He felt no regret, at least at the time. He couldn't let himself feel fear. Yet, that night he could not sleep, or at least he became very confused about what was reality and what was dreaming.

Jerry continued to be angry for two days. He knew that Liz would come back. She couldn't survive without him. He wasn't sure where she went. She was gone for two nights. He probably could have found her, but didn't try. "Let her suffer, she'll be back," he thought. Then the next day, when he came home from work, he found things in the house missing. It was then that he phoned me for an appointment, and I was able to see him later that day. Jerry came in and threw himself in a chair, and while telling me his story, he eventually told me about his sleep during the three nights Liz had been gone. "After I went to bed, I began to hear noises in the house," he explained, "the back door squeaked like it always does when it is opened and closed. She was sneaking back into the house. Then the bathroom light went on and after a couple of minutes the toilet flushed and the light went off. I waited a couple of minutes, but she didn't come into the bedroom. I figured she must have gone into the spare room. I then drifted back to sleep and again woke. The clock read 12:45. I got up to go to the bathroom and looked in the spare room. No one was there. This shocked me, because I was sure she came in. If I was dreaming it was so real.

"I went back to bed wired. I couldn't sleep, but finally I must have drifted off. Again, I heard the toilet flush and the door to the spare room close. It was only 2:00 a.m.. I got up and looked in the spare room. The door was open, and again she wasn't there. I didn't know what to do. I was in a state of panic. I got back in bed, pulled the covers over my head and lay there shaking, hugging myself. I was crying. I remember the dampness on my pillow. I thought I was going crazy. Eventually I drifted off and again dreamt she was in the house before I again woke feeling scared and exhausted."

Jerry finally was able to be honest with himself and admit his fear of losing his wife. He was facing the message offered by the spirits of his dreams, the sounds of Liz coming into the house. Telling this story in such emotional detail was trance-inducing in itself. Being aware of the client's depth of trance in telling such stories is important. Because of the depth of Jerry's trance, bringing him back to this story in future sessions will be trance-inducing.

Though the three children of Loki are separate entities and the feared and respected Jormungand is dealt with first in the mythic narrative, before guilt and obsessive worry, therapy is not in reality linear. Each monster may be faced more than once, and in an unpredictable order. Sometimes, in fact, the three children are inseparable.

ARLENE'S FEAR OF BEING INCOMPETENT

This was the case with Arlene. Her first levels of fear and guilt were impossible to separate. After several sessions of therapy, she came to one session in a state of panic. Besides her two stepsons and stepdaughter, she and Tim together had two smaller children, 3-year-old

April and 16-month-old May. Arlene worked as a receptionist in a dental office three days a week and was a part time student the other two days, working towards becoming a dental hygienist. Tim respected her busy schedule and helped a lot around the house, but Arlene insisted on doing the laundry. It was Arlene's thing. She had always liked dressing up their two girls, and shopping and caring for their clothing. "Yesterday morning when I was getting the girls ready for daycare, I discovered they had no clean clothes. I have such a hard time keeping up with all the laundry. Tim was on my case because, to him, the laundry should be no big deal. To him, a load of laundry should take only a few minutes to sort and put in the washer and then dry. It should be no sweat to do two or three loads of wash an evening and in between do homework or other things."

"The night before, I put in one load, Tim's and my underwear. I then sat down to read the newspaper. I have a right to relax a few minutes before I start my homework. I never got back to the wash. I thought that the girls had enough clothes. Tim eventually went in and put the clothes in the dryer so we would have underwear for yesterday.

"I can't stand Tim's lectures. He thinks the girls have enough clothes, but there was nothing that would fit them or match. I won't let them go to daycare in rags...

"Tim just didn't understand and gave a frustrated sigh. I lost it."

After listening for a while, I finally interjected, "Wow, with the needs of your children, your husband's needs, your own needs, the dental office, school, your house, there are not enough hours in the day."

She was quick to answer, "But there is no excuse for my daughters to not have clothes. The other kids can wear what they want. The girls should come first, and it would have taken me only a few minutes to put in another load."

I hesitated before offering Arlene the excuse of having too much on her plate. She could have used this excuse to avoid taking responsibility for her actions. But, knowing Arlene to be a perfectionist, guilt ridden and very responsible, I knew she would have this paradoxical reaction to my list of her responsibilities.

"Sure, it would have taken you only a few minutes to do another load of wash. But you needed some time for yourself to read the newspaper. You deserve such time, and reading the newspaper only takes a few minutes."

"But that was being selfish." Arlene was becoming more and more agitated in her guilt.

"You're still blaming yourself—so much guilt. You take responsibility for everything."

This was the same route we had taken a couple of weeks earlier to facing her guilt, and then Arlene was determined to let go of it. Now she could see herself being sucked right back into the cesspool of guilt, and it frightened and angered her. The session began with her fear of being an incompetent mother, fear that was now identified in reality as guilt. Her first level of fear included the fear she held that she would be incapable of letting go of guilt. Jormungand and Hel often cannot be separated.

CARL'S FEAR OF THE SIN OF VOYEURISM

We now return to Carl, who had been terrorizing his wife by accusing her of having an affair. Our next session of therapy took another drastic new direction. During the last session Carl had revealed that he knew that Abby was not having an affair, but still the feeling of losing his wife was there and he could not refrain from making these accusations. He did not know why. I suggested that he might be punishing himself for some reason.

Carl was very hesitant at first to open up. I could feel his tension and waited him out. He finally started to talk. "Wednesday evenings Abby goes to her choir practice at church and I am home alone.

Several months ago I went into the bedroom to close the curtains like we do every night. I looked out the window and could see into our neighbor's bedroom. It was only an accident, but I could see they were having sex. I watched. I watched for only a couple of minutes and then went downstairs. But I had to go right back up, but then I couldn't see them. I was relieved, but I have become obsessed with checking that window. I've seen them a few more times. It seems that his girlfriend is there now most every Wednesday night. It's so disgusting but a few weeks ago I even masturbated while I watched them. I feel so terrible about it. I can't stop thinking about them, at work, at night... all the time. Will this ever end? It scares me. I feel so terrible about it."

"Stay with those feelings for a few moments... disgust, feeling terrible, scared. Feel those feelings, realize they are God-given, they're important. Those feelings are thoughts in your head... feelings in your chest...stomach...other places within you. Stay with those thoughts and feelings. They are a message to you, a message that if you listen to it, you will learn something important. Stay with them, your feelings and thoughts. They are God-given."

I might have talked of these messages coming from the unconscious mind, but because of Carl's strong religious beliefs, the use of "God" was more relevant.

Again, it is sometimes impossible to separate fear from guilt (Chapter 9) and obsessive thinking (Chapter 10). These feelings are all very alive inside Carl.

DEEPER LEVELS OF FEAR

After a client faces the first level of fear in therapy, a door is opened to deeper fears. As therapy continues, it becomes apparent that these deeper fears are the result of threats against other parts of the client's self. These threats are the source of the deeper levels of fear. The threatened parts of the client's self may be described as archetypes, subpersonalities or ego states.

Consider the distinction between when a client's problems are due to a trauma caused by someone else such that the client does not need to take responsibility (*Grendel and His Mother*) and when the problem is due to some unwise decision or act of the client for which the client needs to take responsibility (*Loki's Children*). This distinction is generally recognized when the client faces his or her fear (this chapter), guilt (Chapter 9) and obsessive thinking (Chapter 10). This distinction will become apparent for Jerry in the following session.

JERRY'S DEEPER FEAR OF BEING STUPID

We last visited Jerry three days after his wife left. The night she left, he repeatedly dreamt that his wife had returned and was in the house, but each time he discovered she was not. He now could not deny his fear. It was during this earlier session that I had used the Bear Spirit Posture to provide him with increased ego-strength with the suggestion of being curious and wondering about the deeper reason that led his wife to leave. As the drumming played quietly, I had him stand with his hands resting on his center of harmony, feeling it rise and fall with each breath. As he inhaled a sense of increased strength flowed in, and as he exhaled the strength flow throughout his body. I gave him a recording of the drumming and instructed him to practice it at home to help him learn to find this focused and increased strength in facing his wife leaving. During this session his first level of fear had somewhat subsided and he was ready to face a deeper level of fear. As I sat at the edge of my chair with a straight back, grasping my knees with my hands, I suggested that Jerry sit in this way, and asked him what he felt. He reported that he felt that he was anxiously waiting for something. I suggested, "We are going to take your feeling of fear back through time to see where it began, and it is that answer that you are anxiously waiting for." With his fear as the affect bridge,[3] we again stood in the Bear Spirit Posture for a few minutes while he focused on his breathing, inhaling increased strength and allowing the strength to flow throughout his body, before we sat grasping our knees in the Lady of Cholula Posture, (Fig. 1.2). As I turned on the drumming, I suggested, "Carry your feelings of fear with you as you begin to go back through time, curious and wondering. Watch your life go by, year by year, season by season, places you've been, watch your life go by as you carry your feeling of fear with you, curious and wondering. You will soon find yourself at some important place and time in your life. When you arrive at this place and time, lift the index finger of your right hand to let me know that you are there."

When his finger lifted, I asked him of his experience. "I'm sitting in a reading circle in school. I hate to read. The teacher is going around the circle having each kid read a couple of sentences. I'm scared. It will soon be my turn. I hate this. I stumble and stammer over every word. I'm next. Everyone is looking at me. I feel so stupid, dumb..."

He was still in trance, sitting grasping his knees and the drumming continued. After a few moments of silence, I suggest, "Take a few deep breaths. Slowly let yourself again begin to relax. Stay with the spirit of your younger self feeling frightened of reading out loud. Your fear has an important message to you. You may not understand that message now, but there will be a time when its importance will become clear.... Now, they have now passed you in going around the circle. The reading circle is about over. What happens next?"

"Recess. We get to go out to play kickball."

"Go on. What happens?"

"The teacher makes me captain. I get to pick my kickball team. I love kickball. I'm really good at it."

"Enjoy those good feelings of playing kickball. The spirit of your younger self reminds you that he is good at kickball... Now let yourself move ahead in time. You have told me about some of the books you read. Move ahead in time to an early time when you found that you can enjoy reading."

"I think it was the 8th grade, the teacher lets us pick a book off the shelf and read for the last 10 minutes of class. I still could not read out loud. I would stammer and get the words all jumbled, but I picked a Hardy Boys mystery and read the whole book over a week or two. When I finished the teacher told me I could have the book. That was the first time I can remember enjoying reading. But I still enjoy reading. I think I must have read 50 Hardy Boys books after that."

"Good. Okay, with all the wisdom and understanding of your adult-self, your adult-self who enjoys reading, go back to be with the spirit of your younger self in the reading circle. If you feel like it you can put your arm around your younger self and give him a hug. Let him know that there will be a time when he will enjoy reading. You know him better than anyone else. Though he is anxious, even panics when it comes to reading in a circle, you can appreciate his persistence, his willingness to keep on trying. You know that he will eventually learn to enjoy reading. Appreciate your younger self. Help him understand and feel good about himself."

After offering this counter-narrative I could see Jerry's shoulders drop and the tension leave him. Jerry continued to share his experience. "I never thought about it. I know that I practice pitching a lot. I enjoy practicing and I know that is why I'm good. No pain, no gain. I have to work hard to be good. I did work hard in reading too. I hated feeling stupid and wanted to do better." Though the trauma of the reading circle could be blamed on his teacher, it was apparent that Jerry took responsibility for his poor oral reading ability and had worked hard to overcome it. At least he accepted my suggestion to appreciate his persistence. This persistence was one of Jerry's assets, and it would be used throughout the course of therapy. His deeper level of fear was the fear of being stupid or dumb. He was beginning to take responsibility for his wife leaving him because of his stupidity or dumbness. Using the affect of the fear of his wife leaving him as a bridge allowed him to make this connection and take this responsibility.

ARLENE'S DEEPER FEAR OF FAILURE

It is frequently impossible to separate the three monsters of fear, guilt and obsessive worry. This was most evident with Arlene. We left her last feeling the guilt of her "selfishness" in sitting down to read the newspaper and not getting back to the laundry. "You're still blaming yourself," I noted. "So much guilt. You take responsibility for everything."

This was the route we had taken several weeks earlier, and although Arlene was set upon letting go of her guilt, she now could see herself being sucked right back into it. Her panic was a clear reminder of this previous experience. She was a "control freak" but was unable to control her guilt. Her first level of fear included the fear of her incapability of letting go of guilt.

As I stood, I asked Arlene to stand and place her hands on her center of harmony. "Become aware of your breathing. For the next several breaths, inhale a sense of calmness, and as you exhale let that calmness go deeper inside of you. Let yourself begin to relax. Take your time." After a few minutes I had her sit tall, at the edge of her chair, grasping her knees. I asked her what she felt in sitting in this way, and after a couple of minutes of discussion, she concluded that she felt she was sitting in anticipation of something. I suggested that she was sitting in anticipation of the answers to the questions we will soon ask. Then I turned on the drumming and proceeded, "Face and picture your guilt and fear. Let the experience of your guilt and fear grow. Take your time. As this image forms tell me how you picture it."

After a minute or two Arlene answered, "It's black and heavy."

"Does it take a shape or temperature?"

"It's damp and clammy. No shape. It's more like a damp, heavy cloud. It's hard to breathe. It's suffocating." Arlene's chest was rising and falling steadily and easily, so I took the suffocating as figurative and did not attempt to move her away from this experience. In fact, she showed her emotions more in her eyes. A tear was forming.

"Go on. Stay with the black, heavy and damp spirit cloud of your guilt. What are you experiencing now?"

"I'm a failure. I can do nothing good enough."

"Okay. Hold onto that feeling of failure. Connect your feeling of panic and fear to a fear of failure. Your daughters did not have clean clothes. You are a failure. You have two beautiful daughters and a husband who cares. You are a success. In the dental office you sometimes get behind, but they appreciate your work. The office would have a difficult time without you. You are a success. In doing your school work you sometimes get behind, but your grades are very good. You are a success. Who doesn't get behind sometimes? Think of the times you get in the longest checkout line at the market and you say to yourself, 'Why do I always get in the slowest line?' For some reason you only count the times when the line is slow. You forget the times that there is no line or a very short wait. For some reason you feel an overwhelming need to count your failures and do not appreciate your more important successes." With this counter-narrative I planted a seed then ended the session.

CARL'S DEEPER FEAR OF NOT KNOWING WHAT TO SAY IN HIS SHYNESS.

In the previous session with Carl in pain, he had admitted watching the young couple next door having sex. He defined within himself the feelings of disgust, of feeling terrible and being scared, scared with the rhetorical question, "Will this ever end?" He did not use the word guilt, but it is likely that is what he meant when he said, "feeling terrible."

I proceeded, "First I want to teach you a relaxation exercise and then lead you back through time to find where these feelings came from." I stood and motioned for him to stand as I turned on a recording of rapid but soft drumming. I put my hands on my lower abdomen, my center of harmony, and nodded to him to do the same thing. I then suggested, "Feel your hands rise as you inhale and fall as you exhale," saying these words in rhythm of his breathing. "As you inhale feel a sense of calmness enter your body, and as you exhale let that calmness flow throughout your body and to your head where it can quiet the words that flow through your mind." I continued in this manner for a few minutes, and then suggested that we sit down, demonstrating to him sitting at the edge of his chair with a straight back and grasping his knees. "I suggested that in sitting this way, you are waiting in anticipation, in anticipation for an answer." The drumming continued. "As you sit there, take your feelings, feelings of disgust, feeling terrible, of being scared, take these feelings with you as you begin to go back through time, taking with you the words, disgust, feeling terrible and being scared. Watch the months and seasons go by, the years go by, your life go by as you go back through time. As you go back through time carrying your feelings with you, something will soon catch your attention. When that something catches your attention, lift the index finger of your right hand." These words or similar words were slowly repeated. Soon his finger lifts.

"Where are you?"

"I am in my car in front of Abby's house."

"What is going on?"

"I am taking her home from our church youth group meeting. I put my arm around her and squeeze her shoulders. She gives me a kiss on my cheek and gets out of the car. We've done no more than that and it is nice."

"Stay with your feelings: disgust, feeling terrible and scared. What else is going on?"

"I have an erection and there is a wet spot on my pants. I hope my parents don't see the wet spot."

"Stay with those feelings, with the spirit of your erection and wet spot. We can and will come back to this time. Now go back farther in time, carrying your feelings with you." Almost immediately his finger rises. Where are you now?"

"I'm at a meeting of our church youth group and a new girl walks in, Abby..."

"What's happening?"

"I think she is cute."

"Go on."

"Our youth leader is talking to her and I hear her say that her family just moved to the area. They were in church this morning and I noticed her there but I was too shy to talk to her..."

"How do you feel now?"

"Shy, scared, too scared to talk to her."

"Go ahead a few minutes in time. What is going on?"

"She looks at me and smiles. I think I am the only boy in the group. I want to say something but I can't. Then the leader asks each of us to introduce ourselves. I say my name but that is all I can say."

"What happens?"

"I go home after the meeting and all I can think about is her."

"Okay, then what happens?"

"I see her in school, but I am too shy to say anything. She smiles at me and says, 'Hi,' and I say, 'Hi' back. Later one of the other girls in our youth group tells me that Abby asked her what my problem is. I feel disgusted with myself and embarrassed. I avoid her the next few days."

"When do you finally talk to her?"

"After one of the youth group meetings she asks me if I would drive her home. I'm the only person in the group that drives. Most of the others live close by in town and walk home. Our leader takes one or two home and has taken Abby home. I live a couple of miles out of town so my folks let me take the car. They don't want me to depend on others."

"What do you talk about?"

"I don't remember. All I remember is that my heart was racing a mile a minute and I could not catch my breath. But I took her home after that and it became easier. We liked each other."

"What happened then?"

"We graduated from school about a year and a half later and got married that summer. It felt very right. We were both virgins when we got married, not like it is today."

"Wow. You're right, it is not like it is today."

Carl's deeper level of fear was seen in his shyness. In the next session, I asked him to tell me about his childhood.

"I grew up on a dairy farm. I was an only child and spent a lot of time doing farm chores, bringing in the hay, doing the milking and everything else. I didn't have much time to be a kid."

"What was school like?"

"I had good grades, but I was very shy. I'd go to school on the bus, go to my classes and go back home."

"Tell me about your time in classes."

"I was quiet. No one bothered me. I sat at the back of the classroom or on the side. I was a big kid, the tallest in the class. I would do my work and answer the teacher's questions if she asked me anything, but she knew I knew the answers so she rarely asked me."

"What did you do between classes and at lunch?"

"At lunch I sat by myself. In between classes I went to my locker and switched books and then back to the classroom."

"What was going on in your head? You saw other kids talking and doing things together. Did you ever get teased for being so quiet?"

"I might have been teased in the beginning. I don't remember. I was always big, so I don't think others picked on me. I remember seeing other kids whispering in class or passing notes, but I didn't think much about it. I was listening to the teacher or reading."

"You had more time sitting by yourself at lunch to watch others."

"That's where I did most of my homework. I did feel shy. I don't think I would have known what to talk about if I sat with other kids. I was more comfortable by myself."

"What was your school's mascot?"

"I don't remember. Oh! I think it was the Green Dragons."

"Were you a Green Dragon? Did you ever go to any other activities in school?"

"No. I was not interested in sports. I had to get home to do my chores."

"How about after you got together with Abby? Did you go to any school activities with her?"

"No, except for church things. I think she was in the school chorus. I did go to the school's Christmas chorus program when she sang. That was probably the only thing I ever went to. My folks took me."

Carl's shyness and fear of not knowing what to talk about controlled his life. Jormungand was much alive within him, yet he accepted it so it was not greatly painful except when he fell in love with Abby. It is apparent that his deeper level of fear was his fear of relating to others, but he seemed comfortable in his withdrawal from others. His size prevented him from being teased by others, so he was able to comfortably stay to himself.

To this point, therapy has focused on uncovering the deeper levels of fear for each client. Yet, this is not the end of facing fear. Jormungand's head will continue to surface from deeper and deeper depths. For Arlene, her fear was very much intertwined with guilt. In our culture women tend to be more likely than men to openly face and express their feelings, thus these feelings may be more difficult to separate. Carl's feeling of guilt was obvious when he first talked about his voyeurism, yet the two feelings were easily separated in therapy, likely because his guilt was the more painful of the two. Jerry had yet to identify his feelings of guilt. Guilt will now become the focus of therapy in this next chapter.

CHAPTER 6

HEL: DEALING WITH GUILT

Loki and Angrboda give birth to a daughter, Hel, whose disposition is gloomy and whose body is half rotten with decay. Odin wisely recognizes that Hel, like her brother Jormungand, could be a terrible threat. He acts quickly to rid the world of this danger by casting her into the dark realm of Niflheim, the lower world occupied by those who lack the honor of dying valiantly in battle but who instead died of illness or old age. Hel represents our guilt. Born out of an illicit act of Loki, she is that part of us who suffers in gloom because of our injudiciousness. She acts penitently in caring for the needs of the aged and infirm after death. Her acts are a means to relieve guilt.

HEL'S SUFFERING

Odin commissions Hel to care for the dead and share whatever food she has with those who are sent to her. She builds Eljudnir, a great hall with high walls and huge gates. Within the gates of Eljudnir, Hel is given over to the gloom and doom of endless suffering. She names her bed Sick Bed, and her bed hangings Glimmering Misfortune. Her servants are called Borders-of-sorrow. Those who see them report that they move so slowly that they appear not to move at all.

The gods occasionally journey to Hel's hall to seek wisdom and advice from the dead because of their wealth of knowledge. Travelers who return from Niflheim relate vivid descriptions of Eljudnir. As recorded in *The Prose Edda*, Odin, Baldr's father, ventures to Hel's kingdom in an attempt to seek the interpretation of his son's dream from a long-dead seeress who resides there. Odin's quest takes him into the "gloom and swirling mist" of Niflheim. He finds the great gates of Eljudnir guarded by Hel's hounds, ferocious animals with "hair caked with blood." One of these hounds we will meet in the final chapters of this book. Crossley-Holland recounts the journey of Svipdag[1] as he braves the terrors of Niflheim in search of his mother Groa who could answer Svipdag's question. As Svipdag draws closer to Hel's hall, "the ghastly rotting smell rises towards him. The cold begins to burn him. The darkness reaches up to him as he draws near to the place as dreadful as the worst of fear, the worst of dreams."

While suffering penance in this disgusting world, our temptation to behave in our wrongful manner, without the honor of valiant fighting, may be diminished. In fact, we may be disgusted by such behavior. While disgust and guilt can eat at us just as half of Hel's body is eaten with rot, we feel safe from temptation while doing penance, and penitential deeds may become a major portion of our life.

On the other hand, the other half of Hel's body is healthy, and pictures of her portray her as being beautiful. Half of her body is sexually tempting. Within the confines of Hel's hall, this temptation would function only as a reminder of the deed for which we are doing penance. One might think that the rotten portion of her body, when paired with the tempting portion of her body, would act to decondition or eliminate our feelings of temptation just as a hypnotic suggestion to experience nausea when smoking a cigarette might for some decrease the drive to smoke. However, such negative reinforcers to change behavior are generally considered ineffective just as guilt is generally ineffective in changing Loki's or our behavior.

Similarly, the ineffectiveness of negative reinforcers is also seen in the disorder of bulimia, when the vomiting and suffering of a person does not decrease the person's drive to binge.

HEL'S AUTHORITY

Hel is given the authority over nine worlds. The upper realm of the Norse universe includes: Asgard, home of the warrior gods; Vanaheim, home of the fertility gods; Valhalla, home of the slain warriors, and Alflheim, land of the light elves. Located in the middle world are Midgard, world of the humans; Jotunheim, land of the giants; Nidavellir, land of the dwarfs, and Svartalfheim, land of the dark elves. Niflheim, the dark world of the dead and Eljudnir, Hel's great hall, are in the lower world.

The number nine, the last or end number of the initial sequence of numbers, represents the concept of death and rebirth in Norse mythology. Hel was given extraordinary power, which exceeds that of the gods. She was able to determine life, death and rebirth of residents in all nine worlds. Following the death of Baldr, Odin sought his son's release from Niflheim by petitioning Hel, but Hel offered an impossible proposition for his release as we will see again near the end of this book. Showing no remorse, Hel clings to her commitment and authority by refusing to release Baldr. Although she leads a penitential existence serving the dead in Niflheim, Hel achieves considerable authority, fame and glory.

However, this fame and glory are hollow rewards for Hel's penitence or suffering. Her feelings of guilt and suffering remain unabated in spite of her deeds of penitence. Why? Because of a double bind, she has to suffer even more to find relief from the increased guilt she experiences because of her fame and glory.

DEVELOPMENT OF GUILT

Parents and other parental figures who discipline children use a variety of words and phrases with the hope of eliciting appropriate behavior. Many of these terms generate an atmosphere in which the child reacts with fear or guilt.[1] Threatening phrases that engender fear may include, "Go to your room and don't expect dinner!" or "Do you want a taste of leather?" Shaming phrases that make the child feel guilty are, "Where have I gone wrong?" "This is going to hurt me more than it hurts you," or "After all I have done for you!" Children who experience guilt may develop one of two responses. They may learn to assume responsibility for their actions and make efforts to change their behavior. On the other hand, when parents use shaming words, the children may resent their feelings of guilt and grow angry with their parents for "making them feel guilty." Children may not change their behavior but may feel more guilty for becoming angry. The child's anger can escalate the feelings of guilt. This escalating cycle of guilt-resentment-anger grows and becomes the force that in adulthood drives husbands or wives to explode in abusive rage.

FIRST LEVEL OF GUILT

The first level of guilt is the guilt experienced because of the dysfunctional compulsive acts of the individual. Such acts as an extramarital affair, overeating, an explosive temper or overspending would logically trigger feelings of guilt. This guilt might be sufficient to bring the person to therapy. On the other hand, this guilt might diminish an individual's feelings of self-worth such that it might prevent the person from entering therapy. Moreover, some individuals are effective in rationalizing their behaviors, thus diminishing the experience of guilt. Beyond these superficial aspects of guilt, an underlying insidious dynamic exists where guilt works to promote the behavior and the behavior promotes more guilt. As we shall see, in therapy, it is important to clarify feelings of guilt and lead the client to experience and own this guilt.

CARL'S GUILT OF VOYEURISM AND HIS DAUGHTER'S PREGNANCY

Carl's first level of guilt was very clear. What initially appeared to be delusional, his thoughts that his wife was going next door to sleep with the neighbor, was triggered by his guilt of voyeuristically watching the next-door neighbors having sex. As we continued over the next couple of weeks, I learned about how shy he had been when he met Abby and that she took the initiative when they first got together. They got married right after they both graduated from high school, and he started working in a factory where he now was the quality control engineer and would soon become the plant manager. He was not shy but very proud in his work. During the first ten years of their marriage, he went to college part time to earn his BS in mechanical engineering.

Carl and Abby have a daughter, Angie, who is now married and has two children. Angie and her family live in Virginia. Carl talked of worrying about his daughter as she was growing up because she was not shy and he was afraid that she might become pregnant before she got married, which is in fact what she did. He was both worried about and envious of her self-confidence. Though he hated his own shyness, he also noted the advantage of being shy. It had prevented him from having sex before marriage. He expressed confusion about right and wrong. "Abbie isn't shy. She always seems to know what she wants and gets it. She got me. In that way Angie and Abby are alike. I learned that 'the meek shall inherit the earth.' Angie is not meek, and I hated being meek. I've worked hard and I'm proud of owning our own home and saving enough to retire comfortably. I've not been meek at work. It hurt when Angie got pregnant, but I'm proud of her family now."

Though Carl expressed confusion about the value of meekness and self-confidence, he did not express this confusion with a sense of guilt. The guilt became evident in the deeper narrative of a dream. This session happened early in January. I had not seen Carl over the holidays since he had been busy with his family. His daughter and family had visited for a couple of weeks. As he reported: "Angie and the family went with us to the Christmas Eve service at church, and we had a very pleasant evening. This was the first time she has been to our church since she met Steve and they got married. Yet, the other night I had a dream that Angie refused to go, claiming that the children would be too much to handle in church. In the dream I knew the real reason she didn't want to go was because she was too embarrassed, because she was pregnant before she was married."

"Remember that each part of the dream, each character or action in the dream, each spirit of the dream can be part of you. What part of you is Angie?"

Carl had to admit that the Angie spirit was that part of him that continued to be embarrassed that she was pregnant before she was married. He admitted that at the Christmas Eve service, when he looked around the room, he wondered how many of the people there were remembering or thinking about Angie's premarital pregnancy. This embarrassment, and in fact guilt, was still alive within him. He still harbored some anger when thinking about Angie's "self-confidence," or that she showed so little guilt in telling people that she was pregnant. She had telephoned several of her high school friends telling them with a sense of pride that she was pregnant and going to get married. He had heard first about her pregnancy from Abbie who had heard about it from the mother of one of Angie's friends. He still felt very guilty that he raised Angie with so much arrogance, and he considered her behavior arrogant. Yet he loved her, her husband and the children. Thus, Carl's guilt was not only caused by his voyeuristic obsession but for his failure to teach his daughter humility. But, his wife, too, lacked humility. He commented that Abbie seemed to have totally forgotten about Angie not being married when she got pregnant and seemed most happy about becoming a grandmother.

ARLENE'S GUILT OF NOT PLEASING MOMMY

Arlene's fear was also intertwined with guilt. In therapy she went back and forth between experiencing the two feelings, but for Arlene it was the guilt that drew her to the core of her problems. During the last session Arlene had described her feeling of guilt as "black, heavy, clammy and suffocating," a feeling that, "I can do nothing good enough." It was time to use the Jivaro Underworld Posture, Fig. 1.3. After we stood for a few minutes with our hands on our center of harmony, Fig. 1.1, I suggested that she lay back on the couch with her back of her left hand resting on her forehead, explaining that this posture would take her into the underworld of her unconscious mind. I then turned on the drumming. As we began, I offered the simple suggestion for her to let the drumming carry her back through time to the source of her black, heavy, clammy and suffocating feeling, the spirit of guilt. This feeling again took her back to her childhood. "We are trying to leave the house to go somewhere, probably Gram's house, but Mom can't get out the door. Stuff is lying on the couch and she has to put it away even though it had been there probably for weeks. Part of it is a pile of clean laundry. I start folding the towels, and some of my things are mixed in, so I take them and put them away."

"How old are you?"

"Oh, probably thirteen."

"Good, go back to your 13-year-old self, you are folding the towels and putting away your things." My question probably was not necessary at this point, and for some people or in some situations this distraction takes them away from the regression experience. But the continued drumming kept Arlene in the moment and at the same time being her adult-self. She was able to maintain this double awareness and go back and forth between her younger and adult selves with no problem.

"I run to my room to put my things away and I bump into Mom coming around the corner. She yells at me to keep out of the way, that she can't stand the mess any longer and has to put the stuff away. I guess I am just like her." Arlene says this with sort of a laugh but also with a shiver. This sets the stage for a counter-narrative while still in ecstatic trance:

"Okay, move to your feelings. Be your 13-year-old self. Grab your clothes out of the pile and run to your room. On the way you bump into your mother. What are you feeling?"

"I feel scared. Mommy is angry at me. I didn't put my clothes away. I feel guilty that some of my things were still mixed in with the laundry. I should have put them away days ago."

"Let the spirits of your adult-self be with your 13-year-old self. With the wisdom of your adult-self, help your younger self understand."

"When Mom is racing like this, if she found my clothes in this laundry, she would yell at me, 'Why haven't you put away your clothes?'"

"Can your adult-self see that Mommy is unfair? She hadn't put her things away either."

"Yeah."

"Tell that to your 13-year-old self. You don't have to feel guilty. You didn't see your couple of things mixed in with your mother's things. It was unfair for her to be angry at you."

Arlene half smiles.

"Children and adolescents don't usually understand these feelings but they feel intensely. Your 13-year-old self has learned to react in fear and is quick to blame herself. She is quick to feel guilty. That way maybe Mommy won't be quite as mad. You have carried that fear and guilt with you even up to today. Somehow, if you always do the right thing, then Mommy won't be mad. If you do something wrong, then it is your fault that she is mad. You just can't be a kid who sometimes makes mistakes."

JERRY BEGINS TO TAKE RESPONSIBILITY FOR HIS WIFE LEAVING

Jerry was the one client for whom guilt was not greatly evident when he expressed fear, in this case fear of his wife leaving. Anger sometimes rises to the surface, but not guilt. Two things alerted me to Jerry's potential areas of guilt. The first was noted when his 4th grade teacher selected him to be captain of his kickball team. The second, which we will get back to when considering his deeper levels of guilt, is his history of asthma.

In Jerry's regression experience of the hated reading circle and going out afterward for recess, the teacher chose him to be captain of the kickball team. As Jerry described his experience, "I picked the class nerd who couldn't kick the side of a barn. I felt bad for him so I picked him. I was always doing that, befriending the underdog. But I remember having an asthma attack when he ran up to kick the ball, missed it and fell on his butt." Even though Jerry's experience was told as a memory rather than relived, what he remembered demonstrated his sensitivity to the pain of others and a desire to rescue them.

"Stay with that experience. You rescued the nerd from the hurt he must have been experiencing. It would have been nice if someone would have been sensitive to your feelings in the reading circle. Let your adult-self understand your feelings in picking the nerd."

"Yeah, I was hurting for him, thinking about how he must feel always being chosen last."

"You were always doing that, picking the underdog."

"Yeah, I remember becoming friends with the new kids in class. I guess I wanted to be accepted too. I had a lot of friends even though I felt dumb in school. I guess I had no close friends that I spent all my time with, but everyone was my friend."

"You felt something was missing in having no close friends that you did everything with."

"Uh huh. I wanted a close friend. I'm thinking about one new kid in elementary school I saw just a few weeks ago. He stopped me to talk, and he remembered how when he came to the area, I was the first one to talk with him, but I don't remember a thing about him in high school, though he must have been there since he is still in the area. It felt good that he remembered me, but I don't know what happened in between. I have no idea what happened to the nerd. I bet he went on to college and is a doctor or something."

"Hum. You reach out to people in need, but for some reason the relationship does not continue."

"When I met Liz, she was a secretary and struggling to pay the bills. She had recently moved out of her parents' house into an apartment. I don't know how a single woman can make it alone on a secretary's salary. One day when she complained to me about her bills, right away I wanted to help her. I thought us living together would make her life a lot easier. She wanted to get married, it didn't take us long. But again, something happened and the relationship crumbled. I guess I haven't been thinking about her for the last several years. The baseball team seems to need me more as a pitcher. Every time I wanted to do something else, the captain would call me and tell me that they needed me that night. I guess Liz needed me but didn't tell me. I guess she did tell me but I wasn't listening. I guess that after I made her life easier by paying her bills, I took her for granted. She would love me because I reached out to her, but then I didn't do anything else."

"You didn't do anything else to keep the feeling of love alive. You rescued her, you rescued the baseball team, you rescued the new kid in school, you rescued the class nerd. People appreciate you for rescuing them, but then nothing continues after that. Love is when people appreciate you, but something is missing after that."

Jerry had become very quiet, very introspective. The session began with a brief ecstatic trance induction and regression experience, but the trance flowed into this introspective experience. By my continuing the *yes-set* and reflecting his introspective experience, the trance was continued and Jerry was taking responsibility for his relationships not continuing. We did not talk about his feelings of guilt. Talking about his guilt was not necessary; it was just there. Somehow, for him, love was experienced in the process of rescuing and giving, but the continued experience of love as experienced through equal sharing and just being together was missing. Recognizing this now brought about a feeling of guilt. He has had to run off to rescue others in order to feel fulfilled.

DEEPER LEVELS OF GUILT

The deeper levels of guilt are not a direct result of the client's behavior but are part of a deeper personality pattern that repeats itself over and over again in the person's life. This personality pattern is an automatic unconscious response to life's situations triggering feelings of guilt. Though this guilt may be legitimate, it also may be illegitimate or unnecessarily held by the client. Uncovering this guilt involves uncovering these personality patterns and automatic thoughts. Some of these patterns that are driven by feelings of guilt and are found frequently in our culture include the codependent, the perfectionist and the suffering servant. Example of these patterns will be examined in the remainder of this chapter, but first we will return to Carl's struggle with his obsession with voyeurism and the related guilt. His guilt at first seems legitimate to the problem at hand and not related to a deeper personality issue driven by guilt.

CARL'S GUILT IN HIDING HIS GOD-GIVEN FEELINGS

Carl's second level of guilt began to emerge with the deeper narrative found in the following ecstatic experience. We began with our usual trance induction procedure using the Bear Spirit Posture and then went into the Jivaro Underworld Posture of lying back with the back of our left hands resting on our forehead as the drumming played. Carl reported at the conclusion of the drumming, "I was watching a rat creep along. I saw it sneak out of the barn near the house in which I grew up. It crept along the culvert along the road. It didn't seem to try to get away from me. I followed it along the culvert until it disappeared into a culvert pipe under the road. I waited for it to come out the other side but it didn't."

"Is that the end?"

"Not quite. I got down and looked into the pipe. The rat was just sitting near the middle of the pipe, looking like he was hiding."

"Tell me more about the rat, your rat spirit guide." I turned the drumming back on.

"It was gray and it crept with its head down. Its tail was dragging."

"What can you imagine it was feeling?"

"It looked like it had been doing something it shouldn't and it was sneaking away like a dog with its tail between its legs."

"What feeling would that suggest?"

"I guess guilt."

"You were also in this experience following the rat. What were you feeling?"

"I don't know. I was just following the rat. I guess curious."

"Take a few moments to put yourself inside the rat, an important spirit guide, hiding in a culvert pipe. Can you find that part of you that is hiding?"

"I can't hide. Maybe I feel like hiding from Abbie or from people at work, but there is no way I can hide or even get away from any of them. I guess I am hiding from the neighbors, hiding behind the window shade. I wouldn't go out in the yard if they were out there but that's not a real problem. They wouldn't know that."

"Take that feeling of hiding from your neighbors. Can you think of when you have had that feeling before?"

"When I first met Abbie I wanted to see her at school, but sometimes I would hide around the corner or somewhere so she wouldn't see me. Or when I went to class, I would often be the last one in and sit in the back row. I didn't want to be seen. I didn't want to talk to anybody."

"Stay with that feeling of wanting to hide, of not wanting anyone to see you, of not wanting to talk to anybody. Stay with that feeling and see where it takes you."

"I never know what to say to people. But that is not true. At work I have no problems with what to say. I have plenty to say."

"At work you have been trained as to what needs to be said. With your neighbors, with your early relationship with Abbie, with kids at school, you did not know what to say. On the farm you had only your parents and the cows to talk to."

"I don't think I ever talked at home. I must have talked at home because I remember my mother saying, 'I don't believe you said that.' I have no idea what I said, but I remember feeling like I had nothing to say to anyone."

"If teachers asked you questions, you knew the answers."

"Yeah, I was smart and knew the answers, but at other times I would not know what to say."

This feeling of not knowing what to say is quite common and is likely what is behind most shyness. It is more of a feeling of anxiety or fear and humiliation. We needed to continue but use as the affect bridge the feeling of guilt. "Okay, when you looked in the culvert pipe and described how the rat felt, you said he was feeling guilt.

Let's go back in time again, but this time carry the feeling of guilt with you as you lay on the couch with your hand on your forehead."

Carl was quick to go back to when he put his arm around Abby and she kissed him on the cheek while they sat in the car, his erection and the wet spot that appeared on his pants. The wet spot was also something he wanted to hide.

"Feel what is going on inside of you, the excitement, your erection and the wet spot on your pants. Besides feeling disgusted and terrible, there are other words to better describe how you feel."

After a few moments Carl did mention the word "guilt."

"Say those words again."

"I felt guilty."

"Hang onto that feeling, feeling guilty. Listen to those words. 'I feel guilty.' You feel guilty for what? For having an erection and the wet spot on your pants? Stay with that feeling and thought. You feel guilty about a normal, God-given reaction of being turned on sexually? Take those thoughts with you this week." As this session came to an end, Carl was left examining his sexuality and his deeper level of guilt.

THE CODEPENDENT

As mentioned above, there are a number of personality types that are driven by guilt including the codependent, the abuser, the perfectionist and the suffering servant. The typical codependent person needs to be needed and seeks other people to fill this need. The codependent person is frequently the rescuer, the person who marries an alcoholic with the hope of rehabilitating him or her, or the nurse who wants to help everybody. Jerry in seeking to rescue Liz early in their relationship and rescuing his baseball team can be considered codependent.

THE PERFECTIONIST

The perfectionist is not perfect but feels he or she should be perfect. The word "should" is the red flag, a flag of guilt. For some reason, often because of conditional love, such individuals feel a need to prove themselves by trying to be perfect. "If I am not perfect my father won't love me." This person can also become unbearable because of a need to have others also be perfect, becoming intolerant of the mistakes or incompetency of others. Often in reaction to their own incompetency, they become irritated, possibly looking for support from others that they are still loved. Arlene is the perfectionist.

ARLENE REALIZES THAT SHE CANNOT MAKER HER MOTHER HAPPY

The 13-year-old Arlene finds some of her clean clothes in the stack of laundry on the living room sofa. She runs to put it away and bumps into her mother as she goes around the corner into her room. Her mother screams, "Get out of my way." Arlene feels frightened and guilty because she can't do anything right to please her mother. As the therapy session continued, I mentioned, "Sometimes when you put away the clothes your mom might be happy, sometimes she might ignore you, and other times she might be angry. You just don't know what you can do to make her happy."

"I don't remember ever making her happy. All I see her doing is being angry. I guess that in between she was ignoring me, but I don't know what she was doing."

"Wow! You have no memory of her smiling at you or of her being happy."

"I was looking through some old pictures the other day and found one of her smiling, and my first reaction was, 'Who's that?' I didn't recognize her."

"That is so sad...to be that unhappy. Tell me about your father in such a situation as when you were putting away the clothes."

"Dad is sitting in the car. I know he is fuming. The horn honks a couple of time. That is going to make mom even angrier."

Mom feels guilty for not getting everything done, for not pleasing everyone, and for not being perfect. Daughter is feeling guilty for not pleasing mom and for not keeping the peace in the family. Within a family, guilt is passed down through the generations.

THE SUFFERING SERVANT

Many Christians take personally the belief that Christ gave his life to save humanity by believing that they must continually serve others without expecting anything in return. I've heard such phrases as, "If I don't give until it hurts, I have not given enough," or "I cannot afford any leisure time because leisure time would show that I am not working hard enough." These same individuals often think to themselves, "I wish I was appreciated more," yet at the same time they feel guilty for such selfish thoughts. This trap of believing in selfless giving and feeling guilty for selfishly wanting appreciation has been referred to as "The Suffering Servant Syndrome." This syndrome is frequently found in nurses and other service-oriented professions. I heard a number of years ago that the autoimmune diseases such as asthma, allergies, arthritis and lupus are associated with this personality type. I forget who the speaker was and have been unable to find the reference, but I have been impressed with how often I have found individuals with this personality type suffering with these diseases. Jerry's mention of his asthma attack when the class nerd he chose to be on his kickball team fell alerted me to the possibility that he might be the suffering servant type, especially since he worked as a physical therapist.

JERRY'S GUILT OF NEEDING TO BE APPRECIATED

So as the therapy session with Jerry continued, I inserted a new word in our talk, "give." "You give so much. In rescuing Liz, your money went to paying her bill. You give your time over and over to the baseball team. You gave your understanding and emotional support to the class nerd you chose for the kickball team. You gave your friendship to the new kids in school. You give every day to your patients as a physical therapist. You give and give, and what do you receive in return? Your wife leaves. Though your patients may show improvement, they still leave with some pain and generally don't express their appreciation for what you did for them. The new kids in school and the class nerd vanished in time. None seem to greatly appreciate what you gave and give. Everyone vanishes from your life, including your wife, with no appreciation."

"Appreciation shouldn't be important. I should give to others just for the sake of giving, just because it is the right thing to do."

"Uh huh. But it still hurts when you are not appreciated. Everyone needs to be appreciated. It's the appreciation that gives them the strength to continue giving." I now deliberately began to move away from him, creating some tension by opening an argument, which started to bring Jerry out of trance in order to defend himself. Though reframing can be trance inducing, the shock of a new way of thinking can also bring a person out of trance.

"I work. I get paid. I don't need appreciation."

"Even so, a little appreciation would feel good, and make your day."

"Yeah, it would be nice, but I don't need it."

"You don't need it; it shouldn't be important. Why shouldn't it be important?"

"When you give, you shouldn't expect anything in return. It feels good to give just for the sake of giving. Giving should be fun."

"That sound like something a mother would say."

Jerry laughs quietly to himself. "That's what Mom often said. She was always giving and with a smile. People loved her."

"People loved her. She was appreciated. What did you dad think about all she did? Did she have time for him?"

"Oh, he thought it was great. He was proud of her."

"You have made Liz's life much easier, yet she doesn't appreciate you. She doesn't appreciate how hard you work for her. She doesn't appreciate how good you are as a P.T. and how you help your patients. She doesn't appreciate how good a pitcher you are and how much you do for your team. She doesn't appreciate you, and that must hurt. Close your eyes. Let yourself hold those thoughts. Feel the hurt and stay with it."

Jerry looked tense. His breathing was irregular. He looked quite uncomfortable, especially in his breathing. Now we moved back into the trance state. The drumming is still playing quietly in the background.

"Stay with those feelings. You look uncomfortable. Stay with that discomfort. Take your time. Look for the right words to describe how you feel. Your wife doesn't appreciate you. You feel hurt, but that thought and the feeling makes you feel uncomfortable. What is that discomfort?"

"I shouldn't expect her to appreciate me. I do those things because I love her."

"You shouldn't expect. Something is wrong with expecting her to appreciate you. You feel guilty about expecting appreciation." I could see Jerry's head nodding slightly in affirmation. "You feel guilty about wanting her to appreciate what you do for her. You are supposed to do those things just because you love her. You shouldn't expect anything in return. Expecting something in return is selfish. Stay with that feeling of guilt.

CHAPTER 7

FENRIR: DEALING WITH THE GROWING OBSESSION

Fenrir, the third child of Loki and Angrboda, the first born is a wolf. Odin allows the wolf to roam freely in the fields and woods around Asgard. The gods, who consider Jormungand and Hel as potential threats, apparently are not especially afraid of Fenrir. Are they in denial that he is a serious threat? Only when he starts to grow beyond the normal size of a wolf do they remember prophecies that a wolf will be the cause of Odin's death.

THE INITIAL DENIAL

Sex addict is a label that could be attributed to Loki, who sired three children during his affair with Angrboda. The sex addict initially says, "I have no problem. I can just stop having the affair anytime." For other addictions the initial fear of Fenrir, when he is young, is also not great. The alcoholic and the compulsive gambler deny the power of their addiction when they say, "I can quit drinking whenever I want. I have no problem," or "I have no need to gamble. I just enjoy it." The abusive husband ends the confrontation with his wife by saying "I'll never abuse you again." Such words are easy to use for an addict who denies the seriousness of the problem. It's easy for the obese person to say, "One more slice can't hurt." Fenrir is no danger, there is nothing unusual about him or about one or two drinks. "A married man is normal if he wants to have a little sex away from the wife." We all know differently. Only when we stop denying the problem do we recognize the real and growing obsession. As we admit to our problem and open ourselves to feelings of fear and guilt, our obsessive worrying then starts to grow and become apparent.

People are normal when they occasionally worry about whether they remembered to turn off the lights or locked the door after leaving home. But, for some people, their obsessive worry forces them to return repeatedly to check to seek if the lights are off or the door is locked, even when the lights and the door were checked just moments earlier. For these people their obsession precedes their feelings of guilt and fear. When such behavior begins to interfere with the normal activities of daily living, then help is needed. Some worrying protects us from making mistakes. Obsessive worry and compulsive behaviors prevent us from living effective lives.

Jerry, just a day or two before he came to therapy, was in denial that his wife was really capable of leaving him. Now Jerry is taking the threat seriously and is in a state of panic. The other two clients, Arlene and Carl went beyond this denial of their problems long ago and are now taking them very seriously. Generally, individuals who come to therapy realize the seriousness of the problem.

THE GROWING OBSESSION

Fenrir grows and grows, and after some time the gods realize the wolf is a problem. Like Fenrir, the usual problems of everyday life can begin to grow to frightening proportions. An unfaithful wife eventually discovers it is much more difficult to end the affair than she had first thought. She may end the affair only to discover that she spends all of her time thinking of her paramour. Such thoughts as "What am I missing?" or "I wish I could share what I am doing with ..." have taken control of her life. The initial fear, Jormungand, and guilt, Hel, seem like small problems in comparison to the thoughts that have grown to an obsession.

ARLENE

The last session with Arlene revealed how much she was like her mother. She had recalled how when she was young she raced around doing everything she could do in an attempt to please her mother, yet her mother was never happy. Her mother could never get everything done and because she couldn't, she would yell at anyone at home to help. Arlene could see her mother in herself and was terrified by this recognition just as she was terrified by her mother. She hated herself for being this way but couldn't seem to do anything to stop it. If she stopped to enjoy the family, then she got behind in her tasks and she knew that she was going to become upset. She did not know what to do.

CARL

Carl's rat dream, the wet spot on his pants and the humiliation he felt in his need to hide, including hiding behind and peeking through a closed shade at his neighbors, only added to his voyeuristic obsession. On Wednesday nights, when he tried to stay away from the window his obsession grew, and when he got to the window he felt extremely anxious and guilty. During the rest of the week as the days passed, getting closer and closer to Wednesday, Carl's obsession, guilt and anxiety grew and grew to where he thought he might explode or could scream.

JERRY

Jerry, during the last session, denied that he wanted people to show him appreciation when he rescued them. He did accept the comment that he had been the rescuer throughout his life, from rescuing the nerd he chose for his kickball team up to rescuing Liz from her financial troubles when he married her. "After all I have given her, I don't know what her trouble is," was something Jerry said in several of the earlier sessions. He had also expressed the belief that Liz should appreciate him for his success as a baseball pitcher, but instead she resented the time he spent playing and not with her.

In this session he revealed another dimension of his resentment for Liz's lack of appreciation: "The baseball team needs me. I made them a winning team." Again he was the rescuer, the rescuer of the team, and Liz doesn't appreciate how he rescues others. In his job as a physical therapist he gives himself to others. It was very apparent that he prides himself on giving himself to others, yet his wife doesn't appreciate this part of him. "Liz is selfish," he said at one point during this session.

Jerry was beginning to accept the fact that he seeks appreciation, though I did not again confront him with this trait. I did mention that he received a lot of appreciation from the baseball team, and he smiled widely. His recognition of his obsession with seeking appreciation was growing. Along with this growing obsession was his growing resentment of his wife for her lack of appreciation.

THE STRENGTH OF THE WARRIOR

As Fenrir grew and grew, soon only Tyr, the god of war, had the nerve to approach Fenrir to feed him. Each individual has an inner strength that, to a greater or lesser degree, enables the person to face life's torment.

The warrior part of the person says "I am not going to let this get the best of me." The warrior, with the hope for victory, has courage to face the obsession. For each obsessive thought and each compulsive act, the integrity of the individual rises and says, "I can beat this." Were it not for this integrity more people would commit suicide. We all have a warrior within who fights with strength or will power, always ready to stand up against the obsession. Sometimes the battle is waged on a cognitive level by the individual who employs the strength of self-talk, a dialogue with oneself in which a person tries to find a way out of the dreadful condition or situation. All of the clients except for Jerry had found sufficient personal strength to deal with their problems on their own for months or even years until their problem reached such a proportion that they sought therapy.

For Arlene and Carl their warrior side eventually admitted that the problem was unmanageable or the power of the obsession too great, and they acted by seeking external support—by making an appointment for therapy. The wisdom of Odin and the courage of Tyr urge an individual to seek help from a therapist. As a psychologist, I have great faith in an individual's will to survive and in the innate ability for self-healing and growth. This will to survive, the warrior part in us all, will continue to grow in strength. The innate ability to heal oneself grows in the subconscious mind. This ability is the Æsir, Odin, Tyr and the entire pantheon of gods within.

ARLENE

Arlene was ready to recognize how much she was like her mother, otherwise she would not have ecstatically gone back to that situation in which she bumped into her mother while carrying her clean clothes to her room. Being ready to face such a fact takes increased personal or ego strength. This realization greatly increased Arlene's guilt and anxiety, as well as her hatred for herself, but she was subconsciously prepared.

A warrior without a war is useless; his weapon rusts, his strength weakens and his courage dissipates. Conversely, warriors need battles to grow stronger. A warrior needs a worthy adversary. Tyr needed Fenrir to feed to keep himself strong. The more Tyr grew in strength, the more he needed the wolf to grow to challenge his strength and to resolve and bolster his courage. The struggles in life provide us with occasions in which we can rise in strength and fortitude. Hercules needed his twelve labors to gain immortality. As Fenrir's strength grew, so did Tyr's resolve to face Fenrir. Many people are inclined to seek challenges to stay fit and ready.

Most people have a protective warrior within, a warrior who seeks battle in order to stay strong. Some individuals demonstrate their inner warrior in their own way by seeking help more quickly. People who have made it through life with minimal or no adversities are more vulnerable to the rapid growth of obsessions than those who regularly face difficult situations in life. In rare cases, they may be so overwhelmed that they commit suicide.

CARL

Of the three clients whose personal struggles are presented in this book, Carl is most likely the one who had experienced the least adversity throughout his life and his experience now was a real blow to him. Three thoughts had surfaced however that gave Carl some strength to face his tormentor. First, he became honest with me that he knew that Abbie was not having an affair and that his own feelings of guilt for watching his neighbors have sex were fueling his obsession. Second, he recognized his struggle between appreciating Abbie's self-confidence and the value of his own shyness, a shyness that had prevented him from getting Abbie pregnant before they were married. He was very confused about shyness vs. self-confidence and the meaning of his sexuality. Third, a seed had been planted that his guilt with regard to his sexuality might be unnecessary, since his sexuality was God-given. I suggested that Carl had gained considerable self-confidence and strength as he aged, especially self-confidence at work, and the strength of this self-confidence allowed him to now face these important questions. This strength became evident in the depths of a dream. As the quality assurance engineer at work, Carl was involved with all departments and almost everyone in the plant. Among these people were several attractive women who were often the focus of attention for many of the men. Carl had always been above such play at work. He had been effective in his work, and he believed the emotional distance he placed between the regular line workers and himself helped when he had to exercise authority and tell employees how to do things differently, especially since he was not their direct supervisor. In his dream, one of these attractive women grabbed his butt has he walked by. He turned and they simply smiled at each other. Nothing was said.

"What do you make of it?"

"I don't know."

"How did you feel in the dream? How do you feel about this new spirit guide?"

"I don't know. I sort of liked it. I didn't feel especially shocked or that anything was wrong."

"Remember, in the dream you created her and she is likely part of you. What is she thinking or feeling?"

"All that comes to mind is that she is saying, 'Pay attention to me.'"

"Pay attention to me. Pay attention to your sexuality." Tyr, the warrior within has an issue in life with which to deal and gain strength. "What is your sexuality all about?" Carl is more open now to deal with this problem with greater strength, gentleness, patience and curiosity.

Fear and emotional pain act as a wake-up call to the warrior within. The warrior within may not be called upon unless a situation has become so grave that it erupts in intense emotional pain. Pain, both emotional and physical, stimulates the flow of endorphins and adrenaline, chemicals which are naturally produced by the body, but when activated to flight or fight can charge a human with nearly superhuman strength.

Some individuals let their inner warrior lie dormant until a problem reaches a crisis. Only when the emotional pain becomes intolerable will the individual seek to "bring it to a head." Some people, who neglect their troubles or disregard stress hoping the situation will improve by itself, respond only when it worsens. Paul Watzlawick[1] describes these as cases in which "the situation is hopeless, but not serious." Only when the situation becomes serious is a person ready to rise to the challenge to change what in the present seems hopeless.

JERRY

Jerry had always prided himself on being self-sufficient. He could take care of himself. His need and ability to reach out to others, to rescue others, depended upon his own self-sufficiency and strength. He denied any personal needs, though this denial did not extend to his need to rescue others. He would not use the word "need" in this case but called it a "want," saying he "wanted" to help others. He was hurt that Liz had left him, but he didn't feel especially needy of her. When Liz left him, he dropped off the baseball team. He was too preoccupied with getting his life together and getting used to taking care of their daughter on visitation days. Now that Liz had been gone for about six months, however, he was ready to call his old friends on the baseball team. Though he was out of shape, he started going to their practices and considered joining the team again next season. He had been away from the team for only a year. He had total confidence in his belief that he could deal with this problem. He was seeing Beth every other weekend. He planned to take her to the baseball games. He could be with her while sitting on the sidelines. He could teach her about the game. It was obvious that we were near the end of therapy. I did suggest that he come back for one last session.

PULLING TOGETHER OUR RESOURCES

The gods' worry grows not only because of the size of Fenrir but also because they remembered a prophecy that a wolf will be the cause of Odin's death. The wise god Odin knows better than to wait any longer, and so should we. It is time to call together all of the gods to decide what was to be done. Our own basic instincts and unconscious awareness provide us with a "prophecy" which warns us we may be involved in life-threatening danger.

Just as Odin regards the individual gods' and goddesses' input as a significant contribution to his council, each person needs to consider the value of each resource in the quest for mental health. We call upon the wisdom of Odin, the warrior strength of Tyr, and the nurturing support of Freyr and his sister Freyja. Loki provides a disruption when the gods and goddesses begin to take themselves and their problems too seriously. This disruption, when taken with a sense of humor, frees a person to change. Laughter is good medicine and a sense of humor is a cherished quality. The maxims "Man plans and God laughs" and "Life is too important to be taken seriously" may help us see our troubles from a proper perspective. These resources are within us, but it may take others such as a therapist, a support group, friends, family and fellow workers to make us aware of our resources.

JERRY

Jerry's strength of Tyr was present. He had thought through his hurt that Liz left him and was making plans for the next years of his life. He found the wisdom to rationalize away his hurt. He was nurturing himself by going to baseball practices, going to the games, and helping out the pitchers in warming up. Beth was old enough that when he was warming up a pitcher, she could sit by herself nearby. One of the other players had a six-year-old son ,and they could play together. He hoped they would become good friends. In that setting he felt very appreciated.

CARL

In therapy, the focus of attention is generally more on feelings than on intellectualizing, but there is a place for intellectualizing. In bringing together one's resources, a major resource is one's intellect. In this session with Carl, the question was raised, what was his sexuality all about? There's a place in therapy to discuss this question from Odin's perspective, calling upon Carl's wisdom. Carl was quick to admit that it was a question that he had not really thought about until I planted the seed a couple of weeks ago.

I pointed out to him, "We are all sexual beings. Our sexuality is God-given. It is the way we are made. If we did not get horny, our species would come to an end. You avoided dealing with sexuality during your youth by being shy. Is that the healthy way to deal with those feelings?"

Putting it that way, Carl had to answer, "No." But he did not know what would be healthy.

"Looking at pornography, having sex with anyone willing, having sex before marriage, are these healthy ways for youth to deal with their sexuality?" Again he had to answer, "No."

"Is masturbation wrong?" I didn't know what he would answer, and he didn't answer at first. He finally answered that he did not know.

I pushed him a bit further, "Is it wrong for a young man to relieve his sexual drive by masturbating so that he does not take advantage of his girlfriend? Is it wrong for a young couple to talk about these feelings?"

To the second question Carl answered, "But talking about these things would turn them on and would lead to sex."

I ended the session with, "A lot to think about. I trust that the right answers are the answers you come up with for yourself."

We had called the gods together, Odin in his wisdom, Freyr in his concern for sexuality, Tyr in his strength and will power. The one god left out was Thor, because he would react to these questions impulsively. I was playing the role of Loki in being provocative, in challenging Carl to think.

ARLENE

The goddess that Arlene needed most was Freyja for her nurturing. Arlene was not nurtured by her mother, and she had a difficult time nurturing Tim and the children. I challenged Arlene to do something each day. It would take only a few minutes, but important minutes, away from her crazy schedule of working, going to school and caring for the house and her family. "Maybe while you are driving home from work or from school, think of Tim and think of the kids. Think of something you appreciate in each, and when you next see them, tell them of your appreciation." The wise part of Arlene was quick to see the importance of this assignment, and she was ready to do it.

THE IMPORTANCE OF KEEPING OUR OBSESSION ALIVE

The gods and goddesses know it is important not to kill Fenrir because blood spilled from the wolf would pollute and desecrate the temple of Asgard. The wise part of us knows that if we could kill our obsessive worry, the symptom of a deeper problem would show up in a different form and would likely be an even greater tormentor.

CARL

For Carl, the potential for growth would have been poisoned by killing Fenrir, by finding ways for Carl to ignore and not deal with his obsession. Carl's thinking and struggle to answer these questions with regards to sexuality would bring Carl to a new place in life. Carl was no longer finding protection from the sexual world around him through his shyness or innocence.

JERRY

For Jerry, Fenrir had died or at least lay dormant. Jerry was feeling strong and good about himself. He believed that Liz was the loser when he received the divorce papers. He went ahead with the divorce with the commitment of getting on with his life and was actually excited about it. He was excited about regaining his pitching arm and getting back into baseball. He dropped out of therapy without really facing his tormentor.

But about three years later Jerry returned to therapy with his new wife. She was unhappy with all the time he spent playing baseball. Jerry was feeling great resentment and a sense of panic, of "here we go again." I expected that he hoped I would try to convince his new wife, Sherry, that he should be allowed to play ball. But this time he was more ready to face the real problem in his life, a problem that he really did not understand, i.e., of his wife's needs and expectations of coming first. Though Sherry and Beth were getting along fine, Sherry's resentment of having to go to the baseball games in order to keep an eye on nine-year-old Beth was growing. She felt she had no time just with Jerry. With Sherry's commitment to Jerry, she prevented him from ignoring the real problem in therapy. Fenrir really did not die.

THE DISRUPTIVE CRY FOR HELP

What is the role of Thor on Odin's council? He is the strongest of the gods, yet he is quite impulsive, a trait that gets him in trouble. Thor's qualities of impulsiveness and disruptiveness could have been disastrous for the gods and goddesses if he had smashed his hammer into the wolf's skull. Fenrir's blood would have desecrated the temple.

The gods and goddesses know the wolf poses a real danger and has to be dealt with carefully and cautiously. They deliberate with one intent. Thor, the alarmist, would have distracted the others from the problem. An individual's impulsiveness interferes with therapy when it causes the client to run away from potential for change. Thor within the client throws up a smoke screen by threatening suicide, by screaming, "I can't stand it!" or by seeking medication as a means to avoid emotional pain which may motivate the client to change. The client who seeks hospitalization as the solution is the client who is not ready to face or deal with the deeper problem. One early goal in therapy is to quiet and restrain Thor—to lead the client to a discovery that these behaviors interfere with real change.

One man entered therapy with constant ranting that he was going to kill himself and that life was not worth living. For most of the first hour he was unwilling to slow down and tell me about what was going on. He continued to express loudly his feeling of worthlessness. His cry for help did not let the door open for help to look in. To counter his disruptive behavior, I had to join the disruptive energy by becoming disruptive myself, stating, "Look, there are two things we can do. I am unable to provide you with around the clock observation to prevent you from killing yourself, so, one option is for me to arrange for you to be committed to the psychiatric ward of the hospital. Or, the other option is for you to cut out all this talk and let us get down to work on the real problem." He immediately quieted down, and I had the opportunity to listen to his frustrations in life.

JERRY

As Jerry was leaving for one of his evening practices, Sherry pleaded, "Do you have to go? I don't want you to go." He just looked at her, took a deep breath of frustration, turned and left. He was angry throughout the practice, and one of the other players asked him what was wrong. He just shook his head and did not answer. When he got home, he and Sherry really got into it. He yelled at her, "Never do that to me again!" Sherry locked herself in the spare bedroom and did not sleep with him that night.

The next session of therapy centered on Jerry's explosive temper. Jerry could not remember ever exploding like this before in his life. The explosion scared Sherry, but it really scared him too. This explosion disrupted the course of therapy for a couple of sessions. It was an effective smoke screen, diverting the issue away from Jerry's inability to understand and meet Sherry's needs. I believed that he likely understood these needs at one level but did not want to have to face them. A solution, having to choose between Sherry and baseball seemed impossible to him. He was married to Sherry. If she really loved him, he thought, she would let him play baseball, knowing that it was so important to him

ARLENE

"My eight-year-old stepdaughter, Jessi, came running around the corner carrying some toys to her room and bumped into me." As Arlene tells this story she breaks into tears. "I at first got so angry for her running in the house. I did not think of thanking her for putting away her toys. When I think back I could see she was scared and in tears herself, but I was so angry I could not see it then." The fact that she could see Jessi's fear now was a great step forward. Arlene could see herself in Jessi, experiencing all the feelings she remembered when she bumped into her mother. Before reliving this experience with her mother she could not have been as empathetic with Jessi. Arlene hated herself, hate that was disruptive or ineffective in the therapeutic process.

"Wow, that is just what happened to you in bumping into your mother. How scary that something like that would happen just now.

It has a real message for you. It is time to be patient, curious and gentle with yourself in listening to that message."

Later that evening, however, she did give Jessi a hug, apologizing and telling her that she very much appreciated her putting away her things.

CARL

Though I had been able to help Carl see the value in facing his tormentor, his condition was still very fragile. His confidence was easily disrupted and he returned to his fragile cry for help. This happened a couple of days later at work when he happened to see the woman he had the dream about. They passed each other, she had a nice smile for him, and this time he noticed and smiled back. A few minutes later he went into a panic, afraid to think about her. I reassured him that the exchange of smiles was very appropriate, and that if he had not smiled she would have felt something was wrong. A smile is an appropriate recognition of recognition. But to Carl, the smile was something more. Feelings were likely rising in him, sexual feelings or sexual thoughts that he believed were wrong and he could not allow to happen. To him it had always been wrong to have sexual feelings or thoughts towards anybody except his wife, and his panic prevented him from recognizing these feelings towards someone else.

These feelings and thoughts presented Carl with more to think about. We spent some time formulating some further questions. In Chapter 4, Moore and Gillette's model of male archetypes was presented. Each of the four male archetypes has a parallel female archetype.[2] Opposite the King is the Nurturing Mother. The healthy King provides for his people, his family. The Nurturing Mother provides by bringing the family to her table and the child to her breast. Opposite the Warrior is the Protective Mother. If your child was picked on by the school bully, the Warrior would go to the school to confront the principal and/or the bully's parents. The Protective

Mother would take her child to the school and by her presence protect the child. Opposite the Magician is the Healing Mother. The Magician heals by knowing what to say or do. The Healing Mother heals just by her love, "I'll kiss it and make it well." In considering the energy of these opposites, the male energy extends outwards in taking action; it is assertive or insertive. The female energy is inward in being just herself; it is receptive. Considering the fourth archetype, that of the Lover, the female counterpart is the Sensuous Woman. While the Lover holds a passion for some activity outside of himself, the Sensuous Woman's passion is for what makes her feel good in the way she dresses or pampers herself. Again, this assertive and receptive energy is God-given; it is the way a person is made; it is hormonal, testosterone and estrogen.

With this last thought in mind, I asked Carl to consider the way women dress. "Dressing-up is not simply to seduce men. Women dress up because it feels good and is a way to please themselves. How should a man react when noticing an attractive woman while walking through the mall?"

Carl's immediate reaction was to think of such a woman as a "slut."

"But how does your wife dress? How did she dress when she was young? How does your daughter dress? They are not sluts. I expect that they take care in how they dress, and that dressing is a sensuous experience. Not that you need to say or do anything, but when you see an attractive woman at the mall, what should you think? Should you quickly look away, maybe feel embarrassed, and look only at your wife? Is it wrong to notice and think that a woman is attractive, is sensuous? It is likely that the woman would want or hope you would appreciate how she looked. What should be your response to seeing an attractive woman?" Again it is important to keep alive Carl's panic at the smile of the women in his dream, to keep alive his tormentor, Fenrir. Seeing this woman in person engendered panic, the disruptive cry for help.

CHAPTER 8

LÆÐING AND DROMI: WILLPOWER IS NOT ENOUGH

THE FIRST TEST

Odin remembers the prophecies that the wolf will be the cause of his death, yet the gods know they cannot kill the wolf because his evil blood must be kept from polluting the temples of Asgard. The Æsir, the council of gods, convenes to determine the fate of Fenrir and decide that the best action is to bind the wolf with a strong chain. To use a chain is to use will power to contain one's obsession. A chain to successfully bind the fearsome wolf would have to be extraordinarily strong; it would take a tremendously hot forge to form its links. Likewise, a person's strength, "heat" and energy must be used to summon the willpower necessary to overcome an obsession. The gods called this chain Læðing. He accepts the challenge and lets the gods bind him in the chain. The wolf expands and strains against the chain and the chain breaks.

Likewise, if we would listen to our inner wisdom we would know that we have insufficient strength or willpower to end our obsession; even so, we must test our strength by mustering the necessary willpower, Læðing, to restrain the obsession. Testing our willpower and failing offers an opportunity for learning more about the nature of our obsession, and what we learn will direct us towards our eventual victory. We need to face our attempts and failures with the therapeutic attitude of patience, gentleness and curiosity in order to learn and gain understanding.

Consider the woman who tries to quit smoking. She has quit many times. Again, as before, she is determined to quit and is able to muster the necessary willpower for success. Yet, part of her knows that she will return to smoking. She gives up the nicotine habit again only to find it replaced by overeating or irritability. In her attempt to use willpower she forgets or ignores the previous pitfalls of weight gain or irascibility. Hopefully, with an open mind and creative thinking, she can go beyond willpower to find new forms of strength to deal with these pitfalls.

Charles Baudouin[1] of the New Nancy School of Hypnosis in France proposed psychological laws which govern the ineffectiveness of willpower. The first law, the law of concentrated attention, states, "The idea which tends to realize itself is always a spontaneous idea. It is not forced attention that produces change." Daniel Araoz[2] restates the law when he says, "It is not will power but imagination that produces change." Araoz replaced the phrases "forced attention" with "will power" and "spontaneous attention" with the word "imagination," an activity of the unconscious mind. The idea that the effort of the will is blocked by something deeper in the unconscious is implied in Baudouin's second law, the law of reverse effect: that is, in Araoz's words, "Conscious effort of the will [willpower] is useless as long as the imagination is adverse to that effort."

What are these unconscious thoughts that block the effort to change? For the smoker there are two common unconscious blocks: 1) Some smokers "wish they wanted to quit." Therapy is used as an excuse that allows them to say, "At least I tried," when they really don't want to quit. 2) Other smokers greatly resent being told what to do by others and even by themselves. This resentment provides another excuse to return to smoking. As long as the individual refrains from smoking, the internal resentment grows until it reaches a sufficient peak and the person starts to smoke again with the angry attitude that "no one can tell me what to do." This block reflects an internal parental voice of the past that was overcontrolling. For each of the three individuals presented in this book, this unconscious blocking language will be uncovered, for some in this chapter, and for others in later chapters.

ARLENE

Arlene apologized to Jessi for her rage when Jessi bumped into her while taking her things to her room. Arlene had gained consider-able insight into the source of her problem. She saw that she was much like her own mother, who would yell at her because every-thing was not perfect. She no longer felt justified when she would become angry at the children or at Tim, but now she would become angry at herself for being just like her mother, something she never wanted to be. This realization gave her the strength to be different, but the problem was that she did not know the alternative, the way she would like to be. I gave her the assignment to express each day her appreciation to each of the children and Tim for something they each did. I hoped this would give her a glimpse of what the alterna-tive would be like. This assignment was a rewarding experience for Arlene. She felt quite positive about the family, and her hopes were high. Fenrir was bound with the chain.

During the next week, however, the chain broke. The family was going somewhere and all were in the car waiting for Arlene. She was racing around the house doing some things she "had to do." Tim honked the horn once, which irritated Arlene, but when she finally got out to the car, "Tim said that my diddling around in the house was going to make us late. I was furious. I went back into the house and just sat there. Finally Tim came in and apologized, but I told him to go without me. He refused and disappointed the kids by missing the movie."

I suggested, "That wasn't very nice of Tim, but he does not yet understand. It'll take a lot of patience and strength to change, but you are on the way." Arlene needed this reassurance.

JERRY

When we were last with Jerry, we were dealing with Jerry's one-time explosion. He had frightened himself by exploding when Sherry asked him to not go to his baseball practice. Though at a deeper level Jerry felt the impossibility of the situation, at a more superficial level he was ready to seek a compromise and felt some strength in that possibility. Sherry's comment that she wanted to spend some time alone with him offered him that compromise. His baseball practices were generally on Mondays and Wednesdays, and games were generally Thursday evenings or Saturdays. This left Fridays as a day of rest, and Jerry offered that on Fridays they could get a babysitter for Beth and he and Sherry could go out somewhere, anywhere that Sherry wanted. He felt pleased with himself in coming up with this plan.

Jerry's new plan worked for a couple of weeks, but then Sherry's parents came for the weekend and arrived Friday evening. The game Saturday was a nice way to entertain at least Sherry's father. The following Friday was the school open house for Beth, and the next was a special practice because there was a game on Sunday, the regional playoff. Jerry's team won the game, thus setting up another game the following Sunday, meaning that there was another Friday practice. Again Sherry complained. It had been a month since they had time alone together. Jerry left the house while saying to her, "the season is almost over." He sat in the car for a few minutes fuming but then left for the practice. The situation did not seem quite as impossible as before because the season was almost over. Yet he knew that soon practices would start for the next season. When he returned from practice he did not lose his temper but was pouting and depressed. This behavior hooked Sherry's guilt and she yelled at him, "Get over it." He kept his cool but went to bed without saying anything to her. The chain was broken.

CARL

The three children of Loki were obviously out of order for Carl. Understanding Carl's fear and especially his guilt derived from his voyeuristic obsession had become most important in therapy, though his obsession with the idea of his wife having an affair came first. Once he became honest about his compulsion and obsession with watching from his bedroom window his neighbors having sex, the obsession over his wife having an extramarital affair disappeared. Carl's first attempt at using willpower was to stay out of the bedroom on Wednesday evenings when his wife was at choir practice. Because he had other things of importance to do, staying out of the bedroom worked for a week or two. Even so, wondering what he was missing caused him difficulty in concentrating on the tasks at hand. This approach was a failure almost from the beginning. On the second Wednesday night, he went upstairs to check the window just as the neighbors' light went off and he kicked himself for not going up a few minutes earlier. Fenrir's chain Læðing was shattered. Though Carl did not feel especially strong as a result of this experience, we shall see that he did learn from the experience and his strength was growing.

Jerry found strength within himself to make the commitment to give his time on Friday evenings exclusively to Sherry. Both he and Sherry learned that such a promise was unrealistic and something else had to be tried. Similarly, Carl learned that staying away from the bedroom window on Wednesdays was unrealistic and caused his obsession to rapidly escalate.

One major task in therapy is to show each client that something is learned from a failure experience. This lesson provides each person with greater ego strength to take risks with new ways to think and behave.

THE SECOND TEST

With Fenrir free to romp in the fields, the Æsir viewed his increasing size with renewed alarm. The Vikings, like their deities, were a strong lot, always testing their willpower, always putting themselves in power struggles or finding new hurdles to prove to themselves that they had the strength to overcome them. It is hard for anyone to admit failure—to admit that something as mysterious or as evasive as an obsession has such great power and cannot be bound by willpower alone. Although their first attempt had failed, at least the gods and goddesses had made an attempt to bind the wolf. The Æsir comes together again and decides to make a chain called Dromi, which is to be twice as strong as Læðing.

While the chain is being forged, Fenrir's size and strength double. Although he realizes that by accepting the gods' challenge to allow himself to be bound with Dromi he will take a terrible risk and expose himself to enormous danger, Fenrir craves fame; he craves recognition. The gods assure the wolf that great fame will be his if he breaks the great Dromi. This time Fenrir thinks, "If I really want to be famous, I must take a chance and expose myself to danger. The greater the danger or the more difficult the task, the greater the fame if I win." Fenrir shares the philosophy of the Æsir.

Fenrir's power struggle is similar to the war within a person who struggles with an obsession. On the one hand the person's willpower is blind to the power of the obsession. Willpower makes a person feel strong, and gives him the strength to believe that he can accomplish the deed. On the other hand, the person has long mistrusted and misunderstood the obsession and its insistence on winning the battle to gain recognition and respect. Although both "sides" represent parts of the individual, they do not communicate or cooperate. Both sides demand victory. The people who sincerely want to quit smoking may not attend to the power of their internal needs or obsessions but believe the habit can be overcome by willpower alone.

Fenrir permits the gods to bind him securely. He strains with all his might, digs his heels into the ground, smashes the links against the rocks and shatters the chain. Fenrir's fame indeed survives, for today, when people accomplish extraordinary deeds, it is said they broke loose of Lœðing or battled out of Dromi.

ARLENE

Arlene continued to beat herself up. She at first blamed Tim for disappointing the children for missing the movie, though she knew that it was equally her fault. Because of her perfectionist tendencies, she considered herself a total failure. I reminded her that this all or nothing thinking does not help and that she needs to be gentle and patient with herself. This language has been used enough over the last couple of months that talk of being gentle and patient calmed Arlene down and was trance-inducing. I continued with the joining of Arlene's feeling but created more distance by creating a story/narrative:

"Close your eyes. Sit back and relax. April is in the playroom watching the Disney channel. You start to walk through the room but then you sit down with her for a moment or two. What she is watching is a Donald Duck cartoon. You know Donald and the way he gets angry, squawking loudly and flapping his arms. Listen to his squawk. Watch and listen to April laugh. But think for a moment, you don't see Donald's temper as funny. You think it is dumb. It makes you feel uncomfortable or anxious. But April and much of the world think

Donald's temper is funny. Watch him with a sense of curiosity. What is funny about him? Stand up, jump around and squawk like Donald. April is quick to jump up and squawk too. See how quickly the two of you are laughing. Take that feeling with you."

Arlene was laughing as she left the office and she commented, "I have wondered why you have the stuffed Donald on you shelf."

I also have a stuffed Daffy Duck, Yosemite Sam, and Tasmanian Devil for the same purpose. In her willingness to jump up and squawk like Donald, even if it was only in her imagination, Arlene took the risk of being playful with her anger, of not taking it so seriously. This playfulness reflected a growing strength within her. I smiled and offered, "You can find strength in being playful with your anger."

Arlene's Fenrir was again bound as she felt somewhat freed from the heaviness of her temper, but the restraint would not last. Sure enough, Arlene returned a couple of weeks later again having lost her temper. This time it was with 3-year-old April, who spilt a glass of milk at the dinner table. Arlene was not too out of control but enough so to start April crying, only adding to Arlene's frustration, guilt and rage. And then Tim, with a disturbed look on his face, took the kids out of the room, only adding to Arlene's guilt and anger. Afterwards she thought of flapping her arms and squawking, and thought that would have gotten April smiling again, but by then April was already in bed.

During the struggle of willpower, three additional ecstatic suggestions are offered, embedded in the language and attitude of the therapist while the drumming was playing quietly in the background. The first is a suggestion that the test of willpower is important and can provide her with even greater strength if she should fail. Second, failure shows strength because it indicates willingness to take a risk. Arlene's willingness to take the risk of jumping up and squawking like Donald was supported and encouraged. Third, with this new strength she is preparing to use new ways to bring about change, ways not previously considered. These three suggestions will be important throughout therapy for all three individuals of this book.

JERRY

The next session Jerry and Sherry came together. Jerry needed to reassure Sherry that he was committed to going out with her on Fridays and that since the season was over, they could get this plan back on track. Sherry was a bit more honest in expressing her frustration that setting aside one evening out of seven made it seem like Jerry was giving her just token time and that he really was not interested in being alone with her. Jerry threw his head back on the back of the couch and laid his arm over his eyes with a groan. Sherry had her head turned looking at him. I asked them, "Stay just as you are, don't move."

I started by talking to Jerry, offering a counter-narrative. "You feel like you can't win, that you cannot give enough to Sherry. Sherry always wants more." I knew that Sherry was ready to jump in and I was quick to put my hand up to cut her off. "You don't know how to please Sherry. But really to please her is not so much about the amount of time you spend together. That is important, but what is more important is the quality of the time together, time when Sherry really feels you are attentive to her, really feels you appreciate her and are able to really make her feel good about herself. With your head back and your arm resting over your eyes, take some time in your mind to shift gears, to let go of your frustration and to be with Sherry. To let go of your frustration may take a few minutes. Be patient with yourself as you slowly shift to Sherry. In your mind pick some place, maybe in a quiet restaurant or just parked in the car somewhere together. Just feel your breathing slow, just listening to Sherry breathing slowly near you. Just feel Sherry's presence near you. Feel her warmth. Feel your love for her. Picture her near you. Feel how attractive she is to you. Really be there with her. Read her mind. Read how much she loves you. Read how much she wants to be with you. Appreciate her love. If she is talking, listen intently to her and understand what she is saying more deeply than you have understood her before. Reflect your understanding back to her so that she knows that you understand. If for some reason you miss in understanding her, listen more deeply and try again to reflect your understanding. Feel yourself really understanding what she is saying and what she is feeling. To do this requires that you step outside of your own thoughts and feelings. Those thoughts and feelings are not important right at this moment. There will be a time for your thoughts and feelings later. Now is the time to selflessly really understand Sherry, and by really understanding Sherry you are showing her how much you love her. You are giving her quality time. When you experience her, when you listen to her in his way, she will know that you really love her and the feeling of love between you will grow and feel amazing."

To Sherry, I continued, "Feel Jerry's love for you and appreciate it. Help him understand you by finding new and gentle ways to express yourself when you feel he misunderstands you. Love takes a lot of patience. Be patient with him in expressing yourself. Now it is Jerry's time to listen to you, to understand you. There will be time for Jerry to express himself to you, and at that time really listen to him, too, and reflect back to him your understanding of what he is thinking and how he feels. You will find that time will be later today and every day."

Returning to Jerry, "But right now, Jerry, and today and everyday it is your time to really listen to Sherry, to experience Sherry. You have learned over your life to give of yourself to other people by doing things for them. You are good at giving your time. Doing for others and giving your time is your strength. Use this strength to do something different, to do nothing but listen actively to Sherry. Feel the strength of listening and understanding. The strength of listening and understanding along with your strength of doing is a much greater strength than just the sum of the two. Giving yourself in listening to and understanding Sherry in this way, though, this is new to you and will take practice, but you are a person who has been ready to take risks and try new ways. When you listen in this way, she will really feel loved by you."

After listening to this counter-narrative they both opened their eyes with a smile. Again Fenrir was bound, though the chain would again break. Both Jerry and Sherry would have times of impatience and frustration in their conflicting needs, but this exercise was a beginning and needed to be practiced. Listening in this way is a new experience for most people, especially men.

CARL

By gaining understanding of Carl's fear and guilt, by learning of his history, his teenage attitudes, his courtship of Abbie, the birth, pregnancy and marriage of his daughter (in that order), and his struggle between shyness/humility and self-confidence, we had gained some links for the stronger chain with which to bind Fenrir. Carl was now struggling with thoughts he had never thought of before, that one's sexuality is God-given, asking himself, "What is the healthy way to think of sex?" Not all women who dress seductively were being "sluts." His wife and daughter enjoyed dressing nicely. How should he react when seeing an attractive woman walking through the mall? Carl was beginning to talk more freely in therapy about these thoughts, thoughts that he used to believe were in themselves seductive and would lead to sex. He was beginning to discover that just by talking about these things, some of the obsessive power that sex had had over his life was diminishing. For years his sexuality had been repressed sufficiently so as not to bother him. But once it was shoved in his face by his neighbors having sex in front of an open window, his defenses crumbled.

During the next session of therapy, Carl mentioned that although he and his wife had not had sex for years, the other evening after his wife put on her nightgown he had reached out and impulsively given her a warm hug. Afterwards she had stepped back and looked at him, blinking her eyes with a smile, but said nothing. But the words came out of him, "We have to do that more." Maybe it was because he had been thinking about sex, but this interaction really surprised him; he enjoyed it and he thought that Abbie did, too. I recommended that he do more of the same.

"You took a risk in hugging Abbie, but what is important is that you had the strength to take that risk, and I am sure that you knew at some level that it would please her. You trusted your intuition."

A session later he announced that Abbie had even initiated some hugs. I assumed that the lack of affection was more Carl's doing than Abbie's. Abbie had always been the self-confident one who went after what she wanted. She also said to him with a smile, "Therapy seems to be doing you some good." Even though their interactions did not go beyond hugs, Carl was feeling more loving towards Abbie, and he thought that he did not need to watch the neighbors. Again he busied himself with other things on Wednesdays and avoided going upstairs. Again this lasted for a couple of weeks but with less obsessive thinking, until one evening Abbie was late for choir practice and ran out of the house without hugging him. That evening he sat by the upstairs window feeling lonely, with a loss of self-confidence. Dromi was broken.

Again, each person had found the strength to battle their obsession, had taken a risk, and had tried something new and different. Each person learned from the experience of failing. I offered an exercise to Jerry and Sherry to illustrate how to be loving listeners. Both were heartened by this and ready to make their Friday evenings more ful-filling. Practicing this exercise would teach them greater intimacy, though the chain would break because the problem was more than a lack of intimacy.

Arlene was offered a lesson on how to "lighten up" by seeing humor in the temper of Donald Duck. On a couple of occasions she did take the risk of laughing at her own temper while thinking of Donald, but the family patterns and ingrained expectations were danced automatically without missing a step so that subtle changes were not appreciated. April's tears, Tim's protectiveness of the children, and Arlene's frustration continued. Carl and Abbie were enjoying each other's hugs. Something needed was coming back into their life because Carl was willing to take a risk. Carl's newfound freedom to think and talk about the meaning of sex in therapy was a help. He failed to stay away from the bedroom window only when he lost confidence in himself when Abbie hurried out of the house and forgot to hug him.

Each person learned from and found strength in their failure. The story of Loki's children suggests that willpower needs to fail twice. In real life, failure likely occurs many more times than twice. Often when the person faces the obsession on his or her own, failure is to be expected because failure is not experienced as an opportunity for learning. Psychotherapy offers the client a chance to experience such failure with patience, gentleness and curiosity, and with this attitude psychotherapy turns failure into an opportunity for success.

Moreover, the three additional ecstatic suggestions mentioned above, embedded in the language and attitude of the therapist, set the stage for change: The first suggests that the test of will power is important and can provide even greater strength if the test should fail. Second, failure shows strength because it indicates willingness to take a risk. Third, with this new strength, the individual is preparing to use new ways to bring about change, ways that they have not previously considered.

At this stage in the process of growth, clients need to test their willpower and fail. Using willpower and accepting failure is done at a conscious level and may to a degree ignore the beliefs and conflicts of the unconscious mind. Trance is a bystander in watching this match between willpower and unconscious beliefs. When willpower fails, the clients may give up for a considerable length of time before they are willing to try again. These suggestions, when offered when the client is in trance, can shorten this time and provide hope that once these tests of the strength of willpower are over, there will be other ways to win in this battle to find peace and freedom.

CHAPTER 9

GLEIPNIR'S POWER: THE POWER OF THE UNCONSCIOUS

The Æsir are afraid they will be unable to find a means to restrain Fenrir. All turn to Odin, hoping for a solution to this problem. Odin sends Skirnir, the messenger of the god Freyr, down into the abode of the dark elves. These dwarfs devise a binding which they called Gleipnir. They consider this binding for Fenrir very special and magical because it is made of substances no one has heard of before. The gods accept the unusual nature of this binding because they realize that it will take something very special, something that no one knows of or understands, to bind Fenrir. The substances used to make this fetter are six in number. They include the noise a cat makes when it walks, the beard of a woman, the roots of a mountain, the sinews of a bear, the breath of a fish and the spittle of a bird. The fetter is as smooth and soft as a silken ribbon.

THE CAVE OF THE DARK ELVES

The cave of the dark elves—our unconscious mind—was the source of the gods' powers. The dark elves gave Odin his spear, Gungnir, which never missed its mark and his golden arm ring, Draupnir, from which eight more golden rings would drop every ninth day. Freyr's golden ship, Skidbladnir, which was large enough to hold all the gods fully armed, came from this same cave. When this ship's sails were hoisted, a breeze would spring up to fill them. Yet, the ship could be folded up to fit in a purse. Freyr's golden boar, Gullinbursti, also made by the dark elves, was always surrounded by golden light to show the way. When Freyr rode it, the boar could run anywhere faster than a horse. The elves also made Mjolinir, Thor's famous hammer. When Thor threw Mjolinir, it hit its mark and returned to Thor's hand. The real powers of the gods, these wondrous treasures, came from the deep understanding of the unconscious mind—from the cave of the dark elves. Loki, our psychologist of Asgard, brought each of these gifts to the gods through his manipulative ways.

The lives of those who dwelt in the cave of the dark elves are generally kept secret from the world above the ground because a dwarf would turn to stone if he were touched by sunlight. The great knowledge of the dark elves is demonstrated when the dwarf Alvis is promised the hand of Thor's daughter Thurd in exchange for making weapons for the gods. Thor, however, regrets the promise. So, when Alvis approaches him, Thor engages Alvis in a lengthy conversation in which he tests the dwarf's vast knowledge. So great is Alvis's knowledge that he is detained through the night and still remains in the upper world at sunrise, at which time he is turned to stone. A person who wants to gain vast knowledge and understanding must access and interpret this deep unconscious world. When this knowledge from the unconscious is brought to light, it becomes permanent like stone in the conscious world.

THE SIX SUBSTANCES

When Skirnir approaches the dwarfs and asks for their assistance in preparing a binding for the wolf, the dwarfs fashion Gleipnir, the magical, unbreakable, silky-soft ribbon. Odin and the rest of the Æsir have faith in the unconscious mind, in the cunning of the dwarfs. The gods now know this silken cord is the only substance with which they can successfully constrain Fenrir. They recognize that the dwarfs possess a knowledge which they themselves do not have. Each of the substances in the cord are a mysterious yet potent power of the world, a power familiar yet hidden from the gods and goddesses. Understanding each of the six substances in the ribbon is essential to comprehend its incredible strength.

The first thread of the ribbon is the noise a cat makes when it walks. We might say, "But a cat does not make a sound. What strength is there in no sound?" The silence in stalking is the cat's strength. The noise a cat makes when it moves is the strength of cunning in preparation to pounce.

The forms of strength, or "Jing," are greatly refined in Oriental martial arts. The book on advanced Tai Chi Chuan by Jwing-Ming[1] lists fifty forms of jing. Modern Western culture restricts the comprehension of strength to muscular force and thus loses knowledge of useful subtle strengths, which are apparent in a pouncing cat's spring. A cat's senses, which are used as it stalks, could be considered Jywe Jing, or sensing jing, with which a person senses an opponent's flow of energy and intent. Ying Jing, or hard jing, is the strength of a cat's pounce or the bear's sinews. Also, one can see a cat tremble or shiver just before it pounces, exhibiting Dou Sou Jing or trembling jing. From the animal's stable stance, the power, Dou Sou Jing, is generated from the inside out, transmitting jing into the explosion of motion and energy, Ying Jing.

The second component of Gleipnir is the root of a mountain. Mountains rest on subterranean rock that provides them with stability and support. These foundations are similar to the complex root structures on which great trees rest in that both are massive and concealed beneath the earth's crust. The substructure of a mountain remains a strong, stable and substantial foundation. The roots of the mountain are similar to Pan Jing, or rooting jing in martial arts. Rooting jing is the energy which results when a person sinks his or her roots deeply into the ground to gain stability.

The third filament in the magical ribbon is the bird's spittle. Many species of birds use their own spittle as a kind of cement to bind mud, branches, twigs or straw. Some mud nests are so strong that they can be reused for many years with minimum remodeling at the beginning of each mating season. Tsan Nein Jing is the adhering-sticking jing which may be equated with the bird's spittle.

Another invisible element in the magic ribbon is the fish's breath. A fish takes in water through its gills and separates oxygen from water in a process that may have been mysterious to the ancient Norse. The ability of a fish to breathe represents the strength seen in the breath expelled by the fish in the form of bubbles rising to the surface of the water, rolling and flowing uninhibited by anything in their path, thus representing the strength of Lu Jing, the rollback or rolling jing.

The fifth ingredient in the binding Gleipnir, the bear's sinews, is one the Vikings and Western Culture greatly respect. Although the bear's sinew is concealed beneath the animal's furry coat, the immense strength of the animal depends on its well-developed invisible muscles and tendons. The bear's sinew represents physical strength to the Norse. One group of famous Viking fighters who were known as the "berserks," or "bear shirts," would play out the bear's physical strength in battle by meeting their foes in an animalistic manner. Fighting with their bare hands, the berserks would battle in a frenzy, snarling and growling like bears. Hard jing or Ying Jing best describes the bear's sinew. Tiger Claw is one martial style which specializes in hard Jing.

The final substance of the silken ribbon is a woman's beard. When the delicate balance of estrogen, progesterone and the male hormone testosterone within a female's body shifts in favor of the male hormone, a woman may produce facial hair. "The male hormones tend to increase aggressive behavior." When a woman reaches menopause and her body produces less estrogen, she may develop external masculine traits. Some women have lived their entire lives without expressing personal feelings on any issue in an assertive manner because being assertive may be considered unladylike. As they grow older, they may feel freer to show an aggressive side, a "male" side. I am reminded of something my mother said. Although I have no memory of my mother expressing her personal feelings on any issue in an assertive manner, she later in life told me how she spoke her mind on some issue at one of her senior citizens' meetings. When I said, "That does not sound like you," she responded, "At my age, who has a better right?" A beard comes to a woman at an older age when she has nothing to prove or nothing to lose in being assertive. A beard represents assertive, persistent strength. Thus, each of the six substances in the ribbon represents a different aspect of strength. The six strengths can be used individually according to one's immediate need, or as in Gleipnir, synergistically for extraordinary strength.

FINDING STRENGTH IN ACCESSING THE UNCONSCIOUS MIND

CARL: USING DREAMWORK AND AGE REGRESSION TO ACCESS THE UNCONSCIOUS MIND

After the Wednesday night of the missed hug, hugs resumed for Carl. Even so, he felt extremely vulnerable and despondent. After listening to his emotional pain with an empathetic ear, I eventually heard him begin to tell from deep within him of a dream. "I was in bed with a naked woman, my wife, the woman next door and the woman who gave me the smile at work, I'm not sure which, a combination of the three or they kept changing. They-she was all over me. It was ... great." Carl was not sure if he should admit it.

"You know that dream can be described with only one word," I said with a smile.

Carl's waited with anticipation.

"Horny!" After a pause I continued, "Sit back and relax. Close your eyes. Take a few moments to get back into the dream." I turn on the drumming to assist him in going into a trance and suggest that he lay back on the couch. He automatically took the Jivaro Underworld Posture. "What are you doing in the dream?"

"Just laying there."

"How? On your back?"

"Yeah?"

"What is she doing?"

"Sitting on top of me. Each time I open my eyes she is someone different."

"Okay. Stay with the feeling. With each breath let the feeling of horniness become more part of you. As you breathe in the feeling, let yourself begin to go back through time. As you go back through time watch the years and the events of your life pass. Let that feeling take you back to some specific time. Be curious and wondering as you go back through time. Soon you will get there. When you get to that specific time, lift the index finger of your left hand to tell me you are there."

I then was quiet and after a short time Carl's finger lifts. "Where are you?"

"In bed."

"What is happening?"

"Abbie walks into the room wearing something outrageous—red negligee."

"Tell me more."

"It was about 12 years ago. We were in New York in a hotel. We were there because of a special awards banquet for our company because our plant was considered the most efficient of the six plants across the country. That night..."

"It sounds like Abbie had planned a special award for you. Go on."

"I just looked at her. I didn't know what to say. She stood there for a minute or two then went back into the bathroom and came back wearing her long nightgown."

"Then what?"

"She got in bed and turned off the light. That was it."

"She didn't say anything?"

"No."

"What was going on inside of you?"

"I don't know. I was tired. It was a long day."

"She didn't show you in any way that she was hurt?"

"No. I guess life went on like nothing happened."

"Let your present self return and be with your younger self and with all the understanding and wisdom of your present self, help your younger self understand."

"I guess Abbie could have been hurt but she is never negative, she never says anything negative about anybody."

"Wow. What a saint. We will come back to your hotel room but first, carrying your feelings of the dream with you, your feeling of horniness with the woman naked sitting on top of you, again go back in time, further back in time." I then was quiet and soon Carl lifted his finger. What is going on now?"

"Abbie and I are in bed holding each other, trying to have sex. I can't hold my erection. After a few minutes Abbie rolls over with her back to me. That was the last time we tried to have sex."

"Again Abbie said nothing?"

"Yeah."

"How long ago was that?"

"I think about 20 years ago."

"It sounds like she just gave up on you. Again we will come back to this, but let's go back further one more time. Again take your horny feeling back further through time. Be curious and wondering as you go back..." Again after a minute or two Carl's finger slowly rises. "What's going on now?"

"I'm just getting home from work and Abbie announces that she is pregnant."

"What happens?"

"We're happy. Abbie wanted to get pregnant."

"Was it hard for her to get pregnant?"

"Not really. It took several months."

"Were you having a hard time keeping an erection then."

"Not then. Not a first."

"Okay, let's come back to this point next week." Carl was already coming out of trance.

The next week felt like the time to try something new, the Feathered Serpent Posture, Fig. 1.4. The energy in Carl towards change was in full bloom. I felt that the inhibited part of him was about to die and his sexuality was about to bloom. He exhibited a real sense of determination for something to happen. I had him stand with the back of his hands resting on his waist with his wrists bent such that his fingers pointed upwards and elbows extending out to each side. I asked him how this posture felt, and he first thought of his mother standing that way, angry that he had not started his chores. With a little discussion of how he felt in this posture, he soon recognized the feeling of determination. I was able to say, "You are ready, you are determined to change the way you think of your God–given sexuality."

I then told him about this posture and the other three that we had been using, that these postures are ancient expressions of certain feelings that were important feelings in the work of the hunter-gatherer shamans or healers in their practice of healing, and that in Felicitas Goodman's research with ecstatic trance, she found that these postures continue to have power in providing direction to the trance experience today. I showed Carl pictures of these postures and named them from where they came. In his determination to change he was now much more open to looking beyond himself and open to expressing this determination in the way he stood as he went into trance. I turned on the drumming CD. The only words I said were, "Carry with you on this journey with the Feathered Serpent your five new spirit guides, the dream of the three naked women, of Abbie in the New York hotel room standing in front of you wearing the red negligee, twenty years ago when you last tried to have sex, and when Abbie told you she was pregnant."

Carl did not interrupt the fifteen minutes of drumming and at the end I asked him what he experienced.

He reported that he went to each of the four experiences of last session, but with each one he quickly went back to Abbie standing in front of him in the red negligee. Each time I saw her standing there I wondered what she was trying to tell me, and the words that kept popping up were, "Let's have fun! We were in the city to celebrate, so let's have fun." I felt very confused, and did not know what to say. Your word of being horny is God-given also was in the back of my mind."

I suggested, "You haven't let yourself feel horny since then until your dream. Your neighbors may be a blessing to get you turned back on to life. The spirit guide of Abbie standing in her red negligee has the message of 'Let's have fun' for you, a message that you now understand and are ready for."

Carl was just standing there with his eyes wide open. He was in a different kind of trance. He was in shock.

Feeling the power of his reaction, I continued. "Getting and holding an erection takes practice, it takes using your imagination, it takes feeling horny. This is something that could bring life back into your relationship with Abbie. It's God-given. It's something that Abbie would have liked and can still enjoy if you practice, if you learn to let yourself feel horny. I'm not saying it is right to watch your neighbors. But what your neighbors are doing is something that should be appreciated in life. Their joy in life can be appreciated, and you can find that joy in your life."

Carl left the session in a state of shock. This experience took away the negative power watching his neighbors had over him. He still watched his neighbors at times and still felt it was wrong, but his feelings were different. He watched with a sense of appreciation. The magical binding was woven.

Both Arlene and Jerry were at similar turning point in therapy and it was time to introduce them to shamanic postures and to the Feathered Serpent Posture. Their determination to change was at a peek.

ARLENE

Arlene needs to lighten up in dealing with her family and almost everything else in her life. After her last explosive episode with Tim, I had led her through an exercise to see the humor in the temper of Donald Duck, and to absurdly exaggerate her own temper by flapping her wings and squawking so that April and she could both laugh at it. But when April spilled her milk, her tears were automatic. Tim was quick to protect the children by taking them out of the room as Arlene imagined Donald and remained relatively calm. Though Arlene was pleased with herself for staying as calm as she did, she was angry this time because the family danced to their expectations without noticing a difference in her.

Arlene was ready to find a deeper, inner strength, a strength that would grow from her unconscious mind and that could change her life. A dream opened the gate to the depths of her unconscious. "My mother-in-law gave us a sterling silver platter for a wedding gift. It was a family heirloom. In my dream I noticed it was starting to tarnish so I took it down to polish it. When I wiped it with the polishing cloth, it shined for a moment then turned blacker than before. If I stopped for a moment to rest my hand it turned blacker and blacker. I was getting nowhere. I finally got so tired of polishing that I just threw it down and watched as it turned black and then it crumbled into nothing but dust. I screamed at Tim, 'What did you do to the platter?'"

"Let's take a minute or two to look at the parts of the dream. First, you notice that the platter is tarnished and you take on polishing it. Second, you need to take time to rest your hand and when you do the platter turns black. Third, you get frustrated and tired, and it crumbles. Fourth, you yell at Tim, blaming him for doing something. What name can you give to each of these four parts? The first part, you take on polishing the platter."

"There is always something that needs to be done, just one more project."

"Okay, how about naming it, 'Just one more project.' The second is that you need to take a rest and it turns blacker. What's a good name for that part of the dream?"

"I'm always tired. There is always too much to do."

"Shall we name it that, 'Always tired.'"

"That's okay."

"Now the third part, you get frustrated and tired and it crumbles."

"I give up. When I give up everything falls apart."

"Good, and the last part, you yell at and blame Tim."

"I never get any help. I cannot keep ahead of Tim and the kids. They make messes faster than I can clean them up."

Reading from my notes, "We have 'Just one more project,' 'I'm always tired,' 'I give up,' and 'I never get any help.' I stand and place my hands at my waist in the Feathered Serpent Posture, Fig. 1.4, and briefly tell the story of Felicitas Goodman's discovery of the power of these postures, similar to the story I told Carl. I then suggest that she stand as I am standing, and as I turn on the drumming CD I begin with, "With each breath you inhale calmness, and as you exhale, the calmness goes deeper inside of you." After these words the only words I said were, "Go back into your dream." I trusted the power of Arlene's dream would lead her to a rebirth experience. At the end of the fifteen minutes I asked her to describe her experience.

"In going back to the dream what stood out was what I felt when my mother said, 'I never get any help.' I saw myself as a little girl. Those words are my mother's. I can clearly hear her voice saying them. I feel myself shaking. I was always trying to help but could never do it right. I could never please her."

"You feel yourself shaking?"

"Um huh. Scared. I don't know what to do. Frozen in fear, afraid to do anything."

"The 'I never get any help' spirit guide from your dream causes you to shake, frozen in fear.

"Bring your kids and Tim into your image. Can you see them shaking?"

Arlene began to cry. She was out of trance and hurting. She was not ready to truly let go, but she had a deeper understanding of how hard she had been on the family and a beginning understanding of the meaning of letting go. She understood the message of her spirit guide.

I added, "Maybe for the family's sake it is important to let go and let the platter crumble." These were the threads with which she would weave the Gleipnir. So often the strength of Gleipnir is found in new insights and understanding.

JERRY

I had offered Jerry and Sherry the exercise of being better listeners. They practiced it with limited success. They still spend much time feeling frustrated and angry with each other. During the next session, Sherry had some other commitment and Jerry came alone. This offered other opportunities in therapy.

Sherry had shown Jerry that she did understand his feelings—that he valued commitment and responsibility to the team and that he in turn was appreciated and respected by them, and that this appreciation felt very good, it was something he needed. On the other hand, Jerry was hurt that Sherry did not appreciate his trait of being a committed and responsible person. She complained that he was committed to the team but not to her. This complaint especially hurt because he felt very committed to her and she was attacking one of his most highly valued traits.

In addition to this discussion Jerry mentioned a brief dream. He was on the mound and receiving signals from the catcher as to what kind of pitch to throw. He shook off the first suggested pitch but accepted the second.

I mentioned that I think he understands the message of this dream's spirit guide, that his communication with the catcher is good. "You know the language and what he is telling you. You take turns in communicating and you are able to disagree without a feeling of resentment, without getting angry. Though you are trying to listen to Sherry, when you disagree the resentment goes to a fight."

Jerry's determination was high and with the insight this dream had to offer, it was apparent that it was time to introduce him to a new posture, The Feathered Serpent, Fig. 1.4. I told him about the shamanic power of this and the other three postures we have been using and the research of Felicitas Goodman with these postures. I then suggested that with this new posture we would explore at a deeper level the meaning of some of these thoughts and his inability to communicate with Sherry. I turned on the drumming CD.

As Jerry stood in the Feathered Serpent Posture, the only words I had to offer were, "Let the spirit of the Feathered Serpent lead you to deeper understanding in communicating with Sherry."

At the end of the fifteen minutes Jerry reported: "I quickly saw this small, yappy dog barking his head off at me. Several days ago I got so mad at Sherry for again telling me that I cared more about baseball than her that afterwards I apologized for yelling. She smiled and said, "I know your bark is much worse than your bite. I rarely yell and the only person that can push my button is Sherry when she accuses me of something that is not true. That is so unfair."

"But you have gone to a baseball practice when she wanted you to stay home."

"I know, but she did not need me at home as much as the baseball team needed me. And I had promised the team that I would be there that night. But when we have a fight like we did, my mind is not on my pitching, though I don't think the team notices."

"What did the yapping dog tell you?"

"That my anger is not a threat and something she could laugh at. I have known a few yappy dogs that I would laugh at. I guess my anger is for nothing and a waste of time. We have talked about how I should listen and let Sherry know that I understand what she is trying to tell me by repeating it back to her in my own words. We have been doing that some, but when she accuses me of not caring, that is too much. I'll have to try harder to listen and not get so angry."

Dreamwork with Arlene's dream led her to a deeper understanding of the pain she caused her family with her perfectionism and began to show her the real meaning of letting go. Attaining this level of letting go is much easier said than done and would take some time, but Arlene's commitment to letting go of her perfectionism had grown sufficiently to bind Fenrir.

Old habits are hard to break, but Jerry committed himself to being a better listener to Sherry, and he let her know that he understood her feelings when she said that she felt that the baseball team was more important than she was to him.

Each found the binding that would work in restraining their Fenrir. This binding still represents the use of willpower, though of much greater strength than the two chains used previously—willpower that is effective in restraining one's obsessions, even if for only the time being.

As we have proceeded to this point in therapy it has become apparent that Arlene, Carl and Jerry are paying much more attention to others in their lives and they are much less self-centered. As they have grown to this point they have been discovering the power of the spirits and their spirit guides found in their dreams and trance experiences. I believe that they are ready to hear the litany of calling the spirits. This litany opens them to a broader doorway to the spirit world, an opening that will allow them to experience the spirits more fully and openly, the spirits that come from their unconscious mind and possibly at times from the beyond, from the universal mind. Thus, in our next session I tell them the story or narrative of this spirit world and the litany for calling the spirits of each direction:

"Spirits of the East, of the sunrise, the beginning of the day, the dawn of spring, and the birth of new life, we honor you. Please join us and bring us your wisdom. Spirits of the South, of the warmth of the middle of the day and of the summer, the growth of our children and our gardens, we honor you. Please join us and bring us your wisdom. Spirits of the West, of the sunset and autumn, of the harvest and productive years of life, we honor you. Please join us and bring us your wisdom. Spirits of the North, of nighttime, of sleep and the dormant months of winter, the time for sleep in preparation for the new birth at spring, we honor you. Please join us and bring us your wisdom. Spirits of the Universe that placed the Earth where it is with respect to the Sun that brings us the seasons of the year, and night and day; the moon the brings us the tides of the oceans; and the stars that bring us all the substances with which we are composed, we honor you. Please join us and bring us your wisdom. Then spirits of the Earth, the Earth that lovingly sustains life through the interdependency of all things, we honor you. Please join us and bring us your wisdom. And finally, spirits of the center, of the heart, of the uniting of all things, we honor you. Please join us and bring us your wisdom."

As we faced each direction I offered the spirits of that direction a pinch of cornmeal. I felt that each person opened themselves more to the spirit world, the world beyond the five senses, realizing that there is much beyond the small world that they had been experiencing.

CHAPTER 10

FENRIR'S BINDING: A NEED FOR SACRIFICE

FENRIR'S BINDING AND TYR'S SACRIFICE

Skirnir brings the ribbon back to the Æsir, who thank him for going on this mission into the world of the dark elves. Odin describes this binding as soft as a silk ribbon yet stronger than one can imagine, the only binding that can hold Fenrir.

The Æsir beckon the wolf to come out to Lyngvi, an island in Amsvartnir Lake. The gods show Fenrir the silk ribbon and challenge him to break it. Although each of the gods who test the ribbon is unable to break it, the gods suggest that the wolf can break it easily. Fenrir answers that the task is no challenge and will not add to his fame. He adds that if the challenge is a trick, he will most certainly not let them wrap the ribbon around him. The challenge of the gods continues, "This ribbon is so slight that you can break it easily and if you cannot, you should not be afraid, because we will be here to free you." Fenrir laughs, "If I cannot break it, you will just go away and leave me. I cannot trust you! But I cannot let you accuse me of being a coward. If one of you will put your hand in my mouth, I will trust that your test is done in good faith."

The gods, looking at one another, realize their dilemma. No one is willing to accept the wolf's challenge until Tyr puts out his hand and places it in Fenrir's mouth. Fenrir then lets the gods wrap the ribbon around him. As Fenrir tugs and strains, the ribbon becomes tighter and tighter. Suddenly Fenrir bites down, severing Tyr's hand from his arm.

The journey into the unconscious has provided each person with the strength to bind their obsessions, but to do so each has to sacrifice something. Any change in a person's life requires giving up the old way, and giving up the old way is painful as each narrative will show; sometimes it seems easy but with time the pain will surface. As we shall see, for Carl the sacrifice at first seemed easy.

CARL

As we began the sessions with calling the spirits from beyond, over the next several sessions Carl told stories of how his love life was changing, stories in which he was at times using his imagination, taking him into his new world of sexuality. I pointed out to him that his imagination came from beyond his five senses and was also of the spirits. But it was my time to listen and provide emotional support. The next Wednesday night after our last session, Carl watched his neighbors with appreciation. While sitting on the edge of Abbie's and his bed, watching, he had the thought of how amazing God's creation is, how two people are drawn together to make love and without this, life would not exist. Though he still felt it was wrong to be invading his neighbor's privacy, he felt truly amazed. When Abbie got home and they went to bed he continued to feel this amazement and reached out to hold Abbie for a while. She had her back to him but he pressed against her and felt her warmth. Nothing was said, but he felt his erection grow as he continued to press against her. The next morning Abbie commented with a smile, "What got into you last night?"

For a moment Carl didn't know what to say and felt a little embarrassed, but then he told her of his thoughts of how amazing it is that one's sexuality is God-given, attributing his comments to what was discussed in therapy. All Abbie did was smile and give him a hug. But that evening, rather than wearing her long nightgown she dug out some lingerie from somewhere to wear. He thought it was the same that she had worn years before in the hotel in New York.

This time Carl was able to grin when she crawled into bed. They hugged and he fumbled around awkwardly. He got on top of her but was disappointed for her because he came too quickly, though she later mentioned, "That was a good start." Carl mentioned in therapy that he felt like a teenage boy.

I suggested that Carl and Abbie were adults and could and should talk more about the experience, especially what each liked about it. I suggested that coming prematurely is quite common for men and told him of Helen Singer Kaplan's book, *The New Sex Therapy*[1] and how the ejaculatory reflex can change for the man with practice by stopping before he feels himself coming, and in this way prolonging the experience. With practice he can become sensitive to that point of loss of control and just imperceptibly hesitates or slows down enough to prevent himself from coming. The suggestion made sense to him and he was ready to practice. Telling his wife about what we talked about in therapy was becoming easier and now made talking about sex easier.

In one of these sessions he told of how his wife was the one to generally close the window curtains or shades each evening. He had never thought about the possibility that Abbie might have seen the neighbors making love on other nights. On one evening he happened to come to the bedroom when she was closing the shade and noticed that she could see the neighbors too.

I asked Carl how she reacted to seeing them.

"She just grinned and said that they should close their curtains but that she was giving them their privacy. She made no big deal about it. But we had a good time in bed that night."

Then on another occasions their daughter Angie and her family came to visit. "She suggested that we watch a video together and she had one in mind. I was shocked that she would want to watch such a sexy movie with us but Abbie did not seem to think a thing about it."

"Maybe she is trying to educate you about sex too." We both laughed.

Carl's education was opening his mind. He was for the first time in his life enjoying sex. Yet he was still obsessing about watching the neighbors and still felt it was wrong to be watching them. He felt guilty when he saw how casual and unobsessed Abbie was about them. These experiences did not give him the strength to end his voyeurism, but at least his guilt now was not all-consuming, and it did not interfere with the rest of his life. He accepted sacrificing the high moral expectations he had of himself for his improved sex life.

ARLENE

For Arlene, calling the spirits, opening her mind more to the world beyond her five senses made sense and opened more doors for her. Planning and rehearsing what she is going to say to the family that she appreciated is from beyond the five senses, thus also of the spirits. Her family appreciated her changed behavior, of telling them how she appreciated them. Work was a different story. Her impatience and driven perfectionism was appreciated, especially by her dentist boss, though it sometimes alienated her from others not so driven. In school these traits made her a good student and impressed her instructors, but they also set her apart from other, younger students who were seeking to have a good time as well as study. School, then, was not so much of a problem.

The day after our last session the tone in the house changed, a change initiated not so much by Arlene as by Jessi. Jessi ran into the house after school, threw her book bag and jacket on the floor and started running towards the kitchen. She looked up in time to see Arlene frowning. She quickly turned to grab her bag and jacket with a "Woops, I'll get them." Arlene's quick smile made the rest of the evening pleasant. When Josh ran in a minute or two later she was quick to hug him and direct him to his room with a lightness in her voice before he let go of his book bag. She was generally not home when the kids got home from school. This day was an exception. Usually when she got home the book bags and jackets were already on the floor and getting the kids to put them away became a bigger issue. This time the smile, hug and lightness in her voice made the difference, and best of all, Arlene realized it.

The next night, when she got home later, with the same smile, hug and lightness in her voice she asked the kids to put away their school things, and this approach worked without a problem. Arlene was on a new track. She was a good student and learned quickly what was effective. A somewhat bigger problem was Tim only because Tim was not as trusting and forgiving as the children, but Arlene's commitment was strong.

Tim's work was taking him out of town the next day, so he had to get up a couple of hours earlier than usual. Needless to say, he wanted to go to bed early, but Arlene was busy with her homework. "You can go to bed without me."

"You know I don't sleep well when you are up and around. Come to bed."

Arlene started getting irritated because her homework was important, even though others might think that she over-studied.

Tim called out a second time, "Come to bed."

Arlene stood up, ready to rage into the room, but then she remembered she had an hour before class tomorrow, thought of Tim's feelings, and started getting ready for bed. Tim was tense, and Arlene had not totally let go of her anger. When she got into bed the tension was thick. Tim let out a sigh and Arlene said to him, "Get off it, I'm in bed where you want me." She couldn't yell because the children were already asleep. Such a fight would usually escalate, with Arlene getting back up and Tim's frustration making it impossible for him to sleep. This time Arlene rolled over to massage Tim's shoulders and suggested that he relax because everything was okay. He took a couple more deep breaths and began to relax. The next day in class, though she did not feel as prepared as she usually did, she had no problem holding her number-one spot.

Work was another story. One of Arlene's jobs was to make sure work done was recorded in the patient record in order to validate billing. One hygienist, Amy, tended to be sloppy in record keeping, and Arlene had to keep on her case. The dentist appreciated Arlene's perfectionism, but Amy wasn't so appreciative: "I have someone waiting. I'll get to it after I finish with him."

To Arlene it made so much more sense to record the work right then. It would only take a moment and would leave less room for mistakes. The dentist happened to walk by at that moment, and Arlene, looking up, shook her head in frustration. The dentist said to the hygienist, "The patient can wait." Amy felt criticized and blamed Arlene for getting her in trouble. This tension between Arlene and Amy was ongoing but did not mean much to the dentist.

What could Arlene do? If a mistake in a record happened, it could be a problem for everyone. I suggested that the hygienist is also a professional and should be respected. "What if you don't file the record until the note is completed? Leave the record where Amy will find it and trust her to eventually write the note. If the chart is still out at the end of the day when she is ready to leave, then there is a real problem, but you are not responsible for or to blame for her problem."

Arlene saw my point, though the suggestion ran against her need to keep things organized and have things put away. This work situation offered her a clearer picture of what she had to sacrifice, her perfectionistic organization and her compulsion to keep things where they belong. This sacrifice allowed Arlene to show appropriate respect for others. The spirits of her perfectionism and her ability to show appreciation to others were alive within her and struggling with each other.

JERRY

Jerry showed a deeper insight at the end of the last session when he realized that he could gain Sherry's respect by becoming a better listener and by appreciating her, but acting on this insight would require sacrificing his attempts to impress her with his success in pitching. Thus, during the next session I offered Jerry a new narrative to improve his listening skills with her. We had called the spirits and I had him stand in the Feathered Serpent Posture as I turned on the drumming:

"To many men intimacy means sex. To many women the same word means a deep level of communication requiring trust and honesty and, more concretely, talking about feelings. For men to learn to be intimate in the ears of a woman takes beginning at the concrete level of talking about feelings, and that means using feeling words, "I feel hurt," "I feel happy," "I feel humiliated," etc." This was as difficult for Jerry as for most men. It takes paying attention to each sentence, each word he speaks, making sure the sentence includes a feeling word. "It hurts when you don't seem proud of my baseball accomplishments, the one thing in my life that I have succeeded at." "It is humiliating and embarrassing when I miss a practice because my wife wants me at home." "I am most happy when my wife is in the stands cheering for me." We spent considerable time during the next several sessions of therapy framing such sentences. "I feel inadequate when I can't make you happy." "I feel adequate when I'm pitching." It was apparent that the spirits of my counter-narrative continued to be alive within him.

Speaking intimately takes concerted effort (willpower) and practice, but it was paying off for Jerry. Sherry would smile happily when she heard Jerry trying. I had a therapy session with Sherry and gave her a brief lecture on how difficult it is for a man to learn to talk intimately. She didn't believe it at first because she was raised to talk intimately. It came naturally to her. Jerry was raised to do things, to accomplish things, and not to express feelings. She finally accepted the fact that Jerry had to really concentrate to talk intimately. They made a commitment that for a half hour each day Jerry would practice speaking intimately, though this sometimes did not happen on the evenings of baseball practice. I suggested that he talk about incidents of daily living, not just his feelings about playing ball, using the language of intimacy. His ball-playing feelings were especially heavy, even to Sherry, and I couldn't recommend dumping them on her all at once. I pointed out to him that everything one does has a feeling associated with it, no matter how simple. "I felt happy to fill your car with gas. I thought it would please you." "My mouth felt clean after I brushed my teeth."

This active listening worked for a while. One evening Sherry came home from work with complaints about her boss. Jerry listened well and added, "I feel frustrated because there is nothing I can do to solve your problem except suggest that you quit, and I know you are not ready to do that." Sherry smiled and told him all she needed to do was to ventilate, to express her own frustration and anger, and there was nothing she expected him to do.

Sherry's problem at work continued to escalate, however, and a few days later Jerry in frustration said, "Why don't you just quit." With a raised voice, Sherry said, "You know I can't do that." Jerry's level of anxiety shot up with the tension in the air of Sherry's frustration at work and Jerry's frustration with not knowing what to do. Sherry added, "You know Jill (Sherry's boss) and I have been through this before. It will blow over." Jerry began to relax.

Jerry soon noticed that the hassle of his going to practices had diminished. Sherry seemed genuinely happier now when they were together, and she did not complain much when he had to leave. They talked about what they could do together when he was not going to practices or games, and he even missed a few practices when she had something special she wanted to do. Beth was now 11 years old and was still visiting on weekends, but as an 11-year-old she was much more independent and not a big strain on Sherry. Having developed a friendship with the daughter of another member of the team, she often went to games with her dad. Other times she would ask to stay with another friend, so she was not home a lot with just Sherry, so Sherry could not complain.

Jerry still longed for Sherry to be at the games and cheer for him, but she rarely went because she valued her weekend time to get things done at home. Jerry was quick to express his happiness on the rare occasion that she would go to a game, yet she spent much of her time in the stands working on whatever project she brought with her, knitting or reading some book. She did not seem to pay much attention to the game. Jerry learned to accept her disinterest with little or no complaint but was still disappointed that she showed no enthusiasm for baseball. He felt that he made a real sacrifice in order to make Sherry happy. He no longer demanded that she be his number-one rooter, but at this point he was able to admit that it was worth giving up this demand for the sake of his love for her.

For each of the three people in therapy the sacrifice had been made and the obsession was bound, at least for the time being.

FENRIR'S HOWL

When the gods are certain that Fenrir is securely bound by the ribbon, they fasten a chain to the ribbon Gleipnir. They draw the chain through a boulder which is then driven deep into the earth. A huge stone is then used to plug the hole, thus holding the boulder in place.

As Fenrir struggles, he widely opens his mouth. When he does, the gods quickly gag him by placing a sword in his mouth with the point wedged against the roof of his mouth and the hilt propped on the lower jaw. The bound and gagged Fenrir howls horribly, the saliva from his mouth running to form the River Von.

Though each person in therapy has found the strength of Gleipnir to bind their obsession, on the distant Island of Lyngvi in Lake Amsvartnir their obsession howls in captivity. Each person has taken his or her obsession to a distant island, either in denial or to make it easier to ignore the problem, yet its howl can be heard at times as a reminder that the problem has not gone away.

Though Jerry was happy with the respect Sherry had for him in his ability to communicate intimately, he still hurt because she had little or no interest in his accomplishments as a baseball pitcher. Carl's sex life had come alive and he felt closer than ever to Abbie, yet on Wednesday nights he still was obsessed with the howl from watching his neighbors in their bedroom and felt guilty for his voyeuristic weakness. Arlene had found greater peace at home because of the rewarding response of her children and husband to her more loving behavior, though her need for the howl from her need for perfection still was strong and showed itself mostly in her work. She had found the strength to be more tactful at work, yet her frustration still howled within her and drooled for the day she could speak her mind.

CHAPTER 11

BALDR'S DREAM AND DEATH

BALDR'S DREAM

For each of the three clients in psychotherapy, Fenrir's howl can be heard in the distance. Back in Asgard, a new event is developing. Baldr the good, the most loved, innocent and gentle of the gods, has a dream predicting his death. He reports this dream to the Æsir who, fearing his death, take counsel together to decide what must be done. Their decision is to request an oath from all substances on earth that none will harm Baldr. Frigg, Baldr's mother, goes on a journey to request this oath from fire, water, iron and all kinds of metal and stone, the earth, trees, diseases, all animals, birds, snakes and poison. When she returns with these promises, everyone rejoices and begins to celebrate by testing these oaths, throwing at Baldr every imaginable substance they can find. Yet he goes unharmed.

With our tormentor-obsession restrained in the distance, we begin to regain our confidence and feelings of innocence. Subconsciously we know that the threat to our confidence and innocence is still alive, but we want to believe in our strength over our dysfunctional behavior, and we seek to test it.

ARLENE

Arlene's confidence was rapidly growing. The positive responses from her children and Tim were very rewarding and in turn, her positive attitude towards them increased daily. The children were trying hard to please her, and the good feelings were spiraling upwards. At work, her frustration with Amy, the hygienist, continued, even though she had followed my suggestion to leave the unsigned records out on the counter until they were signed. Then one day the expected happened.

On the day before, Arlene had had to leave early because she was having a final exam in one of the courses she was taking. The next morning, when she came into the office, several charts were still sitting on the counter unsigned. Amy came in just a few moments behind her and Arlene said nothing; she didn't know what to say. When the dentist came in she only had to nod her head towards the charts and raise her eyebrows. He motioned for her to leave the room and then had a few words with the hygienist. Arlene felt great satisfaction. Her change in routine of leaving the charts on the counter paid off. From then on, at least for the next couple of months, Amy's notes were written and signed immediately after the patient was seen. Though the feelings between Arlene and Amy were not great, the two were able to work together comfortably.

Arlene's perfectionism was appreciated at work and at school. At home, her perfectionism was taking a different form. She was quick to learn that by keeping a positive attitude, by rewarding the children for picking up their things and by letting Tim know she appreciated his patience with her, things were going as she liked.

CARL

Carl's life had come alive with his new understanding and openness in his sexuality and sexual experiences with his wife, creating a life that apparently his wife Abbie always wanted. During the summer months the church choir did not practice, since too many members went on vacations, so Abbie was at home on Wednesday nights. Though Abbie had always gone upstairs to close the bedroom curtains, Carl now occasionally would go up before her to do it and he would sometimes take a few moments to watch the neighbors if they were in bed. One night, Abbie came upstairs just behind him and came in while he was watching. Carl reported, "I stayed cool this time by saying, 'They're at it again.' I was a little surprised when Abbie smiled and said, 'They know how to have a good time. There are things we could learn from them.' I asked her, 'What have your learned?' and she answered, 'I'll show you,' as she started taking off her clothes. We got into bed and this time Abbie got on top. It was great, but I couldn't help myself. I came too fast."

Some things can change in life like an avalanche, starting slowly with hesitation and then moving such that they cannot be stopped. Carl and Abbie's life had changed like an avalanche. Carl's only comment was, "Why couldn't I have discovered these things sooner?" Though Carl "was cool," at the beginning he was hesitant and scared, with a possible nightmare of death when Abbie walked in and saw him watch through the window. But he was quick to learn that nothing could harm him, and even coming prematurely was not a big deal.

JERRY

Jerry was smart and still very much a "doer," "a human-doing." He had become skilled in active listening just as he became skilled in pitching. Sherry had been very impressed by his ability to learn to listen actively, and their relationship was going smoothly. He was playing baseball as he would like, going to the games and most practices. He was taking his daughter when he had her, and she enjoyed this time with her father. Sherry still did not go to the games, but now said she liked this time home alone. Everything was going well.

Jerry's confidence was high that his problems felt solved. His innocence was still alive.

BALDR'S DEATH

When Loki sees what is going on in this assembly of gods, he is angered. He thinks the god's hypocrisy is ridiculous. "What do the gods really love the most, Battle or Baldr, fighting and strength or the epitome of gentleness and innocence? It's hypocrisy for them to say they love both." Thus, this shape-shifter shifts his shape, assuming the shape of a woman and visits Frigg. While being questioned about this assembly, Frigg happens to mention that she missed getting an oath from one thing, mistletoe. To her the mistletoe had seemed too young or small to cause any harm.

Loki then leaves Frigg, finds a piece of mistletoe, and carves it into the shape of a dart. Returning to the assembly, he finds Hod, Baldr's blind brother standing at the edge of the crowd. He suggests to Hod that to honor his brother he should throw something at Baldr but that since he is blind, Loki himself would help him in his aim. He puts the mistletoe dart in Hod's hand and turns him in Baldr's direction. Hod throws the dart. It strikes it mark and Baldr falls dead.

Again it is the Loki within that brings things to a head. A part of us knows that our problem is not totally resolved. Though our torment is restrained and held at a distance, it is still alive and we deceive ourselves in claiming our innocence. It is time for Loki to act, time for something to happen in our lives to force us to be honest with ourselves. As blind as we are, we need to see the death of our innocence.

ARLENE

With Arlene's perfectionism still reigning, her life could not continue to run smoothly. This personality trait was bound to cause another crisis in her life, and it didn't take long for it to happen, this time in school. Her instructor in one of her dental hygienist classes gave out a new assignment for a term project, and Arlene was randomly assigned a partner. When the pair first met, her partner's resentment was quick to emerge: "How can I work with you? You're such a 'brown noser.' You're going to have to do this by yourself."

Arlene was dumbfounded, so shocked by such directness that her mouth just hung open. Her partner turned and left.

As Arlene told me this story, I felt a need to offer some sort of explanation. I feebly suggested, "Your partner sounds self-destructive, like someone who is afraid of success and needs an excuse to fail. This could be an opportunity for her to get a good grade, but she is sabotaging the possibility."

What Arlene wanted, however, was a solution. "I can't tattle to the instructor. That would probably make things worse. I can't do the project by myself because the project depends upon the two of us working together. Half the grade is on how well we work together, and anyway my partner doesn't deserve a good grade. I told Tim about it. He was no help. I mentioned it to the dentist. He had confidence in me that I would work it out by myself." This crisis brought Arlene's perfectionism back to the front. Her innocence was dead.

CARL

Carl was able to watch his neighbors having sex and had learned that to Abbie it was no big deal, though he was on guard for Abbie walking in, when he had to make his watching look brief and casual. But then Abbie went to stay with their daughter for a couple of weeks. Angie was pregnant and about due. She wanted her mother there to help when the baby came. While she was away Carl "spent too much time at the window masturbating. I'm so horny and I feel terrible about it." His voyeurism was still alive. Carl's awakened sex life was fulfilled with Abbie. When she was away his story was different. His innocence was dead.

JERRY

Jerry's confidence was high, but then came one evening before practice. Sherry came home from work very upset and was really looking forward to telling Jerry about her bad day. Jerry listened and reflected, but as the time drew near for him to leave, Sherry still had much to say. Jerry became preoccupied with leaving. He continued to reflect Sherry's feelings but in a mechanical and somewhat impatient manner. Then he looked at his watch.

Sherry was quick to pick up on his impatience and started getting irritated. "Your practice is more important than me."

"But I was listening and reflecting."

"You were getting impatient and angry, looking at your watch, sighing. I need you tonight."

"I told the guys I would be there. They're counting on me."

Everything broke down. After weeks of good feelings, everything felt lost, back to the way things were when the couple first came to therapy. Jerry's newfound innocence was dead and his anger and frustration were back.

BALDR'S FUNERAL

Though the gods know that Loki had something to do with Baldr's death, they can do nothing about it. The sanctity of Asgard needs to be protected and not defiled by an attack on Loki. The gods fetch Baldr's ship, the largest of ships, and prepare for the funeral by building a pyre of wood on it. They attempt to launch the ship, but it will not move. So they send to Jotunheim, the land of the giants, for help. Hyrrokkin, a giantess, returns to help, riding her wolf and using vipers as reins. It takes four berserks to hold her mount. As she pushes on the ship's prow it begins to roll, with flames shooting from the rollers and the earth quaking. Thor is angered and ready to swing his hammer at the head of the giantess, but the gods beg for his mercy.

As Baldr is carried to the ship, his wife Nanna collapses in grief and dies. She, too, is carried to the funeral pyre along with Baldr's horse. Thor, still angry, kicks at a passing dwarf and knocks him into the fire so that he, too, burns.

We know that our innocence is dead, that we are unable to deny our obsession; still, we attempt to deny its death, but we fail. Besides the denial of the death of our innocence and our failure in this denial, there is also within us that impulsive anger, like Thor who wants to hurt or to fight against our honest acceptance of this death. It takes great strength to lay our innocence to rest.

ARLENE

With Arlene, I needed to lead her to make a connection between the problem that existed with her school project partner and her perfectionism. She had come to value the spirits that would come to her when in trance and listening to the counter-narratives I would tell her. Calling the spirits at the beginning of a session seemed meaningful to her. She could feel the beginning of a counter-narrative as I suggested, "You have an advantage over most of the other students in your class because you already work in a dental office. Take a few moments to think of the dental patients that come into the office. Probably most of them are no problem. A lot, if not most, of them would say they don't like dentists, but they cause you no problem. There are a few, though, that are a problem, patients who are difficult to work with because of their fear of the dentist. Probably a lot of children are afraid of the dentist, but pick an adult and spend a few moments thinking about that adult and how he or she makes life in the office more difficult. Take a few minutes to think about that person. Okay, now describe that person to me." Simply using such phrases as "take a few moments to think," moved these words into the realm of trance, especially for a person who has had as much experience with trance as Arlene. Even so I did turn on the drumming CD to add to the depth of trance. She was sitting and moved forward to grasp her knees in the Lady of Cholula Posture.

Arlene answered with her eyes closed. "She's a woman about 70 years old. She first came in way before my time, but I understand that she would shriek as soon as the dentist would ask her to open her mouth. Now, when she has an appointment her husband comes in first and she waits in the car. When it is her time he goes out to get her and she walks in holding his hand. By the time she is sitting in the chair tears are running down her face, but she no longer screams out. The doctor is so gentle and patient with her, and with all the things he has at his fingertips there is no longer much pain. I can't imagine why she still cries."

"Okay. Her husband leads her past your desk and to one of the rooms where she sits in the dental chair. As she passes out of your sight, take a few moments to think about your feelings towards her. What are those feelings?"

"I just sort of shake my head. I don't understand her. The word is too strong but what comes to mind is 'impatient.' She seems so weak or fragile, even though she is a strong and fairly large woman. She looks silly being led across the room by the hand, with her head down, like a little girl about to cry."

"Okay, then how does the dentist relate to her?"

"Oh! He is very patient. He doesn't seem bothered at all by her tears but just talks to her with confidence like he would talk to anybody else, explaining to her what needs to be done and how he is going to do it with as little pain as possible. He is good with her."

"Okay, take a little time to compare your feelings or attitude to the dentist's feelings or attitude. Think of the time when you will be a hygienist and she could be your patient. Think of how she would react to your feelings and how she would react to his feelings... Maybe the key words are 'impatience and patience.' The patient's impatience is your spirit guide, the spirit of your impatience." After a longer pause, I continued, "Think of your impatience as part of your perfectionism, and how that interferes with the feeling of confidence you would want to show the patient. One of the reasons you're in school is to learn such confidence and patience. This situation is different from the situation in school with your project partner, but it is also the same, and again your perfectionism is getting in the way." Arlene got the point—I could see her deflate. The spirits of self-confidence, patience and impatience were alive within her.

CARL

Returning to Carl, until now we had focused in therapy not on the problem of voyeurism but on opening up Carl to a healthier and more satisfying sexual life. With this new strength, now was the time to help Carl face his obsession with watching his neighbors making love. I suggested that as he sits that he closes his eyes and take a few moments to go into a trance. Automatically his back straightened and he reached forward to grasp his knees as I turned on the CD player. After a few moments, when I could see Carl's breathing change, I suggested, "Let the observer part of you stand in the doorway of the bedroom and watch yourself watching your neighbors and masturbating. Watch, and in a little while images will come to you, images of what you're watching and masturbating remind you of."

Carl was quick to describe a dog he used to have that after it ate would lick its genitals until he got an erection even though the dog had been fixed. "It was disgusting. He would walk around awkwardly with his back legs spread because of the erection, dripping and looking uncomfortable. If I was sitting nearby he would come over and try to mount my leg. I would just get up and leave the room. Abbie would say he was just being a dog. I guess I'm just being a dog, no self-control. I hate it. It's so disgusting." In this case, Carl was not trying to find justification to protect his innocence. His more virtuous side hated his animalistic/sexual self, the spirit of the dog. His innocence was dead.

Both Jerry and Arlene had learned to value the spirits that came to them when in trance. This was somewhat of a problem for Carl because of his belief in the Holy Spirit. He found that talking of the spirits was more acceptable when I would talk of the spirits coming from the Holy Spirit. He seemed to accept me saying that the spirit of this disgusting dog was shown to him by the Holy Spirit. The problem though was that he understood it as something that the Holy Spirit found disgusting. It would take some time for Carl to accept that horniness was God-given and to be enjoyed.

JERRY

Jerry was feeling hopeless. Sherry again had exclaimed, for the first time in several months, "Your practice is more important than me."

"We are back to where we were quite a few weeks ago. If only Sherry would appreciate you as a baseball pitcher, become excited by your success, but she still hasn't. You've, or at least you had, gained her appreciation for your ability to listen, but not for your life on the diamond." In joining Jerry's feelings to induce trance, I was able to draw upon information provided months ago in reflecting his frustration, "Sherry doesn't appreciate your skill as a pitcher, a part of you that you are very proud of. She just doesn't appreciate that part of you."

Jerry groaned, "Yeah!" He was looking very despondent. "She said, 'When are you going to grow up.' I told her, 'What do you mean? Look at all the professionals that make big money.' But I'm not professional."

"She sees it as a kid's game. But look at all the men who watch baseball on television for hours at a time. Yet many wives gripe about that, too, and see it as childish. Baseball is very important to you. You love the game. It has been a very rewarding activity in your life and given you great self-esteem. Sherry's appreciation for you was lost, was dead.

"You know, you want your mom with you in this..." What happened next is most appropriate for the next section of this chapter, the journey to Hel, the unconscious mind.

HERMOD'S JOURNEY TO HEL

Frigg calls to those present that whoever would be willing to ride the road to Hel's hall to find Baldr and offer Hel a ransom for his release would earn all her love and favor. Hermod the Bold, a brother to Baldr, agrees to ride the road. He takes Sleipnir, Odin's horse, and leaves. After traveling nine days and nine nights and longer, he comes to the golden bridge. When he crosses the bridge over the river Gjoll, the guardian maiden questions his lineage and his reason for riding the road to Hel's hall. Hearing his purpose, she reports that Baldr had already crossed the bridge. Hermod comes to the gates of Hel's hall and spurs the horse to jump the gates. In Hel's great hall he sees Baldr sitting in a seat of honor. Hermod spends the night, and the next day he asks Hel for permission to take Baldr with him back to Asgard, mentioning that everyone is weeping for his return. Hel offers one condition for Baldr's release: "everything upon the earth, alive or dead, must weep for Baldr." Before Hermod returns to Asgard, Baldr gives him the golden arm ring Draupnir for Odin, and Nanna sends other gifts, including a linen robe for Frigg.

A nurturing part of us believes that there must be a way to regain our innocence. We hope that in facing our guilt, our remorse will be sufficient to release us from our inner hell. But our remorse has to be total, with no reservations or excuses. The journey to Hel represents a journey into the unconscious mind, just as the journey into the cave of the dark elves was such a journey. The dark elves gave each client new strength. This journey will lead each client to face a part of themselves that is hard to give up but is causing great emotional pain and grief. Because of our resistance to giving up this part we resist remorse. Therapy to initiate this journey begins by joining the client in his or her feelings as a means of trance induction.

ARLENE

Though Arlene realized that her impatience was part of her perfectionism and that it got in the way of gaining confidence, she still asked in frustration, "But what can I do?" This question began her journey into hell.

I knew it would make her angry but I had to say, "Your frustration is also a part of your perfectionism." I could see her fuming, so I let her go for a few moments so that she could kick that weak dwarf part of her into the fire; then I added, "It is just that perfectionistic energy that has put off your project partner. She needs to see, just like you see in your dentist, a sense of relaxed, patient confidence in you. Such patient confidence can melt most any tension or fear.

It was time to offer another counter-narrative, one that would show her the power of self-confidence and patience rather than impatience and frustration, though we had been through this before and intellectually she knew the difference. It was time to plant a seed deeper within her. We had already called the spirits. I suggested that she stand in the Feathered Serpent posture as I turned on the drumming. After a few moments of focusing on our breath, I began the counter-narrative:

"Let's face the feelings of frustration and impatience you feel because of your project partner. What is your partner's name?"

"Valerie."

A hypnotic counter-narrative was forming in my mind. In offering a counter-narrative I automatically turn on the drumming that helps put me in a trance in telling the story as much as it helps the client. I hoped that this counter-narrative would provide her with a new spirit guide or spirit guides: "Okay. Close your eyes and relax. Try this exercise on to see how it fits. Be curious and wondering as you listen to these words. It's after class and you are usually in a hurry to get home, while many of the students have the freedom to go to the snack bar in the Student Union. This time you head towards the Union. As you enter the snack bar you see Valerie sitting by herself at a table. You go over to the table, pull out a chair and sit down. Valerie starts to get up but you put your hand gently on her wrist and look her in the eyes. She sits back down. You start talking, 'You know how different I am from most of the class. I'm older. I have a husband and children. I've worked several years in a dental office. I don't have the life you do with a lot of other interests. I'm envious of you and the freedom you have. I usually feel I have to rush home after class. You can come here to relax for a few minutes. Besides my family, my whole life is dentistry. But I want to be more than a receptionist. My experience in the dental office makes this class somewhat easier for me and all I have to do with any extra time is to study. That may not seem fair to you when you have a full load of classes. I would like to work with you on this project. If you are at all interested, we can spend some time in a real dental office. The dentist I work with is real nice and a good resource. His input is often very useful."

"Take a few moments to feel yourself saying those words or similar words to Valerie. As you feel yourself saying those words, consider such feelings as patience and impatience, self-confidence and frustration. When you are ready you can tell me about these feelings. It is sometimes hard to let people be different from you."

Arlene took a deep breath and opened her eyes. "You're right. People are very different, and I do become impatient. The words you said felt good. I could see what you were doing. I'd have to practice to say them, but I don't know if Valerie would sit back down if I put my hand on her wrist. My first thought was that she would have jerked her hand away."

"She might have jerked it away and left, but at least you would be showing her a patient and self-confident side of yourself, like the dentist showed the 70-year-old patient."

"I don't know that I would feel that confidence. I felt very anxious when I saw her in the Union and started towards her table."

Arlene was clearly experiencing the distinction between the feelings of the spirits within her of patience and impatience, and of self-confidence and frustration.

CARL

Carl, in his pain and self-disgust, asked, "What can I do?"—a logical question to accompany the death of innocence. I sensed that he wanted me to rescue him, to tell him again how what he was doing was okay. His pain was a call for sympathy, something I was not ready to give.

I reflected, "You feel like a disgusting dog. But a dog does not have the conscience to think, 'What can I do?' You, on the other hand, know what you're doing. It is important for you to hold this image of the disgusting dog that the Holy Spirit brought you, the disgusting dog within you, and with patience, gentleness and curiosity you will find some deeper understanding."

What happened next was not at all what I had expected, but maybe it needed to happen. I continued, "Think for a few moments, what is the opposite of your disgusting dog?"

Carl soon answered, "A proper dog, a show dog, well-trimmed, a poodle, a well-trimmed poodle standing with its head up."

I laugh, "I like that. Okay, these dogs can talk. These two dogs meet on the street. The disgusting dog goes over and starts sniffing the poodle. It sticks its nose in the butt of the poodle. What does the poodle do or say?"

"It jumps, 'Get your nose out of there.'"

We were both laughing, and I add, "Huh? What kind of dog are you? You don't even smell like a dog. Oh! I bet you can't smell anything anyway because of all the perfume!"

Carl continues to play the role. "Yuck! I can smell you from here. You stink."

"You got something against being a real dog, smelling like a dog? What's your problem?

"Let's bring this back to humans. You can picture your disgusting self, sitting on the edge of your bed masturbating. What is your proper self? Putting on your Sunday clothes and sitting in church? How does your proper self look at work?"

"Sitting in my office with the door open so people can come in, sitting there working so people can see that I have work to do. I think some people think that the plant manager has nothing to do. If I walk through the plant I nod or say hello to the people as I walk by. Sometimes I stop to talk to someone. I need to make them feel important." Carl was promoted to plant manager about a month ago and expressed pride in this promotion. He is much more open and spontaneous in therapy than he was during the first few sessions.

"You probably employ all kinds of people. Probably some of them are kind of disgusting."

"There have been a couple of alcoholics that have come to work drunk. One was eventually fired. The other went through rehabilitation and is a good worker now. There is always someone, but they don't last. The lucky ones get their lives together. I have respect for most all my employees."

"How about in church, what is the proper person?"

"Wearing my Sunday clothes and sitting in church. Greeting people after church."

"The people in church would probably be disgusted if they caught you and Abbie in bed. I don't get it. You probably still think of sex as not proper and even disgusting even though you have been enjoying it, but from what you say about Abbie, I don't think she would use the word 'disgusting.' Yet she is the good church-going Christian. I think you think she is proper, but how do you explain her ability to enjoy sex? Can that perfumed, ribbon-wearing poodle be a real dog, enjoy sniffing and humping other dogs?" I added as I had before, "Your sexuality is God-given."

Carl had to agree with my evaluation. He went home thinking, seeking to understand the apparent inconsistency, an inconsistency that could prevent him from weeping. His disgusting spirit guide has brought him to feel this inconsistency.

JERRY

Jerry's and Sherry's needs collided. She came home after a bad day at work and needed Jerry to listen, but Jerry needed to leave for a practice. She again complained that baseball was more important to him than her. The feeling of appreciation because of Jerry's new ability to listen was dead.

I joined this feeling of grief by suggesting, "Let's go back to the six months, the season that you dropped out because of your separation and divorce. That was a very painful six months because of the failure of your marriage, but also because you were not playing baseball. You felt very empty. Sit back and relax." As he relaxed to quiet his mind I soon reached over to turn on the CD player and drumming. When he heard the drumming he automatically sat up and grasped his knees in the Lady of Cholula Posture.

I continued with the counter-narrative: "Close your eyes. Turn you mind inward to experience that feeling of emptiness. Imagine your empty self sitting in one chair and your fulfilled self sitting in another, of your empty spirit guide and your fulfilled spirit guide. Take your time to let these images form: the empty self without a wife and without your avocation of playing baseball; your fulfilled self with a wife and pitching for your team. Let these two images form, and when they are there let me know by lifting the index finger of your right hand."

Jerry's finger lifted.

"Now tell me what the empty Jerry looks like."

"He is small, about half the size of the other Jerry. His clothes are baggy and the chair he is sitting in is too big for him."

"Okay, now tell me about the fulfilled Jerry."

"He's big, fills the chair, and is sitting tall."

"Okay, you might want to tell me more about how these two spirit figures look as we go along, but now let your fulfilled Jerry tell your empty Jerry what he needs."

"You need a girlfriend and you should get back on the team."

"What's so important about each? Explain that to the empty Jerry."

"A woman in your life can make you feel good about yourself, someone to appreciate you for what you are able to give her. Baseball can give you excitement. You are a good pitcher and you can make the team a winning team. The team would appreciate you."

"Okay, you said that so clearly, so openly. Many months ago you were denying that you needed to be appreciated, or at least you said that giving should be fun and you shouldn't expect appreciation. The empty Jerry needs to be appreciated. We've used that word, appreciation, a lot over the last few months. You've come to accept it. It's become clear to you that you depend upon appreciation."

This caused dissonance in Jerry, especially the word "depend." The thought of dependence is a negative thought to Jerry. He seeks to be independent. We've come back to facing an issue that surfaced much earlier in therapy. This time he admits it but will seek to justify it.

HERMOD'S RETURN

Upon Hermod's return to Asgard the gods send messengers to every person, animal, plant and stone. All weep, with one exception; the giantess Thokk has no tears for Baldr. We do weep for the death of our innocence, but after searching deep within ourselves, we find that a part of us holds back and refuses to express remorse. That part of us continues to justify or defend our obsessive and destructive behavior and refuses to weep.

ARLENE

Arlene was able to value the patience and self-confidence of her dentist and the patience and confidence expressed in my words that she could say to her project partner, Valerie. Though she valued these qualities, she was not greatly confident that expressing them would improve her relationship with Valerie. Her perfectionism was very much alive inside of her, and the imperfections in others still frustrated her and caused her to feel impatient. Her impatience and frustration were unable to weep.

CARL

Carl returned the next week announcing that he was a new grandfather. Angie had a daughter. Abbie was still at Angie's to help with the baby. Carl had thought some about the images of the disgusting dog and the perfumed, ribbon-wearing poodle, but he had not come up with any sort of resolution to his dissonant thinking or feelings. He hoped there would be some sort of magic revelation to relieve him from his burden, but this did not happen. He seemed just as confused as when he left the last session.

With this experience of the previous week I decided it would be a good time to try a new posture, the Olmec Prince Posture for shape-shifting. I sat on the floor cross-legged and indicated for Carl to do the same. We place the knuckles of our hands on the floor in front of us, and I asked Carl what it felt like. He was quick to suggest that it felt like his arms became forelegs. Then before taking this posture for the fifteen minutes of ecstatic trance we stood in the Bear Spirit Posture to relax and for ego-strengthening. I then turned on the drumming and we sat on the floor in the Olmec Prince Posture.

At the end of fifteen minutes Carl reported: "I knew I was going to become a dog, but I didn't want to become the disgusting dog, so I turned to the poodle. I did not know what to do as the poodle, nothing felt right. I did not know who or where I was. All I could smell is the perfume and could not identify anything around me. All I knew was that I was at the end of a leash at my master's heels and would go wherever he led me. We went back to his house and I felt equally unhinged. I just followed him around. He would tell me to lie and I would lie where he told me. I ate when he told me to eat, and at night he took me to a place where there was a soft blanket, but all I could smell was the perfume. When he left in the morning I would lie by the door until he came home. My life felt very empty."

What this experience showed him was the emptiness in being proper, but this now only added to his confusion, because he did not know how to relieve the feeling of emptiness. He could see the problems with his narrow image of being proper, but it had been part of him all his life and he was not ready to say it was wrong. There was no weeping about it. He did not know how to integrate within him the belief that his sexuality was God-given. The fifty minutes was about up and I suggested he take this experience home with him. No other words were necessary.

JERRY

Jerry was more ready to face his dependency upon appreciation. Earlier he had sought to deny it, believing that dependency upon appreciation was weak. Now he was saying, "Everyone needs to be appreciated and everyone is dependent." In his attempt to justify his new thinking, he showed strength by not shedding tears in remorse for being weak. Jerry's continued need to show strength and his lack of tears will be an ongoing issue in therapy.

Each client had identified an important issue in their way of thinking that lay behind each obsession, as subtle as the way of thinking might be. Each had their own words, their own language to describe their way of thinking. This language uniquely defines each person and each person's narrative provides the unique language for the counter-narrative. Though there are similarities, each has a unique way of expressing their story. For Arlene, the issue was of control, of her impatience in wanting things a certain way. For Jerry the issue was his need to be independent and the recent discovery of his dependency upon women to appreciate him. For Carl it was his need to be proper, and his finding disgust in that which was not proper. These core issues, issues that had prevented them from weeping, from feeling remorse for their behavior, had become evident to each client, causing them some degree of torment. At first this torment did not seem great, but it was growing. The Loki within had caused them to experience this torment, and as the torment grows they will go after Loki for causing them such grief in life. Their Loki, however, will be one step ahead of them and will attempt to hide.

CHAPTER 12

LOKI'S ESCAPE AND CAPTURE: BINDING OUR COMPULSIVE BEHAVIOR

LOKI'S ESCAPE

The gods know that Loki is responsible for Baldr's death and Loki is aware of their anger. He runs away and hides in a mountain cabin, built with four doors so he can see out in all directions. During the daytime he leaves the cabin, shifts his shape to that of a salmon, and hides at the base of a waterfall.

Our confronting/trickster part, the Loki within, forces us to recognize something about ourselves that makes us exceedingly uncomfortable. We are now painfully aware of a personality trait or way of thinking that prevents us from resolving the problem that brought us to therapy. We struggle to change but feel hopeless in our ability to change. As our struggle continues, our frustration increases. We eventually become angry for being challenged to change and reach the stage of struggle where we don't want to be reminded or confronted by this challenge. So the confronting part of us runs and hides as we attempt to deny the need to change, but the denied/

confronting part of us still can see, is still conscious and knows what is going on from all directions.

This part of the story, of Loki's escape and capture, demands being handled differently from the previous part of the story. Why? Because this part of the story is told from Loki's perspective, the part of us that we do not want to face and are trying to deny. Loki, the trickster and confronting part of us, can also be considered our shadow, those needs that we seek to deny, those traits that we don't want made public that reflect our dysfunctional thinking: Carl's enjoyment of sex and his struggle to be "proper;" Jerry's dependency on being appreciated; and Arlene's need to be in control and anger when things are out of her control.

This part of the process of overcoming our obsessions has been unconscious, and when it is brought painfully into consciousness we struggle to deny it. Thus, the dream narrative, triggered by this denial, becomes more evident as a way to keep alive these hidden feelings. Because of this greater prominence of dreams, dreamwork becomes the most effective way to remain in touch with the denied aspects of the self. For some of the clients the process of Loki's escape, evasiveness, capture and restraint was gradual and seen over a period of time or a sequence of dreams, and for others the process moved very quickly and might be revealed in just one dream. In order to accommodate these individual differences, the story will be presented in its entirety, and the dreamwork will follow. Thus, we continue with the story.

THE EVASIVE LOKI

Loki spends much of his time pondering how the gods might catch him. While in the cabin he ties a net made of linen thread, like the nets still used today for fishing. When he sees the gods nearby he throws the net in the fire, changes himself into a salmon and jumps into the river. Odin is able to find the cabin because he can see the travels of Loki from his high seat in Asgard.

The confronting part of us that is forced to run and hide is very much necessary for our emotional growth and health, so it plots its own survival and will eventually return to facilitate the necessary change for our rebirth of innocence. We cannot let that part of us die, even though for the moment we seek to deny it. On the other hand, the wise and conscious part of us remains aware of and can see what we are doing. Though we may try to suppress these uncomfortable feelings, we are very aware of our needed confronting self. We can see our trickster/confronting self from our high seat in Asgard just as our confronting self can see our public/conscious self from the doors of the cabin. Because of this dual awareness, this part of the process can be considered an act of denial or the creation of a false public image of ourselves rather than suppression. It's a time in our lives when we can really feel like we're going crazy.

LOKI'S CAPTURE

Kvasir, the wisest of the gods, sees in the ashes in the fire the shape of the net and realizes that it must be a device to catch fish. So the gods make a net just like the shape they see in the ashes, go to the river and throw it in. With Thor holding one end of the net and the other gods holding the other, they drag it the along the river. Loki first swims along in front of the net and then lies down between two stones so the net goes over him. The second time the gods drag the net they weigh it down so that nothing can go under it, but Loki jumps over the net and swims back to the waterfall. On the third attempt Thor wades down the center of the river so that when Loki jumps over the net he is caught by Thor. Thor's hand slips along the salmon but his hand catches it at the tail, thus salmon have bodies that taper towards the tail.

The wisest part of ourselves knows what is going on and uses this knowledge to assist in the capture or denial of our need to change. With this knowledge and the knowledge of all parties, it is difficult to deny this confronting part of ourselves and the knowledge we have learned from it.

LOKI'S RESTRAINTS

The gods take Loki to a cave to hold him. They then fetch Loki's two sons, Vali and Narfi, and turn Vali into the form of a wolf. The wolf savagely tears his brother to pieces. The gods then use the entrails of Narfi, knowing that Loki can be held by nothing else, to tie him to three boulders, one under his shoulders, one under his loins and one under his knees. His bonds then turn to iron so that Loki cannot escape. They fix a poisonous snake above Loki so that its poison drips onto his face. Sigyn, Loki's faithful wife stands besides Loki with a bowl to catch the poison. When she leaves to empty the full bowl, the poison drips on Loki's face, causing him to jerk so hard that the earth shakes. That is what we now call an earthquake. There Loki stays bound until Ragnarok, the final battle.

In order to restrain the confronting part of ourselves and deny what it has tried to teach us, we need to again sacrifice something, our offspring, the compulsive behavior that we hate. By restraining our behavior we attempt to prove to ourselves that we are okay and can deny our shadow or automatic dysfunctional thoughts that have been part of us for much of our lives. Our will power is now much stronger, it turns to steel, and we go on with our lives believing that we have succeeded. Yet there are those quaking moments that shake us, and we realize that the struggle is still alive within us.

CARL

THE ESCAPE

Carl's images of what was proper and what was disgusting still caused him to feel disgust for masturbating while watching his neighbors. Though he had learned to enjoy sex he had to dissociate himself from his proper self. If he let himself think too much about what he was doing, he found sex disgusting. When he was having sex with Abbie, he was quick to lose his erection if he let himself think about what he was doing.

He still did not understand how Abbie reconciled her proper self and her sexual self. Carl had to learn to live with his inconsistency. Reconciliation seemed too out of reach, but in order to live with this inconsistency, masturbating while watching the neighbors had to end. In the process of escape Carl offered the following dream:

"I dreamt that I was watching the neighbors from our bedroom window but hiding by wrapping myself in the drape. That window does not have drapes. It was a drape from a downstairs window. My hand was on my penis but I couldn't move. I was wrapped too tight."

I often ask a client to give the dream a title. Carl's title to this dream was, "Wrapped too tight," a perfect description for his state of mind. The spirit guide emerging from this dream might be best described as the "hiding spirit." In the next four dreams he is in the dream and plays the role of his own dream spirit, "hiding spirit." His bedroom was dark, and in the past he had never felt a need to hide from the neighbors other than to hide in the darkness, knowing well that they could not see him from their well-lit room. In this dream he found that he needed to hide himself wrapped in a drape too. As the discussion continued, I asked him, "What else are you hiding from, then, wrapped in the drape?"

"I guess I must be hiding from myself."

"You don't want to see that disgusting part of yourself that watches the neighbors and masturbates."

"Uh huh. To live with myself I have to stop doing that. Having sex with Abbie is okay because she seems to enjoy it so much. Thinking about the neighbors sometimes distracts me from enjoying sex, from making love with Abbie, and I lose it."

THE EVASION

"In the dream I had last night I was watching the neighbors have sex from inside their room, from the top corner of their room as if I was invisible, and I could see over into our bedroom window. It was dark. I could have been in there watching, but I couldn't see anything. I haven't watched the neighbors or masturbated in about three weeks. Will dreaming about it go away?" Following the suit of the previous dream, the spirit guide of this dream would be the "invisible spirit."

"That's hard to say. You are still struggling. You still are in a conflict about what is proper and what is disgusting. You were invisible and you couldn't see yourself in your bedroom window. Two weeks ago your disgusting self was hiding from your proper self wrapped in a drape. Now you are invisible and you can't see yourself. Take a few moments to put yourself in those two situations. Experience them and notice the differences in feelings."

"I don't feel wrapped so tight. I'm just seeing them from the corner of their room. I don't even feel like I'm there, just my eyes."

"It sounds like you are hiding the disgusting part of yourself more effectively from your proper self. You're not even sure that you are in your bedroom watching. But dreams often reveal that part of you that you would like to hide." The dream itself was the ashes of the net in the fire.

THE CAPTURE

"I dreamt that I was dreaming that I was watching the neighbors."

"How did you do that?"

"I was watching the neighbors, but I knew it was only a dream."

I gesture with my hands for Carl to tell me more.

"I really wasn't watching them. It was only a dream."

"This time the spirit of the dream is the "dreamt spirit." Do you find that as disgusting as really watching them?"

"Not really. It was only a dream."

I flipped back through my notes and found what I was looking for. "'A few weeks ago you said that to live with yourself you would have to stop watching your neighbors while masturbating.' Can you live with dreaming about it?"

"For now I guess. I wish it would just go away, though."

"Maybe there will be a day when you dream about dreaming about dreaming about it. Even that dream would not be proper?" I asked. "Or you will dream about dreaming about dreaming about dreaming about it." I cushioned this sarcasm with a smile and a laugh (Loki's confrontational humor). "Your sexual feelings just won't go away, and they are not proper."

Carl was caught. He just couldn't get away from something as normal in life as his sexual feelings, from his horniness, from the excitement of sex. Such feelings just didn't feel proper, and yet Carl was caught in such feelings. He did feel good, though, that he had not watched his neighbors nor masturbated for about five weeks.

THE RESTRAINT

A couple of weeks later Carl was still successful in restraining himself from watching the neighbors. When he went upstairs on Wednesdays to close the window shade, if he saw the glow of light coming from the neighbor's window as he entered the bedroom he would just turn and leave, and not pull down the shade. He and Abbie had been having sex about once a week, though he would occasionally lose his erection, but Carl woke one morning with semen caked on his pajamas and sheet. He recalled his embarrassment and wanted to hide it from Abbie, the same feeling he had many years before when he was dating Abbie and felt a wet spot on his pants. He didn't remember having a dream. He was just not in control of that part of his body. If we are to talk about a spirit guide from this experience it is the "undrempt spirit."

Though we had talked of a person's sexuality as God-given and though Abbie seemed to have a healthy perspective regarding sex, Carl at an intellectual level accepted this God-givenness but at a deeper level still saw sex as disgusting. He had successfully suppressed his voyeuristic urges and his need to masturbate, sacrificing that excited but disgusting part of himself, restraining his urge with bonds of iron. Even his dreams showed this successful repression as evident in the sequence of spirit guides showing greater and greater distance from his obsession of watching his neighbors. Also sacrificed was the excitement found in making love with his wife. Now he found sex enjoyable, a way to let go of pent-up tension and to relax, but it seemed more of a duty than a pleasure.

Carl's restraint was made clear in the following dream, a dream that took him even further from his obsession by its metaphoric nature: "A raccoon was sniffing at a trap baited with peanut butter. He put his paw out to touch the peanut butter and got caught. He pulled and struggled for a minute or two but then sat down and began to chew on his leg. He chewed his foot off to get free and hobbled away. He didn't seem to be in any pain. My dad was a trapper and I remember him telling stories about animals chewing their legs off when caught. I don't know why it was baited with peanut butter except that I set a mouse trap the other day and baited it with peanut butter. It was strange. I thought it was a raccoon but it also seemed like a coyote. We have both animals running in our neighborhood."

"Okay, let's see. The raccoon or coyote was curious, or hungry in nosing at the trap. He then caught his paw in the trap, chewed it off to get free and hobbled away. Let's play with the words, find the best words for you. You are curious about something that can harm you or trap you, with the result that you lose something or something is taken from you, or you sacrifice something to get free. But the sacrifice is not especially painful. I think I used the word curious. When you told the dream I don't think you used that word."

"Oh! I think it fits, though."

"How about using peanut butter as bait? What does peanut butter mean to you?"

"I don't think my dad would have used peanut butter as bait. I think he would use a fish or a piece of raw meat. I really don't remember what he used. He would leave early in the morning before I got up. I think of peanut butter as something kids like and eat, but I still like peanut butter."

"A kid's food. What other words come to mind? Childlike? Childish? Playful? Not serious? Silly?"

"Yeah. All those. Well maybe not childish or silly."

"Okay. What does that leave? 'Not serious' and 'playful.' You are curious about something that can trap you that is not serious and playful. What in your life are you curious about that can trap you but is not serious but playful?"

"I keep thinking it has something to do with watching the neighbors, but I am not sure if I see it as not serious and playful."

"You have thought of watching the neighbors as disgusting. Is being childlike or childish disgusting? What your neighbors are doing is something grown up, but is what you are doing when watching playful and childish? Kids sometimes think of kissing as silly or disgusting."

"Yeah. I remember when I was young thinking that liking girls was disgusting when the older boys had girlfriends."

"But curious?"

"Yeah. When I was a little older, curious."

"But back then it was not playful but serious. Now you're still curious, but you're grown up, or should be grown up, and being curious in watching your neighbors—Abbie sees them or watches them as 'playful' and 'not serious,' but you are trapped by seeing 'playful' and 'not serious' as 'disgusting'."

"Yeah. Maybe that does fit."

"Well, let's go on, we can always come back to this. You chew off your foot. You lose something or sacrifice something, sacrifice a part of yourself. Does that fit? What of yourself would you be giving up?"

"Watching the neighbors, my curiosity."

"That disgusting part of yourself."

"Yeah."

"Then you hobble away. What does 'hobbling' mean to you?"

"With my feet tied together. I'm not free to run."

"How are you not free to run?"

"Okay, I'm not free to be playful in watching the neighbors. I am not free to really enjoy sex."

"Isn't that hard to say? You are saying that you are not free to do something disgusting."

"I guess so."

"Okay then, you are curious about sex, but think of it as you did as a child, as disgusting. You were trapped by thinking that kissing and whatever happens after that as disgusting, and now when watching your neighbors you think that what you are doing is disgusting, the way you thought in your childhood."

"But you have chewed off part of yourself. Is that the disgusting curious part of yourself, since you stopped watching your neighbors, and that has hobbled you in enjoying sex with Abbie? You just cannot be free sexually like Abbie is free."

With this coyote/raccoon dream, I felt it was time to again return to the Olmec Prince Posture for shape-shifting, the posture he first experiences several weeks ago. After using the Bear Spirit Posture and then the fifteen minutes of sitting with the Olmec Prince, Carl reported: "I found myself hobbling back to the tree where my new family was. I had the responsibility to bring food to my three young raccoons and their mother, but this time I was without food. When I got there I found them scampering around their mother at the base of the tree, a relief because I did not think I could climb the tree. I then though about what this had to say about sex with Abbie and the raccoon story made a lot of sense. I feel a responsibility to have sex because it makes Abbie happy, but lately I am hobbled by losing my erection." I didn't need to say anything, but simply nodded and smiled as we stood to end the session.

With this summary of what Carl has learned from these dreams and this last dream and ecstatic experience with his raccoon spirit guide we can see that Loki was bound. Such dreams, ecstatic experiences and nocturnal emissions though cause earthquakes, letting Carl know that his sexuality was still alive. It was interesting that Carl's dream was of a racoon and/or coyote, the trickster animals to the Native American just as Loki is the trickster to the Nordic people.

ARLENE

THE ESCAPE

Arlene was struggling with being patient and confident. She thought frequently about talking with Valerie, her project partner, in the manner suggested by me, but each time she would feel anger rising inside her. Then Arlene made a decision that she thought made sense.

She asked the course instructor to meet with her and Valerie, asking the instructor to invite Valerie to the meeting.

The night before this meeting Arlene had a dream: "I went into a restaurant, rather a small deli. There was a fan on the ceiling just above the table where I sat. There were some kids sitting at the next table being rowdy. Somehow one of the kids threw a tomato into the fan." Arlene laughed, "Where do these dreams come from anyway? The tomato splattered everywhere but especially all over me."

"That's it? What did you do then?"

"I just got up and angrily walked out the door. I didn't pay my bill. I don't think I should have to, but that wasn't part of the dream. I just walked out in anger."

I laughed with Arlene and asked, "What do you make of the dream? What are your first thoughts?"

"I can now visualize what would happen when shit hits the fan. I don't know."

"Did you have any special feeling when you went into the restaurant?"

"I went to bed feeling anxious. I think I felt anxious going into the restaurant. I didn't know the place and it was kind of grungy, not very attractive. I think there were a counter and only two or three tables. I took the table closest to the door. I felt like I wanted or needed a quick way to escape. Come to think of it, I don't think I even got my meal."

"You went in and sat down. You noticed the rowdy kids next to you. Tell me about them."

"They looked like they might be in middle school, maybe 14 or 15, three boys. They were just talking loud, laughing and punching each other. I think I saw one of them throw the tomato out of the corner of my eye. I think I saw it coming and started to duck. It splattered everywhere."

"Like shit hitting the fan."

"Yeah."

"You were expecting that something was going to hit the fan when you first walked in. You were a little anxious about going in."

"Yeah."

"Does that feeling and expectation trigger any thoughts."

"Yeah. I was anxious about the meeting the next day I was going to have with Valerie and the professor."

"And you expected to walk out of the meeting angry?"

"Yeah."

"Because the shit was going to hit the fan?"

"Yeah. Even though I knew what I should say, I kept hearing myself saying, 'What's your problem? Don't you want a good grade in the course?' That's pretty much what I did say in a roundabout way."

"You as the spirit guide in your dream were anxious, had no control over what was about to happened and then left in anger. The spirit guide was either a good predictor of what was to happen in your meeting with the professor and Valerie, or it set the stage for what would happen. What happened is what you expected would happen."

"The professor understood the situation and I left her office in anger. With her there, I felt more like just being honest with my feelings more than being the patient hygienist. Valerie said, 'I just can't work with her.' I felt trapped, like something was wrong with me. The professor said, 'Why not?' and she said, "I have my personal reasons, I just can't.'"

"You assumed the professor would think something was wrong with you, too."

"The professor said that she would arrange to change partners. I felt relieved but was still angry with Valerie when I got up and left. I didn't argue or defend myself. I just stood up and said 'okay' and walked out. I don't know if the professor had anything else to say or not. I was just too angry to stay. I got an email from the professor the next evening letting me know about my new partner. I talked with her. She should be okay."

"So everything seems okay. You controlled your anger. It didn't seem to get you in trouble, but on the other hand you didn't become a friend of Valerie's." Arlene found an effective way of channeling her anger in the form of assertiveness. Her feeling of anger was no less, but she was effective in resolving the problem at hand. She had found a way to escape from her inability to let go of her anger, her impatience, with her public self intact.

THE EVASION

"I don't want to be her friend. I know I put her on the spot. The only thing she could say is what she said. I don't need everyone to like me. I don't need Valerie to like me; I don't need Amy to like me. At least I was honest with my feelings." Arlene was very aware of the limitations of her assertiveness and found a way to justify or evade what she knew would have been a better solution, the real winning solution.

"Channeling your anger by being assertive in some ways is a strength, but in some situations patience would produce more effective results."

Arlene answered irritatedly, "I know."

THE CAPTURE

Arlene, Tim, April and May went on a three-day vacation to the shore while the other three children were with their mother. Arlene reported in therapy upon their return, "I didn't feel free. I felt all tied up, not like a vacation should feel. I just couldn't let go."

I was a little surprised that Arlene was aware of this tension, a tension she had lived with all her life. She had to have experienced the carefree feeling to realize that it was missing. I asked her, "When have you felt really carefree?"

"In some of the relaxation exercises we have done, and when things are going well at home and I'm getting a lot of help from especially Tony, Josh and Jessi. April and May are too young for me to expect much from them. We had a good time at the shore, but I always had the two girls to think about. We were playing in the sand. I was building a sand castle with April, but she wouldn't let me finish it. She thought it was more fun jumping on it. I felt irritated and finally stopped trying to build it like when I was a kid. I think I felt carefree when I was building a sand castle as a kid. I used a sand pail filling it with damp sand and then dumping them out stacking them higher and higher. I would try to see how high I could make the castle. That was fun."

"It sounds like you were a competitive perfectionist even in building sand castles."

Arlene smiled. "But April wouldn't let me do it there. But I didn't get angry. I just stopped trying to build it. I even dreamt about it that night, of building a sand castle and getting irritated when April jumped on it."

"Was April disappointed or upset because you stopped? You ended her fun of jumping on the castle. It sounds like the spirit of the dream was reminding you of your frustration, something I expect April felt. Just stopping was an expression of anger."

"I don't know, maybe. I was feeling frustrated and angry."

Arlene was very aware of being trapped/captured by her perfectionism and her inability to relax and let go of it. Yet she was also aware of how showing her irritation and anger would make the situation much worse.

THE RESTRAINT

Arlene was doing much better in all walks of her life. She was vividly aware of how she lost personal power through becoming angry.

Though it still took will power to restrain herself from becoming angry, the benefits of restraint were such that she was able to control herself, at least outwardly. The restraining bindings were strong, yet the irritation and tension she felt in those frustrating situations that are bound to occur in life were the earthquakes that made her so aware of her inability to really let go.

Another dream, not unlike the earlier dream, kept this awareness alive within her. "We were planning an open-house picnic at our place for friends and family. I always find preparation for such affairs very stressful. I always want it to be perfect. This time I was determined for it to be different. It was going to be potluck and I was not going to let myself worry about the food. Tim was making our contribution by grilling hamburgers and hotdogs. In the dream, I sat in a lounge chair just relaxing and watching the people around me, it really felt good. But then, one at a time, first each of the kids came to me with some complaint, 'someone won't play with me,' or 'someone took a bite out of my hotdog.' I don't know what they were complaining about. I just know they had complaints. Even Amy and Valerie were there and had complaints. I somehow was responsible for everyone's complaint. No one would let me relax and enjoy the picnic. I felt so irritated that I wanted to yell, 'leave me alone and take care of your own problems.' My moaning in the dream woke Tim."

"Even though it seemed like you had everything together, you still felt responsible for everyone's complaints. In building the sandcastle with April you took on the responsibility of building the castle, but April would not let you finish it. It is so hard to let go and smile and tell yourself, I'm building the castle for April. It's hers to do as she pleases or at the picnic answering each complaint with, 'You're having a rough time,' without feeling you have to do something about it. You are your dream spirit in this dream telling you what you already know, that your feelings of being responsible for everything and your frustration are still very much alive even though you have found control for expressing your anger outwardly."

Though Arlene found a way to have effective control over becoming angry, her frustration was intense when things were not as she hoped or not perfect. In these dreams her own dream spirit is her spirit guide showing her her problem in needing to control.

JERRY

THE ESCAPE

The last we heard from Jerry was his double chair conversation between his fulfilled self and his empty self. From this conversation Jerry was forced to admit and accept that he was dependent upon appreciation. Yet he had been a person who had always wanted others to appreciate his highly valued independence and his ability to fill the needs of others, whether as husband to his wife or as an effective baseball pitcher for the team. In no way did he want others in his life to see his need for dependency. It was this dependent part of himself from which he sought to escape and which he would like to deny.

Jerry offered the initial defining dream in this process of escape a couple of sessions later, "I had the weirdest dream the other night. I was walking from the car to the field around the end of the stands. The large concrete footer that is the back corner support for the stands was crumbling and the corner of the stands was sagging. All I had was a baseball bat to put under the corner to hold up the stands. I knew that would really do no good, but I tried to wedge it in to hold the stands."

"Okay, we need to examine the deeper narrative of the dream. The stand support is crumbling and the stands are sagging. Part of you is crumbling and sagging and you need to shore it up with your bat, even when you know it is not going to work. If you could give this dream a title what would it be?

Jerry was quick in suggesting, "Temporary fix."

It can be as effective to ask him, "What in the dream is your spirit guide?" As in Arlene's dreams, his own dream spirit is his guide, a dream spirit that has only a temporary fix for the problem.

"Again dreams come from within you. What within you or in your life is a temporary fix?"

After a little thought and discussion Jerry suggested, "I can miss an occasional practice to give Sherry my time, and I could even miss a game, but in the long run that will not be enough. She will become upset, like last time when she wanted my time and I had made a commitment to go to a practice. Missing a practice is only a temporary fix. She is a control freak and will want to test my love for her by asking me to miss a practice. I am willing to do it, but why is she so insecure to have to test me? Why can't she just trust me to love her? She never tries to test my love when I need to go to work."

THE EVASION

The temporary fix dream was one of those dreams that might be considered a prediction of the future. Jerry didn't wait long for Sherry's next test. He was experiencing some shoulder pain, and the next week he talked to a doctor at the hospital where he was a physical therapist. Because of his experience as a physical therapist, Jerry knew what the problem was and knew what the doctor was going to say. He had thought it couldn't happen to him, but it did. He had abused his shoulder in pitching, and he knew he needed ultrasound to reduce the inflammation. In addition, the doctor told Jerry to not pitch for a couple of weeks. There were only three more weeks to the baseball season, so he figured he was out for the season. He knew he wouldn't be back in shape for the last game. "I didn't tell Sherry about the pain or what the doctor said. I thought I would surprise her by making plans for a nice evening the next evening of practice. She was impressed that I was missing practice for her. We made up and made plans for a short trip on the weekend. I still didn't tell her that the doctor had ordered me not to play." Jerry maintained his image as an independent person, evading the issue of dependency and Sherry's occasional test, and he made her happy.

THE CAPTURE

The problem occurred a couple of nights later, when one of the team members called Jerry and got Sherry. He asked her how Jerry's shoulder was doing. Jerry was caught in his deception but sort of got out of it by telling Sherry, "I just wanted to do something for you that I knew you would like and I didn't want you to worry about my shoulder." There was not much Sherry could say, though she still felt let down because of the deception.

THE RESTRAINT

Jerry came to the next session with another dream, and as he started he told me, "There is something I never told you, have never told anybody, not even Sherry. When I first met Liz, she had moved out of her parents' home and had her own apartment. She was supporting herself as a secretary and couldn't keep up with bills. I told you how I rescued her by helping with her bills. What I didn't tell you is that the reason she moved out of her parents' house was that she was pregnant and didn't want her parents to know. The father had left to go away to college and he didn't even know Liz was pregnant. Liz was thinking of having an abortion and I encouraged her. We both thought it made the most sense. The baby and Liz would have a hard life because of Liz's inability to support herself and the baby. One of the bills I paid was for the abortion. After the abortion Liz felt some regret and didn't want to tell anybody. That is why I kept it a secret. Yet, she still believed that the abortion was right because her parents or anybody else would never need to know and she didn't want to hurt them. I helped her through that hard time and felt good that she could trust me, the only person she did trust. The dream I had was of holding her as she cried after the abortion and of reassuring her that she did the right thing, telling her that she now had her whole life ahead of her, that she could have a baby when the time was right, and that she could provide for the baby in the right way. Though she lost this baby, she was going to be a winner when she had a baby at the right time in her life.

"It was that same evening that I proposed to her. It really seemed right. I really felt love for her, and the trust she had in me made it really feel right. I told her that we could have a baby together and the baby would have a family like all babies should. It didn't take too long for her to become pregnant with Beth. I'm not sure where the dream ended but it brought back all those feelings. I think I woke and all these memories were so real, that though there was a loss it really was a win."

"You mentioned at least twice the idea of losing something in order to win.

"Yeah. Liz had dreams but a baby would have ended them. Sacrificing the baby to make the dreams come true makes sense like in baseball, the sacrifice bunt to move a player into scoring position, a strategy to win."

"Wow, like when your marriage to Liz ended. You were strong and independent, ready to get on with your life. You sacrificed Liz. You weren't going to let Liz's leaving, the loss of Liz, stop where you were going in life. Now Sherry is rattling your cage. At least Sherry is letting you know how she feels. You were blind to Liz's feelings.

"Though, back to the dream. What are you losing in life in order to win? I don't think your relationship to Sherry is at that point. Close your eyes and take a few minutes to feel a sense of loss within you. Where does feeling that loss lead you?"

After I repeated the words of loss a few times I gave Jerry some time. He answered, "I used to feel so free when I was with the team.

Now I feel burdened. I worry about how Sherry is feeling, what I'm going to hear when I get home. I've lost that freedom, the independence. I wish I could not let Sherry's feelings bother me when I am playing. I think it sometimes messes up my form. I'm good enough so I don't think the team notices, but I can feel a difference."

"Sherry's feelings really affect you. How you play is depending on how she is feeling. You've sacrificed your independence to Sherry's feelings. If you can make her happy then you can feel free and independent, your pitching feels right and you are a winner. You missed the last three games of the season and it was the team's first three losses. The team knows how dependent they are on you. The team's loss of being number one has been a win for you and Sherry.

"It was nice that Sherry sat with you at the last game. She knew you were hurting and she wanted to be there for you, not for the game but for you, that's love. Even though you really didn't need her there, you still appreciated her presence. She saw your hurt as something she could get close to and comfort. You don't want to depend upon her comfort. You still want to show her and the team your independence. To you rescuing her, providing for her, is love, but you are discovering a new level of love—your sensitivity to her feelings is love, and now your ability to feel her love when she comforts you. Now, until next season you will be able to spend the time with her to reassure her of your love, but both you and she know that next season you will be back to where you were last month."

Jerry's dream of holding Liz after the abortion felt free. His dream spirit was reminding him of how good and free it feels to give himself to someone in need. Now that the season is over he can give himself to Sherry and not feel trapped. He can show Sherry his love by focusing on her need to have him home. He will not be trapped by feeling a need to be in two places at the same time and not give himself totally to either.

PART THREE

THE BEGINNING OF REBIRTH

Stories are the units of meaning for a life, and life unfolds through the enactment of those stories… People rarely transform on their own but instead do so in relation to others who support that transformation. Shared stories create healing communities, which is the purpose of ceremony and ritual. … To understand what will work for that person, we need to hear his or her story, to discover what problems the illness has solved and what values their quest pursues.

LEWIS MEHL-MADRONA, MD, PhD

Coyote Wisdom: The Power of Story in Healing (2005), 8-9, 13.

CHAPTER 13

THE ENDLESS WINTERS: DEPRESSION

Once Loki is restrained, tied by the entrails of his son, three years of great battles throughout the world follow with brothers, fathers and sons killing each other, breaking the kinship taboos. After the three years of battle and earthquakes begins three years of endless winter, Fimbulvetr, with no summer between. The snow drifts from all directions, with great frosts and winds, and the sun does no good.

Once we have gained sufficient willpower to restrain our dysfunctional behaviors, struggle and depression in our lives take over. Each of the three case studies presented in this book have their own issues of struggle. These issues begin to define the dysfunctional cognitions that will be resolved in Chapters 18 through 22.

Each client, with the binding of Fenrir, used willpower in an attempt to overcome his or her obsessive worry but quickly learned that willpower was not enough. Finally, when the client gained some unconscious knowledge and strength, the binding of the worry was effective. But it took another journey into the unconscious, with the journey to Hel, to attain additional knowledge and strength that led to a more lasting binding of Loki, though this would not last either. From what we have learned we have gained limited control over our dysfunctional compulsive behavior, though, without Loki to confront us, our unconscious or automatic dysfunctional thinking has not been resolved.

Arlene found greater peace at home through the power of accentuating the positive with her family, a peace that provided her the strength to control her impatience at home, but her continued struggle with controlling her frustration for imperfections at work and school still haunted her and caused her to become depressed. Carl found a new strength when his mind opened to the enjoyment of sex, a strength that gave him some power over his voyeurism, yet he was still haunted by his conviction that his sexual feelings were not proper. Jerry had found strength in his discovery that Sherry respected him for learning to be a better listener and communicating more intimately, but he was still vulnerable to his dependency on appreciation.

The pain of grief experienced with the loss of their innocence gave each individual the strength and new resolve to bind their compulsive behavior. Yet, the thoughts and feelings driving the dysfunctional behavior had not died and now brought about a sense of hopelessness and depression. Only with the binding of Loki did the behavior end, but again the dysfunctional behavior was bound by willpower, and in the long run willpower is not enough. Using the language of Alcoholic Anonymous, only when a person "reaches rock bottom" is he or she forced to face the real, deeper excuses or dysfunctional cognitions used to maintain the behavior (Chapters 16 and 17). Letting these excuses/cognitions die (Chapters 18 through 22) allows the rebirth of innocence.

What did each client learn in order to bind Loki, their dysfunctional behavior?

WITH NEW DEEPER UNDERSTANDING
LOKI'S BINDING HOLDS

ARLENE

Arlene had been learning useful skills to cope with her perfectionism. At school and work she had become assertive without being too abrasive. She had lost some friends but had been effective in getting done what needed to be done. At home she had found that being positive with the kids, complementing and expressing her appreciation to them, was the most effective way to get them to help. To stay on the track took work, took struggle. With the skills she had learned and with willpower she was able to control her angry outbursts, but she is still a perfectionist at heart and feels irritated when things don't go as she would like. She still cannot let go, cannot let people be people.

JERRY

Now that it was off season and Jerry was not playing baseball, he had the time to give much of his attention to Sherry. Though she was happy with the attention, she was still apprehensive about next year. She worried that the problem would return next season. Jerry could feel Sherry's resistance to accepting and appreciating his attention unconditionally. Yet through willpower he continued to give her loving attention without becoming irritated with her. He found strength in knowing how he was needed and appreciated by his baseball team; thus Sherry's apprehension was not off base, but the strength he had gained in learning how to be sensitive and pay attention to Sherry bound him to staying on the right track. On the other hand his feelings were still fragile. He was still dependent upon others appreciating him, but he still thought of himself as strongly windependent. More importantly, he has lost independence by becoming sensitive to Sherry's feelings. This was love, but Jerry resisted, wanting to believe that love was rescuing and giving. He still wanted to deny his dependency on others.

CARL

Carl was having sex with Abbie about once a week, and both enjoyed the experience. Yet to enjoy sex Carl had had to build a partition between his sexual self and his proper self. He still did not accept the excitement of his sexuality as proper. He had stopped watching the neighbors, successfully repressing this need. The sequence of dreams in the previous chapter nicely showed the process of repression, from hiding wrapped in a curtain, to being invisible, to dreaming of dreaming, to dreaming metaphorically of a trapped racoon. He had a great need to repress his sexuality. Yet the true solution to his problems could not come through repression. He needed in some way to change his way of thinking, to appreciate sex rather than experience it as disgusting.

The clients have had various mechanisms to achieve control over their dysfunctional behavior. Carl used repression fueled by disgust and guilt. Arlene and Jerry found other behaviors or learned new skills to effectively deal with at least part of their problem. Arlene refined being assertive and appreciative, and Jerry learned to listen actively. Yet in each case a deeper conflict still existed that would cause periodic earthquakes, struggles and "three endless winters" of depression in each life.

THE STRUGGLE

CARL

To this point Carl was satisfied with what had been accomplished in therapy, and after one last session, therapy ended with the understanding that he could phone me any time he felt a need. I agreed with this hiatus in therapy knowing that the deeper problem had not been resolved and that he would eventually phone. About two months later he did just that. He had lost his ability to maintain an erection while making love with his wife. He had become quite anxious and frustrated. Since Carl had repressed his sexual feelings, repression that allowed him to refrain from his voyeurism, I expected that other sexual problems would develop. We made an appointment. I suggested that he bring Abbie, but he wanted to see me alone.

Carl wanted a quick fix. I tried to bring up his belief and feeling that a person's sexuality was disgusting, but he was quick to change the subject. He was too sensitive to this topic, and I expect that at some level he feared that this talk would bring back his obsession with watching the neighbors. Thus, I offered the suggestion that he not attempt to have sex for a couple of weeks but spend those sexual times stroking, caressing, and massaging his wife and enjoying her doing the same to him. "Let these sexual times be times of deep relaxation and pleasure, and don't think about sex. You need to talk to Abbie, to tell her what you need and to let her know that the experience is for relaxation and pleasure and not the arousal and excitement of sex." This, too, would prove to be a big threat to Carl.

He attempted my suggestion of massaging Abbie. Watching her moan in ecstasy was too erotic. He admitted it felt too much like watching the neighbors, too voyeuristic. He had massaged her for only about 10 minutes. He got an erection and had to stop. He needed to roll over so Abbie couldn't see his erection. It wasn't relaxing as I had prescribed. He felt very anxious and confused. That night he had another voyeuristic dream and was scared. It was of two dogs, one mounting the other. That was all, something that he had seen many times throughout his life, but this time he felt very anxious.

Carl had been sexually open for a few months, during which time he had learned to appreciate sex. What had caused this big reversal? I reviewed my notes before the next session and noted the turning point. His disgust for his voyeurism and masturbating came alive with new strength after the session in which he had pictured a dog licking his genitals and forming an erection. He vividly remembered that session, even though it was about four months ago. Carl was not free. He hated this animalistic/sexual side of himself. This hatred prevented him from bringing together and reconciling his "proper" and his "sexual" selves. I again asked Carl if he would bring Abbie to the next session. This time he agreed.

When they came in for the next session, Abbie looked to me with an expression of great concern on her face. "What's happened to Carl? He has become so uptight the last few weeks. I can't get near him. He tried to show me some love the other night a week or so ago, but he then just flopped over and would not talk."

I looked to Carl. He just shook his head. He took a deep breath. He was on the spot. Finally he asked Abbie, "How can you be so comfortable with sex?"

"How can you be so uptight? Sex is beautiful. Look what it gave us. Angie is beautiful. I know you've always been uptight about sex. There was a time when I though having Angie would change that. You've always been uptight, but for a couple of months this last year I thought you had changed. What is your problem?"

Carl just looked down and shook his head.

"We pretty much stopped having sex after I got fat with Angie. I felt great, but you had a problem. I didn't know what to do."

I interjected, "Carl learned early in his life that sex is disgusting. That's what so many churches preach and so many people believe."

"That's crazy. I know some churches preach that, but that's crazy. Our preacher does not believe that."

Carl was quick with, "But our preacher before did."

"I don't know about that. I don't remember him condemning sex. Maybe premarital sex. He wasn't uptight about it. His wife sure wasn't, but I guess you never really talked to her." Abbie was sounding frustrated. "Angie did. Angie liked her. She gave Angie a lot of support during her first pregnancy when you didn't. Angie was quite upset with you. She loves her children and thinks they're beautiful, thinks sex is beautiful. What's your problem?"

Carl was silent. I could guess what he was thinking, that Angie was not married when she got pregnant. I let the silence continue for a while. I then mentioned that Abbie might help Carl relax with massage. He hadn't told her about my suggestion. She agreed, but the silence pretty much continued. We ended the session and Carl made another appointment.

When Carl returned he was still quiet. The little he had to say was that Abbie's thoughts about sex and her bonding with Angie was a woman's thing, a mother's thing, and that he didn't think that Abbie being fat in her pregnancy was at all attractive. He was very depressed, very negative about everything. Though we made another appointment, he left a message on my answering service a couple of days later to cancel it and said that he would get back to me if he wanted another appointment.

JERRY

It was late summer, and the news in Central Pennsylvania was that a tornado had come through and knocked down a few trees. This happens every so often. Jerry had a friend, one of the guys on the team, whose garage was damaged by a fallen tree. He had gone over that Saturday to help the friend clean up the mess. There was no game that weekend.

In the meantime Sherry was at home, excited about plans for the evening. It was their second anniversary and they were planning a nice evening on the town. As the day went on she began to worry, "Jerry will be so tired and dirty when he gets home, where is he?" It got to be four o'clock, five o'clock. No Jerry. Six o'clock. No Jerry. She decided to start getting ready, but she was feeling very agitated, very disappointed. Finally at about 6:30 he came in—as expected, dirty and tired. She was about in tears by then. "Where have you been? I have been so looking forwards to this evening and you are filthy! Hurry and get cleaned up!"

Jerry could feel the tension. He knew he had blown it. He didn't say anything but took off his clothes on the back porch and went right into the bathroom.

"Your friends are so important to you. I am nothing." Sherry was stomping around the house. "Don't you think at all about me? What happened to our plans? Did you forget?"

Jerry quickly got ready, but the atmosphere was black. He finally said, "Okay, I'm ready. Let's go and have a good time."

They got in the car but Sherry was in tears. "I can't go like this," she cried, and ran back into the house.

Jerry just sat there, not knowing what to do.

Sherry eventually came back out with, "Let's go," about the only words she said the next hour. By the end of the evening she was smiling, but what a terrible anniversary. When they got home Jerry just flopped into bed.

Jerry knew that he made a mistake in taking so long to get home. He was feeling hopeless. The struggles were not over, and visions of the endless winters lay ahead. Jerry was coming to therapy about once a month. We talked of ending therapy for a while, but he needed to tell someone such stories, so we continued.

On Beth's 10th birthday, Jerry took her out shopping. When they came home to a small party planned by Sherry she was wearing a baseball jersey and ball cap. Beth was happy, but Jerry received a dirty look from Sherry. "All there is is baseball." She shook her head in disgust. The party went well with Beth's few friends, but after the friends left, Sherry asked, "Don't you have anything to say about what I did for Beth?"

"You didn't give me a chance. I thought what you did was great. Beth loved it." But Jerry guessed that was really not enough. Sherry was acting grumpy, but there was nothing else he could think to say.

After telling this story in the therapy session, Jerry added, "Is this going to go on forever? Is Sherry ever going to be really happy?" Though Jerry was really trying to show Sherry his love and was trying to be the good listener, he was feeling down, discouraged, and depressed.

ARLENE

Though Arlene was still a perfectionist and became frustrated with those around her who did not meet her high standards, rather than expressing her frustration in anger she had learned to express it assertively but tactfully. Such tactful assertiveness was not the solution to her problem, but it was at least a more effective response for the time being. Occasionally she did "lose it" in her struggle for perfection, and then the earth quaked.

During one session of therapy she told of such a quaking incident. "What a day. Tim had to work late. I raced home after class. We had a test and I hope I did okay. It was hard. I was up late the night before studying, but still I think I missed some points. When I got home the kids were already there, racing around and making a lot of noise. April and May's sitter had dropped the two of them off five minutes before I got home. She was in a hurry and couldn't wait for me. She phoned me when I wasn't there, but I told her to ask Jessi to take care of them for a few minutes until I got there. I had to get dinner ready and I wasn't sure of what we were going to have. I yelled at the kids to be quiet and go to their rooms. I wanted some peace and quiet while I got dinner ready. April brought May into the kitchen a few minutes later holding her hand. May looked so sad. She said, 'Mommy mad.' I took her in my arms and hugged her, said everything was okay and sent them back to Jessi. I felt so bad. I just can't keep this up.

"Tim then got home and his three kids went running to him. I heard them whispering to him about how I yelled at them and that I was mad. I went to the door and said, maybe yelled, that I had a bad day. Tim shoved them off again to their rooms and came into the kitchen with a big sigh. That was it. I yelled at him to get out and do something with the kids while I get dinner. He stood in the doorway for a minute looking pained at me and then left. When dinner was ready I wasn't ready to face them, gave a look to Tim and told him that I needed to be alone. I took my dish into the living room to eat. The rest of the family sat around the table in a deathly silence. I felt terrible, felt so guilty I wanted to scream. What's wrong with me wanting some time alone?"

The children were quick to forgive, but Arlene's struggle continued. She knew she should not end therapy, but the race of her life was such that I was seeing her about once every six weeks.

On another occasion she came in all agitated. Again at work the hygienist was causing Arlene consternation. She was coming in late and the patients had to wait longer to see her. Arlene thought this behavior was very inconsiderate, but it didn't seem to bother the hygienist. "One day after a patient questioned the receptionist about the delay she made the comment, 'I have to wait when I see a doctor, they can wait a few minutes. No big deal.' The dentist is never late. He is so considerate. I've tried to stay out of it, but he is too considerate of the hygienist. He needs to let her know that she is being inconsiderate and needs to be on time. I'm about ready to lose it."

The next time Arlene came in I asked her how it was going with the hygienist. She reported, "I finally had enough and mentioned it to the dentist how she was always late. He said that he knew and would take care of it. I guess he had a talk with her because she is now only ten minutes late rather than twenty. It's still not right, but I'm trying to not let it bother me. It's not my responsibility." Arlene's struggle was mostly internal, with brewing frustration. She rarely expressed this frustration, but it was seen in her agitated depression, a depression that seems to promise no end.

CHAPTER 14

THE FINAL BATTLE

After the three endless winters something of great portent happens. A wolf swallows the sun, then another wolf catches the moon. The stars disappear from the sky, mountains shake and trees are uprooted. Fenrir the wolf breaks his bonds. The ocean surges and Jormungand crawls onto the land full of rage. The ship made from dead people's nails breaks free of its mooring. Thus the stage is set for the final battle.

After a period of deep depression something happens to force a person to face his or her real problem. Arlene, Carl, and Jerry each reached this point. Using the language of Alcoholics Anonymous, each person needs first to hit rock bottom, and then a solution becomes possible. For some, the depression may last only a few months, for others, years. The narratives of their lives continue. Except for Jerry, who had continued in therapy, Arlene took the least "time off," returning to face her problem after about four months because she was a perfectionist. For Carl it took nearly a year.

CARL

Carl may have suffered from guilt more than the others because the temptation of the open shades was always there. But to fight the temptation he also had to build a strong defense by repressing his sexual needs.

When one night he did watch his neighbors for a minute or two—he felt a lot of anger—"Why do they leave the shade up?" He blamed them at first, but then he left the room, went back downstairs and just sat for a few minutes. He realized that blaming the neighbors was wrong. He could only blame himself. That was something he had learned in therapy from the very beginning when he admitted that he blamed Abbie for having an affair when the problem was really his own feeling of guilt. Now, he was the one who was watching.

The repressed feelings were again out in the open. He sat there and cried, "Why am I so obsessed?" He somehow remembered that he could relax if he masturbated. He went back upstairs, but the neighbors' lights were out. He opened his pants and masturbated anyway and fell asleep.

His wife came home to find him in a mess, semen all over his pants, still dressed and with his pants down around his knees, lying on top of the bed.

He woke to the ceiling light shining in his eyes, jumped up and pulled his pants up.

"What's going on?"

Carl didn't know what to say but started crying again.

"What's your problem?"

Eventually he answered, "I don't know!"

After a few minutes of his wife just looking at him and expressing her concern he finally added, "I just feel so uptight about everything."

She told him that she thought he should go back to seeing me. He then made an appointment. His masturbating was not talked about.

I had known he would be back. "When I saw you last it was so clear that you were repressing all your sexual feeling. Your dreams showed you moving farther and farther from being honest with your sexuality." I took off my shelf the Hopi kachina of Kokopell' Mana lying sexually on top of a Koshari with a smile on his face and his tongue hanging out, her head buried in his belly, one of my favorites in my kachina collection. I handed it to Carl. "Other cultures like the Hopi are so open and celebrate sexuality, celebrate it in a healthy way, placing it in a prominent position in life. Sex is celebrated and fun. Kokopell' Mana is the female erotic counterpart to Kokopelli, the kachina of fertility. She is the only woman kachina to run in a race with the men, but she grabs one of the men, flings him to the ground and imitates having sex with him for the enjoyment of the audience. Sex in other cultures is fun, what it should be.

"Historically, in our own Northern European tradition, on the marriage night and the morning after, the community watch for the bed sheet to be hung from the window with the blood of the wife's first sex on it, again celebrating the couple's sexuality. What has happened to us? Where have we gone wrong? A big part of our culture makes sexuality so difficult, so painful, so evil. Whatever happened to the playful side of sex? For you, why is it so wrong? You both go to the same church, but Abbie didn't take from it such uptight feelings about sexuality. I remember you in trance talking about your mother's shock coming into your bedroom while you were masturbating, the last time you masturbated as a kid. That incident is probably something important to work with. Let's get down to work. What are you saying deep inside of yourself?"

Carl had hit rock bottom and hopefully was ready to work for real change.

ARLENE

At the other end of the spectrum, it took Arlene only about four months to return to therapy. One day, as Arlene walked by the room where Amy, the hygienist was working, she saw Amy drop an instrument on the floor, pick it up and continue using it in cleaning a patient's teeth. Arlene was horrified. She almost barged into the room to grab it away from Amy but caught herself and froze. What should she do? The dentist was busy in an emergency and the day was almost over. Should she tell the patient? Should she call OSHA? All these thoughts went through her mind. She thought of talking with her instructor. But she went home in turmoil and dumped the problem on Tim. She was shaking, almost in tears and full of anger. All Tim could do was listen. After Arlene left for class Tim was almost as shaken as Arlene by her attack on him. He happened to know and work with the husband of the patient of Arlene's concern. Tim took it upon himself to phone the family and leave an anonymous message on their answering service that the wife needed to phone the Occupational Safety and Health Administration office to report this incident.

As it turned out, when the husband got home his wife had him listen to the message and he recognized Tim's voice. The wife was totally unaware that an instrument had been dropped and didn't understand the telephone message. OSHA was not phoned, but she phoned the dentist's office the next day to talk to Arlene and left a message asking why she should phone OSHA. But before she phoned the office Arlene had phoned the dentist. By the time Arlene had gotten to class that night she had calmed down enough to think more clearly, and her instructor validated Arlene's decision to talk to the dentist. She was not working the next day so phoned him first thing.

The dentist expressed appreciation, indicated that he realized that picking up an instrument off the floor should never happen, but he also offered a justification that while the focus of attention is on the patient it is easy to do things such as picking up an instrument off the floor without thinking. That's why the dentist has an assistant to help with instruments. It was obvious that he was trying to calm Arlene, but this justification was not the least bit calming to her. Her agitation came back.

After Arlene's conversation with the dentist, the message from the patient quickly found its way to the dentist himself. He was beside himself and had to call Arlene. The threat of OSHA could cost him a lot and terrified him. When he registered his fear to Arlene, she insisted in reply that this incident could harm the patient, and wasn't the well-being of the patient more important? With this he ended the conversation by asking her to come into the office that evening just before it was to close. As she thought about it she began to worry that this could be the end of her job, but she also realized that if the dentist was not more concerned about the well-being of the patient, maybe this was not the job for her. At this point she called me for an appointment.

By the time Arlene came to her appointment she had met with her dentist. He made the case to her that going to the OSHA could put the whole practice in jeopardy. He had talked to the patient and had been effective in his manner of damage control. The patient was understanding and had no intention of going to OSHA.

The blame for all this commotion fell on Tim. He had over-reacted to Arlene's reaction by taking it upon himself to solve her problem. He "got it" from her when he got home that evening. Tim was mortified, agreed that he had made a mistake and just wanted the incident to be over. In the process of confronting Tim, Arlene terrorized the whole family. The children disappeared in fright to some other corners of the house. It took a while for Arlene to calm down. The kids finally reappeared and it was obvious that April and May had been crying, and Jessi was trying to comfort them. This time everyone in Arlene's life became involved: her family, her colleagues work and even her instructor in school. Arlene realized that she had to do something about her way of overreacting emotionally.

JERRY

Until now Jerry had felt that Sherry appreciated his work as a physical therapist; at least she never complained that he had to go to work, even on the occasions that he had to work at night or on the weekends. A local orthopedic group practice had hired or paid trainers in sports medicine or physical therapists to attend local high school football games to be present in case of an injury. If an injury occurred, the trainer was to assess the problem, offer emergency care within his training, and make the appropriate decision with regard to sending the player to the hospital or making a referral to the orthopedic group. On occasion Jerry had been asked to fill in in this capacity when one of the regular trainers was unable to attend a game.

On one occasion when Jerry was asked to attend a football game, a player was injured, and Jerry saw to it that he was taken to the hospital and admitted. It so happened that this injury was to the son of one of the guys on Jerry's baseball team. Jerry felt that he needed to make a visit to the hospital the next day, Saturday, to see how the boy was doing. On Sunday he went shopping with Sherry. When they were about to return home Jerry suggested that they stop at the hospital for a minute or two to again visit the boy since they were so close. Sherry rolled her eyes but otherwise did not complain. When Jerry returned to the car about twenty minutes later, Sherry asked impatiently, "What took you so long?"

Jerry's response was, "Oh, come on now, visiting was the right thing to do. When you visit you can't just run in and run out."

As Jerry said that, Sherry saw the boy's father coming out of the hospital. "Oh! That's what took you so long. You were talking to his father." She was quiet after that. Jerry knew she was angry. On the way home, she eventually added, "Baseball will always be your life."

Again the right word was "trapped." Jerry felt trapped and angry. In therapy he said, "Anything I do is not enough. I can't make her happy—unless I quit playing baseball, but that probably wouldn't be enough either." He hadn't responded to Sherry's comment, but a seething anger was brewing in him. This frustration and anger came out in his therapy session and was no different than before except in intensity. It was greater, maybe great enough to trigger the final battle.

In the following five chapters Freyr, Tyr, Thor, Odin, Heimdall and Loki all die. Why do the gods need to die? These gods have both exceptional strengths: such as wisdom, strength, vision to see into the distances, the ability to change shapes, etc., and exceptional weaknesses: the overwhelming need to nurture but with a lack of confidence causing him to hide from the one he loves (Freyr); the overwhelming compassion for a cause such that one is willing to sacrifice one's self (Tyr); the overwhelming strength that becomes blind to the facts and impulsive (Thor); exceptional wisdom that becomes overwhelmed and blinded by too many facts thus sometimes leading to the wrong decision (Odin); an unyielding faithfulness that lacks the ability to be critical (Heimdall); and the critical sense that lacks the ability to find balance in appreciating the good (Loki). The gods lack moderation, and it is this lack of moderation and balance that gets them in trouble. Each has their dysfunctional side that causes their death.

CHAPTER 15

FREYR VS. SURT: THE DEATH OF ADDICTIVE AND IMPOTENT NURTURING

In this final battle, Surt marches from the parched lands of the South with his bright, shining sun-sword. Freyr, the protector and nurturer of the earth with rain and gentle sunshine, goes to meet him and is destroyed by the heat of his fiery sword.

Freyr and Surt can be considered each other's shadow, opposites in our world of dualities. Both are important. There is gold in our shadow, but the extreme of either can be unhealthy. Though Freyr nurtures humans by governing the fertility of crops and livestock and also promotes peace, on at least one occasion his shadow showed when he fell in love with the beautiful giantess Gerd, only to become impotent in his loss of manly strength and self-confidence. Freyr's love-obsession keeps him from eating or sleeping, a love that causes him to lose confidence such that he needs to have someone else, Skirnir, his messenger, to intercede for him in communicating his love. Freyr is given this obsession as a punishment for having sat in Odin's high seat. Skirnir, as payment for carrying the message of love to Gerd, asks for Freyr's sword, with its power to fight battles by itself, thus leaving Freyr defenseless in this final battle with Surt. This story is told in the Prose Edda as well as the Poetic Edda, in the poem of Skirnir's Journey.

Though love is a nurturing quality, Freyr becomes impotent in expressing his love for Gerd. As explained in Chapter 7, the bipolar, shadow side of the nurturing mother is either an addiction to the need to nurture or an impotency in being able to nurture. Each of the clients of this book shows some aspect of extreme and unhealthy nurturing. We will see that Arlene's problem was her addiction to nurturing, of trying too hard. Jerry was impotent in his ability to nurture, and Carl was both addicted and impotent. With regard to our obsessions and compulsions, the Freyr within us is nurturing the three children of Loki: guilt, fear and obsessive worry. Each individual needs to recover the ability to nurture in a healthy manner and the nurturing of these monsters needs to end before the monsters themselves can die.

In the language of narrative-therapy the unhealthy aspects of nurturing, the unhealthy narrative, needs to be replaced with a new healthy nurturing narrative. The healthy way of thinking needs to be clarified and presented to the client before the dysfunctional thinking can die, and sometimes it is a slow death.

JERRY

Jerry came to the next session in a quiet and serious mood. He first said that nothing happened during the previous week, but later in the session he mentioned that he had taken Sherry somewhere and when he waved at another team member who happened to drive by, he could feel Sherry give him a cold look. What Jerry then said was nothing new: "After all I do for her, she should appreciate and respect me." At first nothing seemed greatly wrong with this way of thinking, and it had been Jerry's way of nurturing the relationship, yet another way of thinking would have been more effective, helpful and nurturing. The old thinking needed to be replaced. What would bring Jerry to find the more nurturing way of thinking? A lengthy explanation would be ineffective. A minimum number of words that reframes or shocks a person into thinking in a new way is considered trance-inducing by Erickson[1] and can be an effective way of bringing about change.

Thus, I used a trigger word that I knew would push Jerry's button, a word to begin reframing the narrative that had been used by Sherry: "You just don't understand bonding." I could see Jerry begin to bristle, but coming from me the word also elicited curiosity. It caught his attention. After giving him a few moments to brood on it, I added, "Bonding is intimacy, a healthy intimacy that trusts the other person enough to be able to frankly express anger and other painful feelings without fear of hurting the relationship. You feel this trust in communicating with the catcher. Can Sherry trust your love enough to frankly express her feelings?"

I then was silent. Intimacy needs balance between being frank and being considerate, but the first half of the formula needed time to sink in. It was Sherry's frankness that threatened Jerry and made him feel unappreciated. I could see Jerry thinking, so I waited a few minutes before standing to end the session about five minutes early. I didn't want anything else to be said that would distract him from his tranceful thoughts. I hoped that the message he received was that when Sherry expressed her anger she was being intimate in trusting Jerry to understand.

What could be Jerry's new way thinking? What could be his new narrative? Though the specific words would have to come from within Jerry, the new way of thinking would involve a deeper understanding of love, bonding and intimacy. Something to the effect that "Sherry will feel my love and appreciate me if I can be more intimate and feel greater bonding with her," would be a more effective or healthy way of thinking, but those words would have to be felt and experienced at a deep and personal level. "Sherry should respect me for what I do for her" was not as intimate and did not show the two sides of bonding, frankness and consideration, only the one-sidedness of "doing." This insensitivity to intimacy and bonding reflected Jerry's impotency in nurturing. "After all I do for her" was a phrase that ineffectively relied upon guilt in an attempt to influence the other person. Since guilt is at the center of the battle between Tyr and Garm, the battle of the next chapter, there Jerry will find the capacity to gain the necessary understanding he needed to overcome his impotent nurturing.

There are two ways to read this and the next four chapters, reading them in order an entire chapter at a time or reading them as they were written, about each person across the five chapters. Reading them both ways would provide the deepest learning.

CARL

Carl hit "rock bottom" when he masturbated, fell asleep in his relaxed state and woke with his pants down and semen everywhere to find Abbie staring at him. This incident was as traumatic, if not more so, as the incident in his childhood when his mother caught him masturbating. In both cases not much was said, but the shock was there. In this last incident Carl was nurturing his need to relax and knew that masturbating would provide him with that opportunity. His masturbating and his voyeurism were ways of nurturing and satisfying his God-given biological sex drive. Yet Carl's church, and specifically his grandfather who was the preacher when he was young, as well as much of our culture, have created considerable confusion, guilt and other emotional pain regarding this biological drive. Carl had all the information he needed to put this problem behind him, and now his embarrassment had provided him the motivation to do it, but he needed to reorder his thinking in order to make it happen.

First Carl needs to stop the unhealthy nurturing of his voyeurism and instead nurture his sex drive in a healthier way (this chapter). He then needs to lay to rest the guilt he experiences with regard to his sexuality (Chapter 16). In Chapter 17 he lays to rest his fear of going to Hell, and in Chapter 18 his obsession finally is close to death. Chapter 19 reports one last jerk in the death throes of his obsession. The new narrative develops to completion over this and the next four chapters.

"I know my sex drive is God-given, but watching the neighbors and masturbating is not what God would want me to do." Just saying this was a big step in the right direction for Carl.

"Take a moment to sit back and relax." I then motioned for him to stand, and we stood in the Feathered Serpent Posture. I reached over, turned on the drumming CD, and began a new counter-narrative that hopefully would bring about a death-rebirth experience.

"Think about your God-given sex drive. Feel it. Experience it. You are right that masturbating allowed you to relax. Consider how that fits in with your God-given sex drive. Your sex drive is a process. It takes some time to build up, possibly several days, to where you—the best word I know to describe it is you—feel horny. What is the feeling of horniness? It is a tension, a tension that does different things to different people. One common thing it does is to make you very aware of women and of the sexual features of women around you. If you fight to repress those thoughts, your dreams at night are likely to become more sexual. Your dreams may become more sexual, anyway. Those thoughts and feelings can tie you up in knots if you fight them because you think they are wrong. If you fight them, they are likely to come out in all sorts of perverse ways. Since horniness is God-given, it needs to be embraced rather than fought. Look at it for what it is and appreciate it as a God given part of creation. Take time this next few days to watch the feelings of horniness grow inside of you. I expect these feelings are not far from a low point since you masturbated, what is it, about 36 hours ago. Embrace these feelings as they grow. Let them be what they are. Explore in your thinking the healthy ways you can express them."

Carl's nurturing of the healthy side of his sexuality would allow the nurturing of the negative aspects of how he experiences his sexuality to die. Hopefully this counter-narrative would bring his God-given horny spirit alive in a healthy way. The dysfunctional nurturing was both addictive and impotent. His addiction to watching the neighbors caused his impotency with his wife.

ARLENE

When Amy the hygienist picked the instrument up off the floor and continued using it, Arlene was beside herself with not knowing what to do. Her extreme reaction, though, arose out of care, and care is another word for nurturing. When Arlene told the story to Tim, she was so upset that the children ran and hid in fear. I said to her, "You involved Tim, and he overreacted by phoning the patient's husband so that he and his wife were involved too. Your children were involved, as seen in their fear. You upset your dentist. You even involved your instructor. Aren't these dozen relationships more important than any one person's behavior or act?"

"I was worried about the patient. I seem to be the only person who cared."

"And others don't care."

"Yeah, that's what my mother always said. 'Others don't care. You have to take care of yourself.'"

I stood, turn on the drumming CD, and took the Feathered Serpent Posture. So did Arlene. I then offered a brief counter-narrative:

"No one else cares. Your dentist doesn't care about his patients.

Your instructor doesn't care about her students. Tim doesn't care about how you feel. Even the hygienist doesn't care about her patients when she was focusing on her work, on what she was doing and didn't think when picking up the instrument.

"People do care. Tim might say that you don't care about his feelings or the kids' feelings. People care a lot. They may make mistakes sometimes. The hygienist made a mistake. Tim made a mistake. The kids have made many mistakes as they learn. Your mother made a mistake in saying people don't care. You made a mistake in your overemotional reaction. You wear you watch most of the time." I took a sliver of red tape for a role in my desk and reached out for her wrist, putting the sliver of tape on her watch. "For the next few weeks when you look at your watch and see the tape as a reminder, stop and think about what you are thinking. If you are thinking in some way that people don't care, and there may be many different ways you think that, correct yourself and say that people do care. Practice saying, 'People do care.'"

My words were kind of strong, but Arlene was ready to hear them. She was open to listening to the spirit of caring in others. She became very aware of her tendency to overreact, of "caring" too much. Arlene was aware that her tendency to nurture in the extreme needed to die. Focusing on replacing her thought of "People don't care" with "People do care" would bring about that death, the death of Freyr.

This narrative reframing was reinforced the following session. During the past week, in thinking about the dozen people she involved in her concern for one of Amy's patients, Arlene was most concerned about her five children. The others had some reasons to be involved. Her children were innocent bystanders. Seeing April and May red-faced with tears and Jessi's attempts to comfort them were a lasting image in her mind. She was feeling very fragile.

A couple of mornings later she was seeing the kids off to school at the bus stop. Just as Jessi was about to get on the bus, she announced that she had forgotten her lunch on the hallway table. Arlene let out a groan, "How can I bring it to you? I have to take May to a dentist appointment."

Jessi was quick to say, "Oh! Don't worry, I can take care of myself. There is always something that my friends don't want from their lunch. Don't worry."

Arlene was even more upset to think Jessi was mooching food off others. She was also embarrassed. She shouted at Jessi, "You can't do that. Their mothers expect them to eat what she packs for them." She was holding May, who looked at her with big eyes as if she was about to start crying.

As hard as Arlene tried to nurture the children, to really care for them, something always went wrong.

Hearing this story, I offered, "You care so much. You try so hard to make sure everything is perfect, but something always goes wrong. To get everything done at home, work and school you try so hard, but it never goes smoothly. Someone seems to always get upset. You care and try so hard. You care and try too hard."

Arlene could have said, "You can never care too much," but she knew where I was going, we had been there before. "Think of other mothers you know who seem to be more relaxed in what they do, and realize that they care."

"But they don't have five children," Arlene said feebly.

I didn't have to answer that. Again we returned to the Feathered Serpent with another brief counter-narrative.

"Close your eyes and relax as you stand as the Feathered Serpent. Let a mellowness flow through you, a feeling of strength, the mellow strength children need to feel in parents to feel confident and secure. It seems that Jessi has found that confident strength from somewhere. To comfort April and May and to try to comfort you by letting you know she can take care of herself in school, she has that mellow strength. Let that confident mellow strength flow through you. Let it grow." I then was quiet, a quiet that offered Arlene time to experience the mellow strength of the spirit of caring.

Arlene was ready to accept these suggestions. A sliver of red tape reminder on her watch showed her the negative side in her attempt to nurture and care. Being mellow, strong and confident was a positive alternative. The negative side to her nurturing was attacked and mortally wounded. Yet this death was not enough. Guilt, fear and obsessive worry still needed to die before her arguments to support her overreactive caring could die. Such overreactive or overinvolved caring can be considered an addiction to nurturing.

CHAPTER 16

TYR VS. GARMR: THE DEATH OF GUILT

With the death of Freyr the three monster children of Loki can now be faced, the topics of this and the follow two chapters.

Next in this final war Garmr, the monster guardian hound, chained to the massive gates of Hel's realm, breaks free and faces the bravest of the warrior gods, Tyr. Tyr, who has sacrificed his hand to restrain Fenrir, now sacrifices his life to the guardian of those who sacrifice little, those who die not because of bravery but because of illness and old age. Garmr at the same time dies at the hands of Tyr.

Chapter 3 portrays Hel, the daughter of Loki, as the guardian of those who have died of illness and old age. She is our guilt, yet this guilt has continued to grow, and it confronts us now in the form of Garmr, the monster guardian hound of the gates to Hel. For each client of this book, what does this monster that has grown in strength to match that of Tyr, have to protect? As for Tyr, what is the nature of his sacrifice? Why does the guilt-ridden person continue to perform the guilt-provoking act? What is gained in performing an act that is seemingly insignificant to others, yet has such significant payoff that the guilt-ridden person continues behaving dysfunctionally and compulsively? The feelings of inadequacy or insecurity, and the cries of remorse, the self-punishment of guilt, provide the guilt-ridden person with sufficient relief to allow repetition of the act. The pay-off that drives the person to commit the act will be found in their dysfunctional thinking, the person's shadow. Garmr is the growing guilt that comes out of repeated performances of the guilt-provok-ing act that for the Nordic people is their cowardly behavior or the weakness of doing nothing courageous in life. Tyr is the sacrifice of self-punishment, of remorse, that allows a return to committing the act. In considering Moore and Gillette's warrior archetype, one shadow side of the warrior is the masochist and the other is the sadist. The self-punishment of Tyr suggests the masochistic side. Garm is the antithesis of Tyr, guardian of the weak rather than the strong. Yet, as shadows of each other, the two are inseparable and need to die together. With their death, we can begin to move towards regaining our innocence.

JERRY

The next session with Jerry took the words of "bonding, intimacy and love" to a deeper level. Last season Jerry's inflamed shoulder caused the team to lose in the regional finals. This season the team had won. As they left the field the team was signaling "number one" with their fingers with some shouting to the same effect. Sherry had attended since it was so important to Jerry, but these post game antics embar-rassed her. All she could do was shake her head and exclaim, "What foolishness!" The importance placed on the game and the energy put into it made little sense to her.

Jerry's understanding of Sherry's feelings lacked just as much sym-pathy. He added, "She just doesn't appreciate the respect and honor I bring to our family by being number one."

This comment opened the door to a journey of understanding. Even though he had successfully learned how to be a good listener, what Sherry had to say still made no sense to him. What could be said in therapy to bring Jerry to this understanding?

Jerry continues, "Though nothing was said, I thought about her trusting me enough to express her anger and not fear that it would damage our relationship. Honestly, I feel it is damaging our relationship."

I had in the previous session suggested to Jerry that a healthy and real intimacy occurs when two individuals trust each other enough to express anger, not fearing that such honesty would hurt the relationship. I motioned for him to stand as we called the spirits from each direction. After a brief time of silence I continued. "Stand and put your hands at your waist with a sense of determination. I turned on the CD player and spoke in a hypnotic voice, offering a counter-narrative, "It hurts when Sherry doesn't respect your achievements in baseball, but what are you saying? There are two issues here, don't lump them together. One is the issue of bonding and intimacy. We talked about that last week. Apply that thinking to the guys on your baseball team. Male bonding is often seen in one guy punching another. Doesn't that mean the same thing? I could hurt you by punching you, but it isn't felt as hurt but as a sign of trust, a special kind of trust that says, 'I'm not going to let a little hurt take away our trust in each other.' It is a test of trusting each other. Sherry doesn't show trust to you by punching you but by being honest with her feelings in expressing her hurt to you. Sherry is testing your love for her over and over, hoping that her honesty in expressing her feelings to you is going to be accepted lovingly and not hurt the relationship."

"I'm afraid that I'm failing the test."

"What's that have to say about your love for her, your unconditional love? You failed the test once in your last marriage. Is it going to happen again? Aren't you big enough and strong enough to take what she dishes out?" I challenged the same issues of our last session, hoping and expecting to reinforce them.

The second issue Jerry needed to face was that of guilt. Saying "should" as in "Sherry should appreciate the respect and honor you bring to the family," was a guilt trip the same way as saying "After all I do for you" was a guilt trip, both ways of attempting to make Sherry feel guilty. A person who relies upon such statements in his attempt to control another is well aware of the feeling of guilt expressed in such a statement. Jerry could use other such attempts to control as threats, shaming or ridicule[1] but his use of guilt suggested that he was very familiar with guilt. Jerry's experience with guilt was indeed very evident in Chapter 6, as seen in his comment, "I should give and not expect appreciation." He had already begun the journey to recognize his feelings of guilt, and the stage had been set for him to find more effective ways of dealing with it, but only now that he had "hit rock bottom" was he ready to "kill" it.

Thus, I continued with the counter narrative: "The second issue is of guilt. We have talked about this before. 'Sherry should appreciate and respect you.' Listen to the guilt trip you are putting on her. You know how you hate when someone puts a guilt trip on you. Part of you knows that it should feel good just to give, but you would like to be appreciated like your mother was appreciated when she gave so much to others.

"What is love? Think for a moment about two different hugs. One hug she gives you because she wants to, because she loves you. The other hug she gives you when you ask for a hug. Which hug shows more love? The hug she gives you just because she wants to could be considered selfish. It's what she chooses to do. When you ask for a hug, she gives it to you out of love. She wants to give to you what you want. It's not selfish. Both are showing love. Getting a hug and getting a hug by asking for one is no less loving. Think about it, Sherry came to your last game because she loves you, she wanted to share the experience with you. She doesn't have to love baseball to experience it with you. Love is not just giving what you want to give, but giving with sensitivity to the needs and wishes of the other person.

"What is love? Listen to her needs. Listen to what is going on in her life. Occasionally, only occasionally ask her to go to a game with you, only when her day seems not too busy. Appreciate those times when she goes to a game, because when she goes with you it is because she loves you and not the game. Asking her to go to a game with you is a direct way of expressing your wish and is not putting a guilt trip on her."

Jerry was ready to hear this counter-narrative which set the stage for him to find a healthy alternative to using guilt in his attempt to influence Sherry. The spirit guides of the bonding arm punch, and the two kinds of hugs are nestled within him, ready to assist him in the sacrifice of his ineffective guilt-trip weapon.

CARL

Carl returned the following week having followed through on his assignment. His horniness did grow, and he released it by having sex with Abbie. He felt okay about the experience, yet somehow it felt empty in releasing it with the help of Abbie. Abbie seemed to enjoy it, but it did not seem as exciting, not a lot more than a release of tension. Carl was struggling to find the right words to express this experience. It was apparent that he did face his sexual experiences throughout the week with good focus. It was just this focus, however, that took away some of the power or excitement of the sexual experience.

Hearing of his week's experience, I again saw a possibility in using the Feathered Serpent Posture. After we went through our now accepted induction ritual, I began with another counter-narrative:

"Go back to when your mother walked into your room while you were masturbating. Consider the two ways you might look at this experience. One is that your mother was shocked and disgusted with you. She walked out in disgust and you felt humiliated. The other is that your mother said nothing and left to give you your privacy. Maybe she understood that what you were doing was okay. I'm sure either way she would be shocked and embarrassed and would not know what to say. Think about it. If she was just giving you your privacy, she would be considered quite progressive for those years, and you have been unnecessarily carrying a lot of emotional pain. If your mother was horrified, you as a youth reacted very naturally in feeling humiliated. Young people experience what their mother or father have to say as if it is from God. A child in most cases believes that what a parent does or says is right. The parent has total power over the child. As an adult you know that parents are not always right. You are still a human being and can make mistakes, but a child does not know that. Spend some time thinking about both possibilities. If your mother was horrified, you might know rationally that she was wrong in her thinking. You learned from that experience that what you were doing was wrong, but take time to realize that it wasn't so wrong. It is a natural way for a young boy to release his horniness, and probably the only way without taking advantage of some young girl or of messing up your sheets with a wet dream. Take time to ponder and weigh these thoughts. You know that young boy who masturbated better than anyone else. You know how guilty he felt. Help him understand that he needn't feel guilty, that what he was doing was healthy."

Again Carl had the information within him. It just needed to be reordered to help him let go of the guilt feeling and using ecstatic trance with the help of the Feathered Serpent is that help. The guilt will not go away immediately, but with pondering over the next few weeks and months what these spirit guides offered him, the guides to lead him to better understanding masturbation, his guilt would eventually dissolve. The stage was set for the death of Carl's unhealthy thinking and with it, the death of his guilt.

ARLENE

When things went wrong in Arlene's life, her frustration was quick to rise and anger quick to flow because she cared, cared too much. Using the mellow and calming strength that Jessi used in comforting April and May as a spirit guide, my suggestion to Arlene was for her to feel within herself the same calming strength.

After we sat silently for a few minutes, valuable minutes for Arlene to process these thoughts consciously and unconsciously, she blurted out, "I felt so guilty seeing April and May's tears and it wasn't me that was comforting them. I was the one who frightened them."

I smiled and said, "Here we are again, back to guilt."

Arlene had to smile too. She still knew where we were going. The stage was already set for this final battle. It was time for it to happen.

Again with a smile I stood and put the back of my hand on my waist as I had done before. Arlene stood and did the same thing as I reached over to turn on the drumming. After a few initial experiences of longer inductions, it now only took a brief suggestion, calling the spirits of each direction, to induce trance in preparation for listening to another counter-narrative. I then spoke, "In seeing your youngest daughter in tears and knowing it is your fault, you feel so guilty. Your intense caring just doesn't work. Go back in time. See your mother's frustration and anger rise as she tries to leave the house. Feel within you the rising need to do something to please her, to make her happy. Think for a few moments. You know that there is never a time when you can turn her frustration and anger to a smile. Even though you always fail you try and try again. You feel so guilty. As many times as you try to turn her anger to a smile, doing everything you could to please her, it never ever worked. You are a failure. But you know now that it was not your fault. It was your mother's problem. You have put such an unfair trip on yourself. We've talked about this before, but now you are ready to let go of it. Let your belief that you were at fault die and your guilt will die. They will die together, this unfair guilt. You have carried so much guilt, and it is this guilt that powers the vicious cycle of growing frustration and anger. Using your mind's eye, look at your mother and blame her for her anger. There is no reason to feel guilty. Let this break the vicious circle, so when you see April and May in tears, your guilt will not have the power to frustrate you and make you angry. You can look at April and May's tears and resolve to not be like your mother in becoming angry, but instead focus on the problem again and again with a calm strength, a mellow, calming strength, and your guilt and the cause of your guilt will die. Give April and May each a hug. Feel their warmth. Let that hug be a hug for yourself, and smile. Feel the love that comes from a hug. Look for every opportunity to hug your children and Tim, feel their warmth and love." With those opening suggestions I let Arlene experience the rebirth provided by the Feathered Serpent Posture.

The nurturing of Arlene's false belief of what it means to care too much, her guilt and its cause, her frustration and anger, had died.

CHAPTER 17

THOR VS. JORMUNGAND: THE DEATH OF FEAR

Thor, the impetuous thrower of lightning bolts, the greatest of warriors who shows no fear and believes he is invulnerable, faces the epitome of what is feared, Jormungand the sea serpent. After a great battle, Thor succeeds in killing Jormungand but with his foolish hubris he allows the poisons of Jormungand to touch his skin, and after stepping back nine paces, he falls and dies, too.

Thor faces Jormungand on two previous occasions in the Prose Edda,[1] in the story of the giant Utgard-Loki and in Thor's fishing expedition with Hymir in the Poetic Edda's poem "The Lay of Hymir."[2] In both cases he greatly impresses the giants Utgard–Loki and Hymir with his fearless strength, but only this third meeting is a battle to death. Thor's foolishness lies in his lack of fear and lack of respect for the strength of his adversary. For the clients in this book, there is also that time when they lack respect for the fear of their obsession or addiction, behavior that demands respect. Once we have killed within us that which we most fear, we can strut around, but only briefly, "for nine paces," soon realizing that this arrogant, impetuous strutting part of ourselves now has no purpose and needs to die. We can then continue to move towards regaining our innocence.

JERRY

Jerry now showed some sensitivity to when he used guilt trips and recognized the alternative strategy of asking Sherry directly for what he might need or wish. The baseball season was about over and the next game would be the playoff between the regional champions in the state. Winning would possibly mean four more games and some overnight trips. He thought Sherry would enjoy getting away and staying in a hotel, so he asked if she would go with him. She could not go to the first game but agreed to go to the second. I had previously asked Jerry to be sensitive to the differences in his feelings and thinking during the game when she was there and when she was not. I expected that he would experience the games differently. I did not see him until after the second game into the playoffs, a game that his team lost, so was eliminated.

Though the games were exciting, Jerry did experience them differently. "When Sherry was there, I was aware that she was there and felt myself pitching and playing to impress her. When she was not there I felt more part of the team, of working together with them to win. I didn't feel as self-conscious. My feelings were not as extreme. I felt good when I struck someone out, but when someone got a hit I didn't feel as bad as when Sherry was there. When I struck someone out I remember looking at Sherry to see her reaction. When she was not there I don't think I looked into the stands but kept my mind on the game."

"Was one experience better than the other? Did you play as well?"

"I think I played about as well, maybe with less focus when Sherry was there. I think it was a little more exciting when Sherry was there, but we lost."

"The experiences were different, both were good and you can enjoy both, but with Sherry there you lost some focus. You can enjoy the game in a different way when Sherry is not there. Let the game and let life be what it is. You don't have to have Sherry there to make it what you want it to be. With Sherry there you were somewhat distracted by your need to impress her, and you lost some focus on your pitching." Though Jerry did not put much emphasis on his loss of focus, I believed it was a bigger deal to him than he let on. His real fear was that of losing control, especially in pitching. This fear of losing control had been evident in his pitching but also in wanting Sherry's appreciation. In school his power lay in having control, whether of choosing the underdog for the kickball team or in being friends with the new kids to the school. His fear was the reading circle, where he had little or no control.

The next week he opened up to this fear of losing control. He admitted that during the last game he had one wild pitch that the catcher missed, and he realized that the wild pitch was because his focus was on Sherry in the stands. He then forced himself to refocus and finished the game, but that wild pitch moved a runner ahead and set the stage for the other team to score. He was hesitant to admit it openly, but he eventually said, "I lost control of that pitch when I was thinking about Sherry."

"You're afraid of losing control. Last time we talked of how you used 'guilt trips' to try to control Sherry. This time you were not using guilt, but you were trying to impress her, and that got you in trouble—you lost your focus on pitching." To move to the deeper narrative I suggested, "Stand up and place your hands at your waist in the Feathered Serpent Posture and close your eyes as you listen to my words." I turned on the CD player. We had earlier opened the session with calling the spirits. I then offered the counter-narrative: "Take several deep breaths and relax. You're sitting on the bench and Sherry is in the stands. You can see her sitting there. You catch her looking at you, and you both smile. You know she is there because she loves you. She loves you for being you. There is no need for you to impress her. Let love be enough. Let your need to impress her dissolve, let it fade away. Feel her love for you. She is in the stands because of her love for you. Feel the freedom these words can give you. 'She loves you. You don't need to impress her.' With this feeling of freedom feel you fear dissolve. There is nothing to fear—you know she loves you. Okay, it is now time for you to return to the mound. With this freedom from fear let your mind focus on the game and on each pitch." I then was silent, letting Jerry listen to the drumming and internalize my words.

As with Jerry's feelings and use of guilt, his fear of losing control (Jormungand) would take some time to die, and then his need to control (Thor) could die. But he now knew what he needed to know, and he was motivated to change, the spirits of the counter-narrative were alive within him. He needed to practice using the words "She loves me. I don't need to impress her." Though there were many situations in which he could use these words, the real test needed to wait until next season.

CARL

The third step with Carl was to assist him in letting go of his fear of burning in hell. Carl had recently told of his mother's father who was the preacher when he was a child in the same church that he has attended all his life. When he was young he was told that he "should not enjoy earthly pleasures, but keep his mind on Jesus in order to get into heaven." His grandfather preached that the earthly pleasures were alcohol, tobacco and other drugs, gambling, overeating and sex. Indulging in these pleasures would lead to burning in hell. A youth would put the preacher-grandfather in the infallible position that anything he would say would be the truth. Carl needed to realize that his preacher-grandfather was only human and could make mistakes.

Carl reported that he in fact had spent a good part of the week pondering the meaning of masturbation and was now able to say that it is a very natural, important act for a young boy, and he could see it as God-given, though watching his neighbors wasn't. What he has learned he saw as coming from the Holy Spirit. With the spirits of my words alive within him, though his guilt was not totally gone, it was weakened or dissolving. Remembering the "fires of hell" sermons of his grandfather likely slowed this death process. Such fears learned in formative stages of development are difficult to unlearn. Overcoming the fear instilled by his grandfather was very important, thus I followed the same formula as in the previous week.

"Okay, stand in the posture of determination, the Feathered Serpent Posture." I called the spirits and turned on the drumming. "Take a few moments to recall the sermons of your grandfather, the fear they instilled in you about going to hell. Realize that he came from a different era, an era when he was taught to be frightened by hell. Think of your pastor today who preaches the other side of the gospel, the side of love, compassion, forgiveness and understanding. Realize that your grandfather was a human being just as you are a human being, and that he made mistakes. Realize that preaching that your God-given sexuality would send you to hell was wrong. Appreciate, celebrate the compassion and understanding of your current pastor. Ponder these thoughts and beliefs so that you can lay your fear of hell to rest. It has been alive inside of you for a long time. Those feelings may not die easily, so be patient with yourself while you ponder these thoughts and beliefs."

I could see in Carl's breathing that he was letting go of his anxiety and relaxing. Now that he had the spirits of this counter-narrative dwelling within him for the next week or two, the stage was set for the death of the unhealthy fear of burning in hell. The death of the belief of burning in hell could be celebrated, and with this celebration the power this belief had over Carl would also die. With God's forgiveness he could even be forgiven for watching his neighbors.

ARLENE

Arlene again faced and let go of the unreasonable feelings of guilt triggered by her failure to please her mother. Two factors made this narrative reframing more effective at this particular time. First, Arlene had "hit rock bottom" and was open and ready to change. Second, while in the ecstatic trance using the posture of determination for death and rebirth, her thinking was accessed at a deeper and more unconscious level. Though she was still vulnerable to feelings of guilt, these feelings would quickly bring back this ecstatic experience. Afterwards, she hugged her children with a calm, mellow strength, smiled and could feel the warmth and love coming from the hug.

One evening when the kids got home, Arlene was there to give them each a hug, but when she was hugging Tony she felt him whimper. She held him away from her to look at him. In his whimper were the words, "I lost my book."

Arlene immediately felt herself tense and knew that tension was not "being mellow." A shiver of fear went through her, the shiver of fear she felt in her own fear of her mother, and she pulled Tony back into a hug. Again all the pieces were there, and it was time only to put them in the right order.

As Arlene told this story the spirits of the story fell into place. Jormungand (that which is feared) must die before Thor (that which reacts impulsively in anger) can die. What Arlene feared was her mother's—and now her own—anger. With a hug the anger could die, allowing the impulsive or automatic response of becoming angry to eventually die as well.

With this thinking in mind, I motioned for her to stand, and we called the spirits of each direction. After a few minutes of relaxing and quieting her mind I suggested that she stand in the Feathered Serpent Posture as I turned on the drumming. I then proceeded with the counter-narrative, "Go back to one of the moments with your mother. Feel the rush of fear within you. Feel your thoughts start to race. What can I do to make her happy? Now join Jessi. Feel the rush of fear dissolve and feel a growing sense of mellow, calm strength." Arlene needs that new strength to comfort April and May, to take care of herself. Appreciate and respect that calm, mellow strength. Feel it growing within you. When you pull Tony back into a hug, you can feel that calming strength. After all, it was only a missing or lost book. Tony knew it was wrong to lose it. You can appreciate his courage in telling you. You can reassure him with a mellow, calming hug. He did not have to be afraid of you, as you were of your mother. Feel the loving warmth of the hug. Appreciate your positive reaction, your victory. Again look for every opportunity to hug your children, to hug Tim. Feel the loving warmth of the hug. Let it dissolve any feelings of guilt or fear. With each hug, feel your confidence and determination grow in your effectiveness in solving problems."

After a pause, I continued, "Now take these same feelings to work, though it may not always be appropriate to hug others at work. Go back for a moment to when Amy dropped the instrument. Watch her doing her work. Feel how involved she is in doing what she has been trained to do. Appreciate that involvement; in this way you are giving her a mental hug. You know she cares about her work. After she is finished with her patient, approach her and tell her that you were watching her work and appreciate how involved she was with what she was doing. Then gently tell her in a simple way that you noticed her drop and pick up an instrument off the floor without thinking. Watch her reaction. It is likely a reaction of shock, but it is a moment that she will likely not forget, and she will less likely do it again."

Again Arlene knew the importance of what I was saying. Her automatic habits of feeling guilt and fear were close to death. She carried the spirits of this counter-narrative and especially the spirit of feel a calming mellow strength with her to carry them through the week as she left the office.

CHAPTER 18

ODIN VS. FENRIR: THE DEATH OF THE OBSESSION

Odin, the wise god of gods, again meets face-to-face Fenrir, the wolf who has not stopped growing. The result of this meeting is that Odin dies in the belly of the wolf, but then Vidar, one of Odin's sons, takes the wolf's upper jaw in one hand with his foot on the lower jaw and tears the wolf apart to avenge his father's death.

Odin was aware of the prophecy foretelling that Fenrir was fated to do the gods injury and it has now come true. Odin's preemptive strike against Fenrir did not protect him but instead set the stage for his own death. No matter how wise, one cannot circumvent fate. What may appear wise can be foolish, as we will see with each client presented in this book. Obsessions, typically created within us, are based on unconscious beliefs that we believe are wise, and live only because of our belief in them. Yet, obsessions generally have no basis in reality and are foolish, though they take on a growing life of their own. Only when Odin, our initial unconscious belief that we are wise, dies as we discover that this belief has no basis in reality, does our new, younger strength, Vidar, kill the obsession.

JERRY

Jerry's belief that "love is being appreciated" has been confronted and has begun the process of dying. Yet, the next part of this journey of the death of Jerry's dysfunctional belief began when he felt Sherry's irritation when he stopped at the hospital to visit one of his patients, the son of one of his teammates. His need for appreciation was again confronted but this time in a more earthshaking way. Sherry had always before been appreciative of him in his work as a physical therapist. Now, even in this part of his life she expressed resentment. This incident pushed Jerry to "rock bottom."

From this experience Jerry was again reminded that his attempts to control Sherry through guilt were ineffective. Saying that she should appreciate him was a "guilt trip" and not a way to show love. Love is empathetic, not coercive. Thus, his "guilt trips" joined his "need for appreciation" in the process of dying.

Next, Jerry learned that he did not need to impress Sherry for her to love him, but that she loved him simply for him being him. Thus, other aspects of Jerry's need to control, this time his need to control by impressing others and his fear of not being in control, joined his "guilt trips" and "need for appreciation," in the process of dying.

With the following experience, the death of Jerry's obsession with his need for appreciation itself would die. He would learn at a very deep level the meaning of love, unconditional love that does not depend upon appreciation. With the death of his old definition of love as being appreciated and his new understanding of unconditional love, his new innocence would allow his obsession to die.

Baseball season was over, and Jerry had more time with Sherry and his daughter Beth. On this particular Saturday Beth wanted to go see the most recent Harry Potter movie. Jerry suggested that they all go to the movie, but Sherry did not want to go. She had things she wanted to do, so she suggested that Jerry take Beth by himself, saying "It would be good for the two of you to have some time alone together." Jerry resisted. In therapy he had admitted some fear of being alone with Beth. "She somehow seems more distant. She does not have much to say to me. She seems to be excited around her friends but she's so quiet at home." He admitted that he was afraid of silence when they were together. He imagined that Beth was unhappy and would rather be with her friends. But he couldn't turn her down when she said, "Oh come on Daddy, you'll enjoy the movie." I commented that being called "Daddy" was something really special, and he admitted that the word always seemed to melt him.

Jerry and Beth went to the movie. Beth even reached up to take Jerry's hand at one point when they were walking, and he considered the outing a great success. He felt loved by his daughter in a very special and unconditional way. He nearly had tears in his eyes when he was telling me this story.

Again with Beth, as with the last two ball games, he let the experience be what it would be, and he felt freed from his past expectations. His readiness to judge each experience with regard to his need for appreciation had died with the death of his obsession. He felt a new level of freedom and innocence in experiencing the moment.

CARL

Carl for a long time had ignored or repressed his sexuality, and when it finally came back to life, it came back as an obsession. For this obsession to die, it was important for Carl's guilt and fear of his sexuality to die. These deaths were happening, but this process of death needed some help or reinforcement.

When Carl came in for the next session, as we had been doing at the beginning of each session, we first called upon the spirits. I then asked him to review with me his ponderings from the week before. He told me, "It makes a lot of sense that masturbating is a healthy release of horniness for an unmarried man. I'm very happy that Abby enjoys sex and is there for me, but still something seems missing."

"How about your fear of burning in hell?"

"Oh that. I talked to our pastor about it. He just laughed and said that everything that Jesus preached was about forgiveness, compassion, and understanding, and preachers these days know that you cannot win anyone to the love of God by frightening them with the fires of hell. I know he is right. My grandfather was strange, anyway. I didn't feel very close to him."

"But your grandfather also preached about the evils of earthly pleasures. He sounded sort of sour, that it was wrong to enjoy any pleasures. There are many simple and healthy pleasures, like the pleasure experienced in going to a fair or in taking a walk in the woods."

"He enjoyed a walk in the woods, part of God's creation. I don't think he would let himself enjoy going to a fair, though."

"Or enjoy sex."

"Especially sex."

"What will it take to enjoy sex? Sit back, close your eyes and relax. Again, something else to ponder. After a few minutes I had him stand in the Feathered Serpent Posture. After I turned on the drumming, I continued with a counter-narrative: "The hormones triggered in sex are incredibly exciting and were again God-created. He meant it to be enjoyable and exciting. That is what sex is all about and why our species continues. Again, at least in this area, your grandfather was mistaken. Ponder these thoughts this next week.

"Also, take the feeling that something is missing when you have sex with Abby and ponder on it this next week. You know she loves you and you know that she enjoys sex. You have let go of your guilt and your fear of burning in hell, the two things that have prevented you from enjoying sex. But letting go of guilt and fear is not enough. You need to let yourself enjoy the pleasures of sex, too. The next time you have sex, be there in the moment, focus on especially the foreplay, in doing those things that Abby enjoys, and enjoy them yourself. Take your time with them. Think about what would feel good to you and mention it to Abby. I bet she would do it. Be playful in enjoying the experience. Your grandfather was wrong. The pleasures of sex are to be enjoyed."

To overcome obsession, false beliefs that kept guilt and fear alive needed to die first. Only with the death of obsession can new innocence survive. During the following weeks, as Carl dwelt upon the spirits that arose from this counter-narrative, a new innocence was born as he laid his obsession to rest.

ARLENE

Arlene came to the next session both pleased and confused. The mellow, calming strength was growing within her with each hug, and there were many, many hugs. There had been hugs before, but these hugs were made with a new, deeper focus, a new awareness or intent. The spirits of the mellow, calming strength and the hugs were very much alive. They were much more meaningful, and a deeper love could be felt. Watching Jessi in action was a big help and brought a smile to Arlene's face anytime Jessi hugged April when the younger girl started crying for some unknown reason. It warmed her to see April's stepsister love her so much and with such calming strength. She knew that a few weeks ago, if she had reached April first she would have felt frustration with the crying for what appeared to be no reason. A few weeks ago, she would have been embarrassed and/or jealous of Jessi's ability to solve the problem. She now knew the effectiveness of intervening with a mellow, calming hug.

Arlene's confusion was experienced when she was preparing for an examination in one of her college courses. She went over and over the material many times, but she still felt uncertain of whether or not she knew the material and believed that she still could have studied more. She felt the obsession of having to be perfect. She reported two thoughts. One thought was that she again "cared too much," and the second was that there must be a limit to how much she studies, but she didn't know when or how to stop. She thought she could have spent some time with the children, but she also believed that her example of studying was good for the kids. This awareness of both showed her readiness to change.

I told her what I knew from when I taught a course in study skills back when I was in college. "Each time some piece of information is recalled it is more likely to be remembered, but after recalling it three times over three successive days the payoff in the increase in remembering becomes so small that it is not worth the energy. For example, after something is read or heard for the first time there might be a 50% chance that it will be remembered. If it is recalled a day later, the chance of remembering goes up to 80% and recalling it for a third time raises the chance to 98%. After that the increase is next to nothing. The numbers may be different depending upon other factors, such as interest and significance of what is being learned, but the learning curve follows this pattern. Your confusion and questions are important. Rehearsing something three times is enough. You are right in considering what is the most important use of your time, and time with your family is very important. You are right to see the connection between your caring too much and the amount of time you study.

"Sit back and relax to quiet your mind." After a few minutes I had her stand in the Feathered Serpent Posture and turned on the drumming. We had earlier called the spirits to the session in preparation for using ecstatic trance during the session. I then proceeded with the counter-narrative, "Again go back and be with your mother. Feel her obsessiveness in racing to get things done before she leaves the house. Weigh in the factor of your father sitting in the car waiting. What is more important? That question is answered best with a mellow, calming strength, knowing you can say that it is time to stop studying or say it is time to stop racing around picking up things, and spend time with your children or with Tim. A mellow, calming strength in making decisions gives you power over your obsession, a power that lets you take charge of your life.

"The part of you who believes that you have to be perfect, the part of you who wants to control everything, the part of you who studies too much or cares too much, can die, and then your obsession can die. You know that you can care too much. The alternative is to approach whatever you do with a mellow, calming strength. When you make decisions without fear or guilt, you make them with confidence, with a mellow, calming strength. This new confidence and decisiveness will let your obsession die."

All three monsters were close to death as Arlene carried the spirits of this counter-narrative with her into the new week. Arlene was letting go of her guilt, fear and obsessive worry. She was looking at life with much greater confidence and decisiveness. The rebirth of innocence was close at hand.

Arlene was finding that it was more important to nurture her relationships with others than to be perfect. Carl was finding comfort in his sexuality and was no longer obsessed with watching his neighbors in bed. Jerry was finding more enjoyment in the freedom he found in trusting Sherry's love for him and not needing to impress her. All had their difficult moments, but all were discovering real changes in their lives.

CHAPTER 19

LOKI VS. HEIMDALL: THE FINAL ARGUMENT

The battles of Ragnarok end with Heimdall, the guardian of the gods, and Loki, the tormentor of the gods, facing each other. Heimdall always justifies and protects the gods for their behaviors, while Loki scolds them. After a struggle, they kill each other.

Again the nature of this relationship between Heimdall and Loki is best portrayed in the Poetic Edda in the story of Loki's Flytings. At a get-together of all the gods, Loki takes advantage of the situation by attacking the weakness of each god or goddess in turn. When it is Heimdall's turn, Heimdall again attempts to protect the gods by attacking Loki, "Loki, drink has dulled your wits. It is time to leave it alone. When ale begins to take hold of a man he babbles baby-ish nonsense,"[1] Loki responds with, "Enough, Heimdall! I know that fate assigned you a servile task....You are doomed to stay awake to guard the gods." To Heimdall's final excuse or justification of "Just one more time," or "Just a little bit won't hurt," Loki's final challenge is "That's enough," or "Just stop." This final justification must die, an excuse that demands the scolding of Loki. When this final justification dies, so does the scolding.

JERRY

Jerry was experiencing real change in his life, a deep change in the way he experienced the world, a change brought to him by the spirits we have called upon in the last several sessions. Yet his "need for appreciation" had not totally died. Every so often this need raised its head and was expressed in subtle ways, ways that Sherry was very sensitive to. The need had been so much part of Jerry's life and expressed so automatically that its death was particularly slow. Part of him said that he had changed so much that such expression now wasn't a big deal; however, because of Sherry's sensitivity it was a big deal to her.

It was the start of the new baseball season, and over the last few weeks Jerry had been stretching and exercising, preparing for the beginning of practice. He could see Sherry becoming more uptight, even though the first practice was still a week away. One day when she gave him her look as he was doing some stretching, he just had to say, "Don't you appreciate me staying in shape? Look, no beer belly."

"Wow! You are already at it. That word again."

"What word?"

"Oh, you know, I don't have to tell you."

"Appreciate?"

Sherry just snorted and walked away.

In my office Jerry added, "Yeah, she is right. The same old guilt-trip." Jerry gave a self-conscious laugh.

"It'll take Sherry jabbing you at times to help you let go of that old habit." Jerry was able to smile with me. Heimdall and Loki were at it again, but both were near death. One cannot live without the other, Heimdall defending Jerry's backsliding moments, and Loki sneering at him.

With regard to narrative therapy, it needs to be realized that behaviorally replacing faulty beliefs can only be effective if each reason for the old way of thinking can be faced and replaced.

CARL

Carl had found a new level of enjoyment in his love-making with Abbie. It was playful, enjoyable, and exciting at times. His guilt and fear about sexuality had died, and this combination of changes in his life had allowed his obsession to die. What was interesting was his reaction the next time he noticed his neighbors having sex. "As I watched them I felt a warm smile forming on my face. I then closed the shade and went to find Abbie. I put my arms around her sexually and she asked what was going on. I told her that our neighbors were naked in bed and I thought maybe we should be too. We both laughed. Abbie dried her hands, abandoned the dishes and led me upstairs."

Carl came to the next session with an important story that validated the changes in his life. While dressing for church the Sunday after our last session, for the first time in his life he did not put on his necktie. It was summer and he realized how hot wearing a necktie would feel. As they left for church Abbie gave him a look of surprise with a smile, but said nothing. Without the necktie he was very aware or self-conscious at first while sitting in church, but when he looked around he saw no neckties. He then realized how out of place he must have been in wearing a tie and had never before thought about it or even noticed that no one else wore a necktie. This brought over him a smile and a new sense of freedom from what he had always thought was proper.

Both Heimdall and Loki died without much of a struggle a week earlier, when Abbie was out of town again visiting their daughter for a few days. Carl was now very much in touch with his feelings of horniness and began feeling horny. He decided to relieve this tension by masturbating and discovered some feelings of guilt, or maybe just emptiness. Masturbating was not greatly enjoyable. The argument within himself ended, however, with Carl deciding that masturbating was appropriate in that situation and it did not need to be greatly exciting or enjoyable. The thoughts of burning in hell and condemning earthly pleasures seemed ridiculous. The excitement and enjoyment of sex was with his wife.

Carl had found real innocence in his feelings about sex.

ARLENE

Who was left? Arlene came to the next session again with a smile. Things had been going well. She had been looking at many things in life with a mellow, calming strength. One was when her boss asked her if she could work on a day that she was planning to study. In the past she would have been very frustrated by his request because she would have wanted to say "no" but felt she had to say "yes," and she would have resented him for asking her. His request would have made her angry, so typically she would express her anger to Tim, something she knew Tim resented.

This time his request did not anger her. She weighed both sides, at first feeling a little overwhelmed, but she decided that she had studied enough and could work. Another factor in weighing both sides was whether or not the family needed her presence at home or the money more.

"You're doing so well. Asking your mother questions likely would have angered her. You are now facing questions with a mellow, calming strength. When one of the kids ask you where something is, you would have become irritated, thinking that it was the kid's responsibility to keep up with their belongings. But children are children, and it takes time and a mellow, calming patience for them to learn that responsibility. Children automatically believe that parents are supposed to know everything. Now you can say 'yes' or 'no.'"

The battle between Loki and Heimdall with their attacks and rebuttals, the constant vacillation back and forth between "You're right" and "You're wrong," ends with the death of both. Having given up guilt, fear and obsessive thinking, Arlene was free to make decisions with confidence and decisiveness. She was experiencing life with a new sense of freedom and innocence.

All three clients were free of their obsessions and addictions. All three were experiencing a new and comfortable feeling of innocence in their lives. There were no more arguments in defense of their obsessive behaviors. With this new strength and understanding, they were ready to move on to a fulfilling life.

CHAPTER 20

AFTER THE FINAL BATTLE

After the final battle, after the deaths of Freyr, Tyr, Thor, Odin, Heimdall and Loki, after the deaths of Garm, Jormungand and Fenrir, after the world has been burnt by the fires of Muspell, the only gods who survived are several children of the gods: Modi and Magni, the sons of Thor; and Vidar, Vali and Hod, the sons of Odin. Baldr also survives—the gentle and sensitive Baldr is reborn. You already know that Vidar avenged the death of his father Odin by tearing Fenrir the wolf's jaw apart. From the old stories we know also that when Thor killed Hrungnir the giant fell across Thor, pinning him to the ground. None of the gods was able to lift Hrungnir's leg off Thor to release him except for Magni. Thus, two of the surviving gods have exceptional strength.

Now, the rebirth of strength and innocence is finally complete, without the presence of the intimidating monsters Garm, Jormungand and Fenrir. Thus all of the clients of this book are living in a new world of strength and innocence. They have a fresh start in dealing with the stresses of everyday life without the dysfunctional thoughts and feelings that inhibited their previous lives with obsessions and addictions. Therapy for each person has come to an end.

JERRY

Jerry no longer played baseball with the need to impress others and the hope of gaining their appreciation, the death of the addicted lover, the Freyr archetype. He played baseball because he loved the game and enjoyed keeping his skill in pitching well polished, the healthy warrior. There was a difference. He was no longer hurt by Sherry's lack of interest in the game. His and Sherry's marriage had reached an innocent love that was not dependent upon Jerry's need to be appreciated. Their love had a new freedom. They enjoyed their time together and enjoyed doing things for and with the other person simply for the joy in it. They both appreciated their new life together of unconditional love.

In summary, Jerry first gained a deeper understanding of his dysfunctional way of nurturing, the tyrant king archetype. To enable this dysfunctional narrative to die he was led to find the alternative of the trust and intimacy felt in healthy bonding. The trust of healthy bonding allowed for hurt, knowing that the hurt would not threaten the relationship. But for this nurturing dysfunction of needing appreciation to die, Jerry's guilt and fear needed to die. The guilt he felt became clear when he realized the unnecessary hurt of the "guilt trip" he was putting on Sherry for not appreciating him, the guilt/Garm archetype. Sustaining this guilt was the deep-seated guilt he learned from his mother that he should not want or need appreciation. This automatic and unconscious or semi-conscious belief became clear when he recalled his mother's words, "You should give without expecting something in return." The healthy alternative way of thinking addressed the issues of what to give: not giving what one wants to give, but giving with sensitivity to the needs and wishes of the other person. Jerry was highly motivated to save his second marriage. With practice in genuine giving, his sensitivity grew and his guilt died. Jerry could then face the third battle, that of fear.

Along with his need to impress, Jerry was ever afraid of failure, of not having control, the weakling impotent shadow side of the king, whether in his ability to please Sherry or when pitching. With regard to pitching the emotional pressure of seeking appreciation was a distraction and interfered with his performance. With this revelation and the knowledge that Sherry loved him for who he was, not his ability in pitching, Jerry was able to see the importance of letting die both his need for appreciation and his use of guilt-tripping. Thus his fear of not being in control died, and with its death he was better able to focus, and thus came the death of his impulsive emotional distractions, the masochist impulsive shadow side of the warrior.

All these thoughts played together to allow the final death of Jerry's obsession with his need for appreciation and Sherry's irritability and anger. The energy that fostered his obsession was his dysfunctional definition of love, i.e., the love of giving and being appreciated. This need for appreciation is a weakness, thus it is represented by the weakling shadow side of the king. Once his obsessive need for appreciation was dead, the obsessive fear of Sherry's anger, the impotent shadow side of the lover, of Freyr, could die. Jerry now could appreciate Sherry's unconditional love and her occasional expression of anger. Finally, his attempts to justify his need for appreciation, the shadow naïve side of the magician, i.e. the Heimdall archetype and his challenges to those justifications, the manipulator shadow side of the magician, the Loki archetype, could die. Thus Jerry was free to experience unconditional love from Sherry, Beth and in a different sense, his baseball team.

CARL

Carl had found a new excitement in sex with his wife that he had never realized was missing. Though Abbie had known it was missing, she had given up on trying to show it to him. Carl could now watch for a moment the neighbors enjoying their time in bed together without becoming obsessed, but with a smile of joy for them, just as Abbie had been able to smile. He then could close the shade to let them have their privacy. This new innocence in sex brought a new meaning to Carl and Abbie's love for each other.

Carl came to this new place in his life when he finally accepted the fact that his sexual desires were truly God-given. He then was able to let die his nurtured but dysfunctional belief that his sexual thoughts were evil, the addicted shadow side of the love. These dysfunctional sexual thoughts that have died were nurtured by Carl's belief that the thoughts were evil in God's eyes, a belief taught to him by his grandfather. But, before he was able to totally let go of this dysfunctional way of thinking, his guilt and that which sustained his guilt needed to die. Sustaining his guilt for all these years was his childhood experience of his mother catching him masturbating. He had believed that she was disgusted with him. This early disgust that had become an automatic and unconscious thought, the masochist warrior archetype, had sustained his current disgust with his voyeurism and masturbating. Relieving this guilt through hypnotic reframing clarified that masturbation in adolescence is healthy and allowed the current guilt of his voyeurism and masturbating to die. They both died together.

Part of this whole picture was the fear instilled in Carl from his grandfather's preaching that he could burn in hell because of sexual feelings. What sustained this fear that needed to die first was the unconscious nature of the fear, a fear that he was taught in childhood that was never questioned or considered after that, and thus was a self-sustaining impulse. Bringing this unconscious thought of burning in hell to the fore and examining its irrationality with the automatic and unconscious power it had over him, Carl could let it die. Finally, the justification for his voyeurism that was never voiced until now, the naïve magician archetype, Heimdallr, i.e. the repression of sexual desires sustained by his fear and guilt, and his challenges that were loudly voiced by Loki, the manipulating magician archetype, but to no avail now died and Carl was free, reborn in innocence, the benevolent king, Baldr.

ARLENE

Arlene no longer needed to be in a battle with the world around her. She could now greet this world with a mellow, calming strength that allowed her to appreciate and value others even in their weaknesses and mistakes. With these changes in her attitude Arlene was discovering greater effectiveness in her roles as a mother and wife, as a student and as an employee. She was excited about the future.

For Arlene to attain this new attitude towards life she had to lay to rest those dysfunctional beliefs learned during her childhood. One major dysfunctional way she learned to nurture herself was from her mother's words, "No one else cares. You have to take care of yourself," the addicted nurturing mother archetype. She now realized that when she showed she really cared, something seemed to always go wrong. The new words she started saying to herself were, "I'll face it with a calm, mellow strength," words that came to describe what she learned in watching the calm, mellow strength of her stepdaughter. Yet guilt blocked her ability to accept these words, the guilt of failure. She had learned more unconsciously than consciously that whenever she tried she would fail. As hard as she had tried to do what would make her mother happy, her mother was always angry. Arlene now learned that her mother's anger was not her fault. She had felt unfair guilt, the masochist warrior archetype. Understanding this now at a deeper level with the help of trance, Arlene was able to let her guilt die when she stopped taking responsibility for her mother's anger.

Arlene had always been afraid of her mother's anger and now feared her own anger. Again it was her own feeling of responsibility for her mother's anger that maintained her fear, the impotent protective mother archetype. Since she had turned that responsibility over to her mother nothing was sustaining the fear, the impotent protective mother. Yet because she had learned early that she would always fail, she lacked confidence in making decisions, thus fueling her obsession to be perfect. Her indecisiveness in weighing all the facts and making a decision was her dysfunctional way of thinking. Once she let go of her guilt and fear, she was able to face decision-making with a calm, mellow strength, allowing her obsession to die. And again with the death of these gods and monsters, the argument between Heimdall and Loki, the justifications and challenges, died, and Arlene was reborn in the innocence of Baldr.

Each person was in a struggle in life, an unnecessary struggle that was defined by their dysfunctional thinking, thinking that was learned early in their life, thinking that was likely not conscious but was still real, thinking that revealed itself in the form of an addiction or obsession. Each person had to face this addiction or obsession, whether it was a need to protect the self from an untrusted world, a belief that she had to do things the right way in an attempt to keep peace, a feeling of extreme emptiness, a need to be appreciated or a belief that his sexual energy was evil. Each person had to face his or her obsession along with its guilt and fear, an obsession that willpower could never be strong enough to change. Each failed until all defenses were destroyed, until rock bottom was reached.

After journeying three endless winters of depression to reach this rock bottom, each person had to face the dysfunctional way he or she nurtured the obsession (Fenrir) in order to let this dysfunctional way of thinking die. Yet for it to die, the guilt (Garm) and fear (Jormungand) that sustained the dysfunctional ways of nurturing have to die. Finally, then the obsession itself (Fenrir) can die.

Thus Freyr, Tyr and Garm, Thor and Jormungand, and Odin and Fenrir all die. Then each person is free to allow the death of all the haggling, the attempts to justify and the challenges to each justification. With these final deaths of Heimdall and Loki, each is finally able to fully appreciate the end of this final battle and experience the rebirth of innocence and strength. Baldr, Vidar and Magni live.

This process of healing and recovery as revealed in the ancient myth of Loki and his children necessarily involves understanding the unconscious processes of the mind that rest behind conscious narratives as well as the deeper narrative of the unconscious, including the origin of these narratives in a person's past. Though the narrative of their origin needs to be examined, these incidents generally found in childhood are used to bridge or make a connection with present narratives and are not the focus of prolonged attention, as in the process of psychoanalysis.

As we have seen, the spontaneous narratives that arise in dreams and hypnotic experiences are also expressed in a shorthand and follow a different logic than rational thought, as found in the conscious narrative. This different logic, that is characteristic of the processes of the unconscious mind, is also characteristic of ancient myth. This logic is free of the constraints of time, space and causality as described by Matte-Blanco.[1] When we move away from rational thinking and open ourselves to this different logic, the meaning of myths and the processes of the unconscious mind as revealed in dreams and hypnotic experiences becomes transparent, offering us a new and deeper understanding of ourselves and others. It is the power of this transparent fourth dimension of consciousness that allows for deeper levels of change in the process of psychotherapy, change that becomes automatic or unconscious.

The myth of Loki's Children reveals the ineffectiveness of the will to effect such change. Chains or even the magical binding, Gleipnir, in the long run, could not restrain Fenrir. Only with the death of the dysfunctional real but unconscious narrative and the reflexive emotional response to this dysfunctional narrative, i.e. one's dysfunctional nurturing of guilt and fear, can the obsessions and compulsions die. Only with these deaths and the rebirth of innocent Baldr can one's healthy way of thinking and living become automatic. The three clients of this book became comfortable in calling the spirits of each direction, a very Earth-oriented litany. In doing so they began to discover new levels of understanding within themselves provided by their spirit guides. This opened them to the great diversity of humankind upon the Earth, of recognizing that the shamans of pre-history and contemporary communities have something to offer the world that is important for personal health. These clients moved from being very self-centered in their emotional pain into a world beyond themselves, a world in which they were able to effectively influence the lives of family, friends and colleagues in a healthy direction. They became the respected and effective elders of their community in showing others how to live, Arlene in her ability to show love and compassion to others, Jerry in understanding intimacy and how a man can benefit from learning this skill, and Carl in opening himself more sexually to others, not taking advantage of them but respecting their sexuality and affirming their own personhood. This therapy took each person beyond the simple relief of their fears, guilt and obsessions and changed their lives to become more effective individuals in a new world of greater diversity. They discovered that listening to the world through their nighttime dreams and in a state of trance opened to them much that they had been missing when living in the restricted world of their five senses.

ECSTATIC TRANCE RESOURCES

There is a growing body of work available on ecstatic trance, beginning with Felicitas Goodman's foundational book *Where the Spirits Ride the Wind: Trance Journeys and Other Ecstatic Experiences*. A student of hers, Belinda Gore, who has been my mentor in my work with ecstatic trance, has published two books that catalog the ecstatic postures: *Ecstatic Body Postures: An Alternate Reality Workbook* and *The Ecstatic Experience: Healing Postures for Spirit Journeys*. In addition to these three books, Felicitas Goodman and Nana Nauwald wrote *Ecstatic Trance: New Ritual Body Postures*, originally published in German and now available in English. Another German resource is Annette Ki Salmen's *Mohnfrau: Wege zur heilung durch trance*. Salmen taught me the way of soul retrieval using the ecstatic postures in a workshop at the Cuyamungue Institute in New Mexico. Also many papers written about ecstatic trance are available on the institute's website.

I have written five books on ecstatic trance. The first was *The Power of Ecstatic Trance: Practices for Healing, Spiritual Growth, and Accessing the Universal Mind*. This book provides many examples of the power of ecstatic trance, including incidents of healing, time regression to ancient ancestral times, and reading the mind of another person, as so frequently happens in the group setting when in this altered trance state. In this state of ecstatic trance I find myself experiencing the experience of another person who is in my presence. The next two books, *Baldr's Magic: The Power of Norse Shamanism and Ecstatic Trance* and *Beowulf's Ecstatic Trance Magic: Accessing the Archaic Powers of the Universal Mind,* deal with my experiences of going back to ancient times to commune first with my own ancestors and then with the spirits of the land. For the hunter-gatherers, communing with their ancestors was central to their way of relating to the world and learning how to live. My fourth book is *Trance Journeys of the Hunter-Gatherers: Ecstatic Practices to Reconnect with the Great Mother and Heal the Earth.* For the hunter-gatherer peoples, their experience of the earth and nature was quite different from ours. They felt at one with the earth and lived in harmony with everything of the earth without feeling superior to any other life form. This book provides many examples of how ecstatic trance returns us to this experience of oneness with the earth and shows us that we are just one small step in the process of evolution.

The role of the hunter-gatherer shaman includes healing or restoring harmony within the individual and the community; communing with ancestors, the teachers of the community's way of life; understanding and attaining oneness with all life and everything of the earth; and going beyond in accessing information from the trans-sensory universal mind. Each of my books has used ecstatic trance to accomplish these shamanic activities. Though for the shaman many other activities are important. *Ecstatic Soul Retrieval: Shamanism and Psychotherapy* is intended to take the healing role of the shaman to a deeper level in restoring harmony. To restore harmony is to restore a lost part of oneself, one's original innocence. Retrieving this innocence is to retrieve the soul.

ENDNOTES

Foreword

1. As also with my first book, *Grendel and His Mother: Healing the Traumas of Childhood Through Dreams, Imagery and Hypnosis* I generally do not share the story of *Loki's Children* unless the client reveals an interest in these Old English and Nordic stories. I might more likely mention Loki as a trickster if a trickster does show up in the therapy session. NB

Chapter 1: The Tools of Psychotherapy

1. Thompson, "Curiosity of Erickson," in *Eriksonian Approaches*, 415.

2. Erickson, E. Rossi and S. Rossi, *Hypnotic Realities,* 58.

3. Gore, *Ecstatic Body Postures,* 6–8.

4. Gore, *The Ecstatic Experience,* 43–45.

5. Watkins, "The Affect Bridge," 21–27.

6. Castenada, *The Eagle's Gift,* 209.

7. Ibid. 183–184.

8. Gore, *Ecstatic Body Postures,* 12.

9. Waggoner, *Lucid Dreaming,* 78–79.

10. De Quincey, *Radical Nature,* 101.

11. Korten, *The Great Turning,* 52–56.

Chapter 2: The Process of Psychotherapy

1. Davidson, *Gods and Myths of Northern Europe,* 46.

2. Ibid., 180-182

Chapter 4: Loki's Discontent: Beginning the Narrative of Healing

1. Young (Trans.), *The Prose Edda,* 48.

2. Ibid., 55.

3. Johnson, *Owning Your Own Shadow,* 7-8.

4. Campbell, *The Portable Jung,* 144-148.

5. Johnson, *Owning Your Own Shadow,* 4-10.

6. Deer and Erdoes, *Lame Deer Seeker of Visions,* 225-226.

7. Erickson, E. Rossi and S. Rossi, *Hypnotic Realities,* 142.

8. Crossley-Holland, *The Norse Myths,* 48.

9. Hollander (Trans.) *The Poetic Edda,* 90-103.

10. Crossley-Holland, *The Norse Myths,* 15.

11. Erickson, *Hypnotic Realities,* 58-59.

Chapter 5: Jormungand: Dealing with Fear

1. Hollander (Trans.), *The Poetic Edda,* 83-89.

2. Young (Trans), *The Prose Edda,* 72-78.

3. Watkins, "The Affect Bridge," 21-27.

Chapter 6: Hel: Dealing with Guilt

1. Crossley-Holland, *The Norse Myths,* 121-126.

Chapter 7: Fenrir: Dealing with the Growing Obsession

1. Watzlawick, *The Situation is Hopeless but Not Serious,* title.

2. Brink, "Hypnosis and Control," 109-116.

Chapter 8: Lœðing and Dromi: Willpower is not Enough

1. Baudouin, *Suggestions and Autosuggestions,* 114.

2. Araoz, *The New Hypnosis,* 4.

Chapter 9: Gleipnir's Power: The Power of the Unconscious

1. Jwing-Ming, *Advanced Yang Style Tai Chi Theory and Tai Chi Jing,* 100-101.

Chapter 10: Fenrir's Binding: A Need for Sacrifice
1. Kaplan, *The New Sex Therapy,* 302–306.

Chapter 15: Freyr vs. Surt: The Death of Addictive and Impotent Nurturing
1. Erickson, *Hypnotic Realities,* 142.

Chapter 16: Tyr vs. Garmr: The Death of Guilt
1. Brink, "Hypnosis and Control," 109–110.

Chapter 17: Thor vs. Jormungand: The Death of Fear
1. Young (Trans.), *The Prose Edda,* 76.
2. Hollander (Trans.), *The Poetic Edda,* 86–88.

Chapter 19: Loki vs. Heimdall: The Final Argument
1. Hollander (Trans.), *The Poetic Edda,* 99–100.

Chapter 20: After the Final Battle
1. Raynor, "Infinite Experience," 403–412.

Appendix
1. Gore, *Ecstatic Body Postures,* 6–8.

GLOSSARY

Æsir: The race of warrior gods led by Odin that resides in Asgard.

Alfheim: The underworld domain of Asgard inhabited by the light elves.

Alvis: The dwarf with whom Thor debates until daylight and thus is turned to stone.

Amsvartnir: The lake where the island of Lyngvi is located on which Fenrir was chained.

Angrboða: "Anguish-Bringer." A giantess, the mistress of Loki, and the mother of Fenrir the wolf, Jörmungand the sea serpent, and Hel, the being who presides over the place of the same name.

Asgard: The domain of the Æsir in the upper world.

Baldr: The most beautiful and gentle son of Odin and Frigg, who dreams of his own death, a death caused by the trickery of Loki. He returns after Ragnarǫk to become the god of gods.

Bestla: The giantess wife of Borr and mother of Odin.

Bolthorn: The giant father of Bestla.

Borr: The father of Odin, Vili, and Vé, the son of Búri, and the husband of Bestla.

Bifröst: The flaming, trembling rainbow bridge guarded by Heimdallr that connects the upper and middle worlds.

Bragi: A son of Odin and the god of poetry, the husband of Idunn.

Búri: Odin's grandfather who is freed from the salty ice when licked by the cow Auðumla. He is the father of Borr and Moðir.

Dou Sou Jing: Trembling strength as seen in a stalking cat ready to pounce (Chinese).

Draupnir: Odin's golden arm ring that produces eight rings of gold every nine days.

Drómi: The second, heavier chain used in a failed attempt to restrain Loki.

Eljudnir: Hel's hall in Niflheim.

Fárbauti: The giantess mother of Loki.

Fenrir: The wolf son of Loki who continues to grow to become a threat to the gods until it is restrained by a magical binding. This restraining of Fenrir costs the god Týr his hand.

Freyja: The sister of Freyr and daughter of Njord. She is one of the fertility goddesses of the Vanir who goes with her father to live among the Æsir.

Freyr: The brother of Freyja and the son of Njord. He is one of the fertility gods of the Vanir who goes with his father to live among the Æsir.

Frigg: Odin's wife and mother of Baldr. She is originally of the Vanir.

Garmr: The monstrous dog chained to the gate of Niflheim. He breaks loose at Ragnarǫk to battle the god Týr.

Gefjon: The fertility goddess who plows the land from Sweden to form the Danish island of Zealand. She is the husband of Scyld Scefing, the first king of Denmark, and the caretaker of those women who die as virgins.

Gerð: The beautiful giantess, daughter of Gymir, with whom Freyr falls in love but is unable to express his feelings except through his messenger, Skírnir.

Ginnungagap: The land between the North and the South that is mild and green, with soft air that thaws the ice of the North.

Gleipnir: The magical binding made by the dwarfs to restrain Fenrir the wolf.

Groa: Seeress and mother of Sviplag whom he visited in Hel's domain.

Gullinbursti: Freyr's golden boar that pulls his chariot in battle.

Gungnir: Odin's spear.

Gymir: The father of the beautiful Gerð. Freyr falls in love with Gerð but is unable to tell her of his love, so he sends words of love through his messenger, Skírnir.

Heimdall: The Vanrir god who chooses to live among the Æsir, and who is given the position of guarding Bifröst, the rainbow bridge, because of his acute hearing. He could hear the grass growing.

Hel: The daughter of Loki and Angrboða whom Odin throws into the underworld to care for those who die not honorably in battle, but of illness and old age; also the place name of the underworld. Hel (sometimes called Helheim) is also the name of the underworld location ruled by Hel, the being.

Hermod: Son of Odin who rode to Hel to try to bring back his brother Baldr.

Heyoehkah: Lakota clown or trickster (Lakota).

Hliðskjålf: The high throne of Odin from which he can see all that is happening in the nine worlds.

Hǫðr: The blind son of Odin and brother of Baldr. He throws the mistletoe dart that kills Baldr.

Hrungnir: The giant who injures Thor in battle.

Hymir: The giant whose massive cauldron for brewing of ale was won by Thor in a fishing contest when Thor caught Jormungand.

Hyrrokkin: Giantess who drags Baldr's burial boat down to the sea.

Idunn: The Vanir goddess who keeps the gods young by giving them the golden apples from a tree in her garden and who teaches all of the healing powers of plants and trees. Her husband is Bragi, god of poetry.

Jing: Strength (Chinese).

Jörmungandr: The serpent son of Loki and Angrboða, who Odin throws into the ocean, where it grows to surround Midgard by holding its own tail in its mouth.

Jötunheimr: The domain in Midgard that is the realm of the giants.

Jywe Jing: Sensing strength, the stalking strength of a cat (Chinese).

Kokopell'mana: Female Kokopell who runs in a ceremonial race and tackles one of the men and pretends to have sex with him (Hopi).

Koshare: Hopi clown trickster kachina (Hopi).

Koyemsi: Hopi mudhead clown trickster kachina (Hopi).

Kvasir: The wisest of the gods who first brews mead from the spittle of the gods, making mead the drink of the gods. Also the god of the Vanir who is offered in exchange for Mímir, a god of the Æsir, to ensure peace between the Vanir and the Æsir.

Læðing: The first lighter chain used in a failed attempt to restrain Fenrir.

Loki: The trickster god skilled in shape-shifting and the father of Jörmungandr, Fenrir, and Hel. His confrontations with the gods because of their hypocrisy leads to his restraint until Ragnarǫk, the final battle that brings an end to the world. He is the cause of earthquakes.

Lu Jing: Rolling or flowing strength as seen in a bubble rising in the water (Chinese).

Lyngvi: The island on which Fenrir was chained and held captive until the final battle.

Magni: A son of Thor and brother of Moði.

Midgard: The middle world; our world as we know it.

Mjölnir: The hammer of Thor that causes lightening when thrown by Thor and then returns to his hand.

Moði: The son of Thor and brother of Magni who watches Freyja's cats silently land on the earth.

Muspell: The realm of fire in the South, guarded by the giant Surtr.

Nanna: Baldr's wife and one of the Vanir.

Narvi: Son of Loki who was killed by his brother to provide the entrails that would turn to steel in binding Loki.

Niflheim: The realm of those who die of illness and old age and is ruled by Hel.

norns: Analogous to the Greek fates. The three most important norns, Urðr, Verðandi, and Skuld, who can see into the past to learn for the future, are advisors to Odin.

Odin: The god of gods, the Allfather, and the father of Thor.

Pau Jing: Rooting jing as seen in the rooted strength of an immovable mountain (Chinese).

Ragnarǫk: The final battle between the gods and their adversaries that brings an end to the world and the rebirth of Baldr.

Sif: Thor's wife whose famous hair is cut off by Loki because of her vanity. Sif is originally of the Vanir.

Sigyn: Loki's wife who remains faithful to him until the end. When Loki is restrained with a poisonous snake hanging over his head, Sigyn protects him by catching the dripping poison in a bowl.

Skíðblaðnir: The ship of Freyr that always has wind for it sails but can be folded small enough to be carried in his pocket.

Skírnir: The messenger who carries Freyr's messages of love to the giant Gerð, for which Freyr gives him his magical sword.

Sleipnir: Odin's eight-legged horse.

Surtr: The giant who guards Muspell.

Svartafheim: The domain in the middle world that belongs to the dark elves.

Thokk: A giantess thought to be Loki in disguise and who prevents Baldr's return from Hel.

Thor: The son of Odin whose mother is Fjorgyn. He is the husband of Sif. This warrior god brings lightning and thunder with the throw of his hammer.

Thurd: A daughter of Thor and Sif.

Tsan Nein Jing: Adhering strength as seen in the mud nests formed with the spittle of a bird (Chinese).

Týr: The son of Odin and the god of war who sacrifices his hand in order to restrain Fenrir the wolf.

Urðr: One of the three important norns and a goddess of destiny.

Útgarðr: The domain of **Útgarða-Loki**, the giant skilled in deception who repeatedly tricks Thor.

Útgarða-Loki: The giant who challenged and outwitted Thor in several contests through his mastery of illusion.

Vali: A son of Loki who turned himself into a wolf and killed his brother whose entrails bound Loki.

Vanaheim: The upper-world realm of the Vanir.

Vanir: The race of fertility gods and goddesses that predates the Æsir. Because their powers are magical, their battles with the physically powerful Æsir are stalemates.

Verðandi: One of three important norns and a goddess of destiny.

Víðarr: An Æsir god of vengeance. A son of Odin whose mother is the giantess Gríðr. He kills Fenrir the wolf to avenge Odin's death in the final battle.

Ying Jing: Hard strength or jing as seen in the strength of the sinew of a bear (Chinese).

Ymir: The first giant killed by Odin and his brothers from whose body Odin creates the world.

BIBLIOGRAPHY

Anderson, R. (Trans.), *The Younger Edda*. Chicago: S. C. Griggs, 1880.

Araoz, Daniel. *The New Hypnosis*. New York: Brunner/Mazel, 1985.

Barnett, Edgar. *Analytical Hypnotherapy: Principles and Practice*. Kingston, Ontario, Canada: Junica, 1981.

Barrett, Deirdre. "The 'Royal Road' Becomes a Shrewd Shortcut: The Use of Dreams in Focused Treatment." In *Cognitive Therapy and Dreams,* Rosner, Lyddon and Freeman (Eds). New York, NY: Springer Publishing Co., 2004, 113-124.

Baudouin, C. *Suggestions and Autosuggestions*. London, UK: Gresham Press, 1979.

Beck, Aaron. T. *Cognitive Therapy and the Emotional Disorders*. New York, NY: Meridian Division of Penguin Books, 1979.

Beck, A. T.; Rush, A. J.; Shaw, R. F., and Emery, G. *Cognitive Therapy and Depression*. New York, NY: Guilford Press, 1979.

Braden, G. *The Divine Matrix: Bridging Time, Space, Miracles, and Belief.* Carlsbad, CA: Hay House, 2007.

Brink, Nicholas E. "Hypnosis and Control." *The American Journal of Clinical Hypnosis* 7, no. 2 (1981): 109-116.

______. "Loki and Grendel: Imagery Therapy for Two Classes of Emotional Problems." *Imagination, Cognition and Personality* 21, no. 2 (2001): 159-171.

______. *Grendel and His Mother: Healing the Traumas of Childhood Through Dreams, Imagery and Hypnosis.* Amityville, NY: Baywood Publishing, 2002.

______, "Age Regression," in *The Corsini Encyclopedia of Psychology Vol.1,* I. Weiner and E. Craighead (Eds.), Hobokin, NJ: Wiley and Sons, 2010, 46-48.

Brink, N.E. *Ecstatic Soul Retrieval: Shamanism and Psychotherapy.* Rochester, VT: Bear & Co, 2017.

Brodeur, A. G. (Trans.). *The Prose Edda of Snorri Sturlson.* New York: American–Scandinavian Foundation, 1916.

Byock, J. L. (Trans.). *The Prose Edda: Norse Mythology.* New York: Penguin, 2005.

Campbell, Joseph (Ed.). *The Portable Jung,* New York, NY: Viking Press, 1971.

Castaneda, Carlos. *The Eagle's Gift.* New York: Pocket Books, 1981.

Crossley-Holland, Kevin. *The Norse Myths: Introduced and Retold.* New York: Pantheon Books,1980.

Davidson, H. R. E. *Gods and Myths of Northern Europe.* New York: Viking Penguin, 1964.

Deer, J. L. and Erdoes, R. *Lame Deer Seeker of Visions.* New York: Pocket Books, 1972.

Emerson, V. F., "Can Belief Systems Influence Behavior? Some Implications of Research on Meditation," *Newsletter Review,* R. M. Bucke Memorial Society, 5:20-32.

Erickson, Milton H.; Rossi, Ernest; and Rossi, Sheila I. *Hypnotic Realities: The Induction of Clinical Hypnosis and Forms of Indirect Suggestion.* New York: Irvington Publishers, 1976.

Erickson, Milton H. *Hypnotherapy: An Exploratory Casebook.* New York: Irvington Publishers, 1979.

______. *The Nature of Hypnosis and Suggestion: The Collected Papers of Milton H. Erickson on Hypnosis, Volume I.* New York: Irvington Publishers, 1980.

______. *Life Reframing in Hypnosis: The Seminars, Workshops, and Lectures of Milton H. Erickson, Volume II.* E. L. Rossi and M. O. Ryan (Eds.). New York: Irvington Publishers, 1985.

______. *Creative Choice in Hypnosis, Volume IV: The Seminars, Workshops, and Lectures of Milton H. Erickson.* E. L. Rossi and M. O. Ryan (Eds). New York, NY: Irvington Publishers, 1992.

Faulkes, A. (Trans.) *Edda.* London, UK: Everyman, 1987.

Gaddis, S. *Narrative Therapy: The Co-Construction of Preferred Identities,* workshop offered at William James College, Newton, MA. Sept. 30, 2016.

Gazzaniga, M. *The Bisected Brain.* New York: Appleton-Century-Crofts, 1970.

Gebser, Jean. *The Ever-Present Origin.* Translated by Noel Barstad. Athens, OH: Ohio University Press, 1985.

Goncalves, Oscar & Barbosa, Joao. "From Reactive to Proactive Dreaming." In *Cognitive Therapy and Dreams.* Rosner, Lyddon and Freeman (Eds). New York, NY: Springer Publishing Co., 2004, 125–136.

Gordon, David. *Therapeutic Metaphors.* Cupertino, CA: META Publications, 1978.

Gore, Belinda. *Ecstatic Body Postures: An Alternate Reality Workbook,* Rochester, VT: Bear & Co., 1995.

______, *The Ecstatic Experience: Healing Postures for Spirit Journeys,* Rochester, VT: Bear & Co, 2009.

Grammaticus, Saxo. *The History of the Danes.* H. E. Davidson (Ed), P. Fisher (Trans). Cambridge, UK: D. S. Brewer, 1979.

Hall, Calvin; Lindzey, Gardner; and Campbell, John. *Theories of Personality.* Hoboken, NJ: John Wiley & Sons, 1998.

Hill, Clara & Rochlen, Aaron. "The Hill Cognitive-Experiential Model of Dream Interpretation." In *Cognitive Therapy and Dreams,* Rosner, Lyddon and Freeman (Eds). New York, NY: Springer Publishing Co., 2004, 161–180.

Hollander, L. M. (Trans.) *The Poetic Edda*. Austin, TX: University of Texas Press, 1962.

Johnson, Robert A. *Owning Your Own Shadow: Understanding the Dark Side of the Psyche*. San Francisco, CA: Harper Collins, 1991.

Jwing-Ming, Y. *Advanced Yang Style Tai Chi Theory and Tai Chi Jing*. Wolfeboro, NH: YMAA Publications, 1989.

Kaplan, Helen. S. *The New Sex Therapy: Active Treatment of Sexual Dysfunctions*. New York: Brunner/Mazel, 1974.

Kerenyi, C. and Jung, C. G. *Essays on a Science of Mythology: The Myth of the Divine Child and the Mysteries of Eleusis*. Princeton, NJ: Princeton University Press, 1969.

Krippner, Stanley; Bova, M., and Gray, L. (Eds.). *Healing Stories: The Use of Narrative in Counseling and Psychotherapy*, Charlottesville, VA: Puente Publications, 2007.

_____; Bova, M., Gray, L., and Kay, A. (Eds.). *Healing Tales: The Narrative Arts in Spiritual Traditions*. Charlottesville, VA: Puente Publications, 2007.

Larrington, C. (Trans.) *The Poetic Edda*. Oxford, UK: Oxford University Press, 1996.

Laszlo, Ervin. *The Akashic Experience: Science and the Cosmic Memory Field*. Rochester, VT: Inner Traditions, 2009.

Leijssen, Mia. "Focusing-Oriented Dream Work." In *Cognitive Therapy and Dreams*). Rosner, Lyddon and Freeman (Eds). New York: Springer Publishing Co., 2004, 137–160.

Mabie, H. W. *Norse Stories Retold from the Eddas*. Chicago: Rand McNally, 1902.

Mehl-Medrona, Lewis. *Coyote Wisdom: The Power of Story in Healing*, Rochester, VT: Bear & Co, 2005.

_____. *Narrative Medicine: The Use of History and Story in the Healing Process*. Rochester, VT: Bear & Co, 2007.

_____. *Healing the Mind Through the Power of Story: The Promise of Narrative Psychiatry*, Rochester, VT: Bear & Co., 2010.

Moore, R. and Gillette, D. *King, Warrior, Magician, Lover: Rediscovering the Archetypes of Mature Masculinity.* San Francisco: Harper, 1990.

Napier, A. Y. and Whitaker, C. A. *The Family Crucible.* New York: Harper & Row, 1978.

Radin, D. *Entangled Minds: Extrasensory Experiences in a Quantum Reality.* New York, NY: Paraview Pocket Books, 2006.

Rayner, E. "Infinite Experiences, Affects and the Characteristics of the Unconscious." *International Journal of Psycho-Analysis,* 62, (1981) 403-412.

Rosner, Rachael; Lyddon, William; and Freeman, Arthur (Eds.). *Cognitive Therapy and Dreams,* New York: Springer Publishing Co., 2004, xiii-xiv.

Rossman, D. *The Northern Path: Norse Myths and Legends Retold and What They Reveal.* Chapel Hill, NC: Seven Paws Press, 2005.

Sarbin, Theodore. "Introduction and Overview." *In Narrative Psychology: The Storied Nature of Human Conduct.* Edited by Theodore R. Sarbin. Westport, CT: Praeger, 1986.

Sheldrake, R. *The Presence of the Past: Morphic Resonance and the Habits of Nature.* Rochester, VT: Park Street Press, 1995.

Terry, P. (Trans.). *Poems of the Elder Edda.* Philadelphia: University of Pennsylvania Press, 1990.

Thompson, Kay, "Curiosity of Erickson." In *Ericksonian Approaches to Hypnosis and Psychotherapy.* Edited by J. K. Zeig. New York: Brunner/Mazel, 1982.

Waggoner, Robert. *Lucid Dreaming: Gateway to the Inner Self,* Philadelphia: University of Pennsylvania Press, 1990.

Watkins, John. "The Affect Bridge: An Hypnoanalytic Technique." *International Journal of Clinical and Experimental Hypnosis* 19, (1971): 21-27.

Watzlawick, Paul. *The Situation is Hopeless, But Not Serious: The Pursuit of Unhappiness.* New York: W. W. Norton & Company, 1983.

Young, J. I. (Trans.). *The Prose Edda: Tales from Norse Mythology.* Berkeley, CA: University of California Press, 1954.